Twentieth-Century
Ecuadorian Narrative

Twentieth-Century Ecuadorian Narrative

New Readings in the Context
of the Americas

Kenneth J.A. Wishnia

Lewisburg
Bucknell University Press
London: Associated University Presses

© 1999 by Kenneth J.A. Wishnia

All rights reserved. Authorization to photocopy items for internal or personal use, or the internal or personal use of specific clients, is granted by the copyright owner, provided that a base fee of $10.00, plus eight cents per page, per copy is paid directly to the Copyright Clearance Center, 222 Rosewood Drive, Danvers, Massachusetts 01923. [0-8387-5432-5/99 $10.00 + 8¢ pp, pc.]

Associated University Presses
440 Forsgate Drive
Cranbury, NJ 08512

Associated University Presses
16 Barter Street
London WC1A 2AH, England

Associated University Presses
P.O. Box 338, Port Credit
Mississauga, Ontario
Canada L5G 4L8

The paper used in this publication meets the requirements of the American National Standard for Permanence of Paper for Printed Library Materials Z39.48-1984.

Library of Congress Cataloging-in-Publication Data

Wishnia, K. J. A.
    Twentieth-century Ecuadorian narrative : new readings in the context of the Americas / Kenneth J. A. Wishnia.
      p. cm.
    Includes bibliographical references (p. –) and index.
    ISBN 0-8387-5432-5 (alk. paper)
    1. Ecuadorian fiction—20th century—History and criticism.
I. Title.
PQ8212.W57   1999
863—dc21   99-15513
                                                                                         CIP

PRINTED IN THE UNITED STATES OF AMERICA

Jacket photo by Galo Carrión, 1988.

Contents

Introduction. Narrative Theory, Ideology, and Literary Production — 7

1. Anti-Realism before Realism: Pablo Palacio, the Ecuadorian Vanguard, and European Surrealism — 19
2. Social Realism and Early Magic Realism: "Stone-faced Indians and Trees that Scream" Language and Nature as Historical Self-Image in Three Ecuadorian Novels (1933–1942) — 39
3. Early Magic Realism 2: Sterile Fertility/Fertile Sterility—Identity, Negation, and Narrative in José de la Cuadra's *Los Sangurimas* (1934) in a Comparative Context with Gabriel García Márquez's *One Hundred Years of Solitude* (1967). — 65
4. The "Transitional Period" (1950s–1960s) Myth, Nonlinear Time and Self-Negation: Demetrio Aguilera Malta's *El tigre* (1955) and Eugene O'Neill's *The Emperor Jones* (1920) — 74
5. Between Ethnicity and Internationalism: Jorge Enrique Adoum and *Entre Marx y una mujer desnuda* (1976) — 85
6. Two Contemporary Novelists: Dialogic Cycles of History in Eliécer Cárdenas's *Polvo y ceniza* (*Dust and Ashes*) and Alicia Yánez Cossío's *Bruna, soroche y los tíos* (*Bruna and Her Family*) — 103

Conclusion — 119

Appendix 1. Translator's Introduction — 126
Appendix 2. *The Man Who Was Kicked to Death,* Pablo Palacio — 129
Appendix 3. *The Sangurimas* (Excerpt), José de la Cuadra — 137
Appendix 4. *Bruna, soroche y los tíos* (Bruna and Her Family), Alicia Yánez Cossío — 145
Appendix 5. *Polvo y Ceniza (Dust and Ashes),* Eliécer Cárdenas — 150

Notes	159
Bibliography	185
Index	195

Introduction
Narrative Theory, Ideology, and Literary Production

> There are fifty ways of saying Yes, and five hundred of saying No, but only one way of writing them down.
> —George Bernard Shaw, *Plays Unpleasant*

> It is precisely laughter which destroys the epic, and in general destroys any hierarchical distance.
> —Mikhail Bakhtin, *The Dialogic Imagination*

Narrative and ideology interrelate in form and function. Narrative encloses and is enclosed by ideology, and ideology depends on narrative techniques to disseminate itself within discourse. Moreover, their functional effects are achieved through similar processes: both typically involve the acceptance of a unifying "authoritative" explanation of events that orders the chaotic world and secures meaning, often manifesting itself as a form of canonization.

This study examines selected works of twentieth century Ecuadorian literature using a framework of European and American critical approaches whose shifting borders are continually reshaped by local, culturally specific Ecuadorian criticism. These multiple perspectives provide useful insights regarding the specificities of the Ecuadorian situation in terms of the interrelations of history and myth, of realism and magic or marvellous realism,[1] and the problem of whether the dialogic reader may actively undermine authoritative discourse, or if that discourse, by its very authority, predicts, preempts, and contains all potential challenges to it via the machinery of production.

The work of Jorge Enrique Adoum, for example, especially his internationally acclaimed novel, *Entre Marx y una mujer desnuda* (1976), provides an ideal context for the exploration of issues of ethnicity and the writer's struggle to construct a coherent identity within a multicultural society. In this novel, Adoum deftly balances extensive references to major figures, styles, and issues in world literature with numerous, relatively obscure, local references that characterize a certain tendency in much Ecuadorian literature produced for the urban, middle-class audiences from the 1970s onward.[2] The questions that Adoum and other "ethnic" Latin American writers raise about identity and difference subvert the pseudo-hegemony of dominant monovocal and monolithic modes of thought.

The struggle between this *mestizaje* (literally "mixing") of languages and cultures within Ecuador's literary, sociopolitical, and other spheres of discourse, and the dominant minority population's denial of those other voices, is one of the principal themes of twentieth-century Ecuadorian literature.

The work of certain European theorists is relevant to the discussion in this introduction, whereas the body of the text employs a wide variety of approaches—stressing multiple views—to the distinct works discussed in each chapter. Since the general purpose of this study is to introduce selected works of twentieth-century Ecuadorian literature to a larger (non-Spanish speaking) audience, chapters 1 and 2 contain relatively more introductory and background material to help "set the stage" than do the subsequent chapters. Chapter 1 is an examination of the work of Pablo Palacio in the cultural context of the Latin American vanguardist movement of the 1920s, and of that movement's reaction to and interaction with European (particularly French) surrealism. Chapter 2 discusses the mythification of history in three works of the 1930s and 1940s, Demetrio Aguilera Malta's *Don Goyo* (1933), Jorge Icaza's *Huasipungo* (1934) and Enrique Gil Gilbert's *Nuestro pan* (1942). The problematic and distinctly Ecuadorian approach to social realism will be examined in relation to the work of European and North American politically engaged artists of the 1930s, particularly John Steinbeck's *The Grapes of Wrath* (1939). Chapter 3 is a comparison of the early magic realist text, José de la Cuadra's *Los Sangurimas* (1934), with Gabriel García Márquez's *One Hundred Years of Solitude* (1967) that stresses the extent to which de la Cuadra's novel prefigures the latter work in terms of thematic content (patriarchy and family history), fantastic elements (communion with the dead), and narrative style (mutually contradictory versions of events). Chapter 4 explores Aguilera Malta's expressionistic play, *El tigre* (1955), in a comparative context with Eugene O'Neill's *The Emperor Jones* (1920), uncovering the fundamentally different assumptions made by these two authors about the impossibility of surviving in a heavily mythified jungle. Chapter 5 examines Jorge

Enrique Adoum's *Entre Marx y una mujer desnuda* (1976) as a work of Lebanese-Ecuadorian fiction, comparing it to the work of other Latin American ethnic and immigrant writers. Chapter 6 uses feminist and Bakhtinian thought to frame a discussion of the work of two contemporary writers, Alicia Yánez Cossío's *Bruna, soroche y los tíos* (1972) and Eliécer Cárdenas's *Polvo y ceniza* (1979), and their more recent attempts to confront and (partially) deconstruct the suppressive official histories that surround them, either through the mythification of alternative histories or a feminist reconstruction of those histories. An appendix supplies my translations of selections from Palacio, de la Cuadra, Yánez Cossío, and Cárdenas, since none of them are yet available in English.

In *Mimesis*, Erich Auerbach addresses the complex dialogic interrelations between "smooth" legendary narrative and the far more varied events of history: "To write history is so difficult that most historians are forced to make concessions to the technique of legend."[3] This will be a central issue in this study, since many Ecuadorian novels and short stories are heavily laden with historical conditions and consciousness. Whenever one version of the legend becomes history, contradictions remain. The elision of these contradictions is often among ideology's greatest goals, which is perhaps why so much Latin American fiction is considered truer by the general population than the "true" official history. How is this elision accomplished? How does one "narrative" achieve dominance over a multitude of conflicting narratives? (Aside from force and coercion, to use Gramscian terms.) Is narrative therefore an instrument of oppression? The answer, apparently, is that it can be, depending on who is using it to do what to whom.

Narrative is one of our primary tools for interpreting the world. How can this be oppressive?[4] The answer is when one abuses narrative's totalizing power to suppress other narratives in the broad sociopolitical and cultural arena. The post-1970 Ecuadorian authors whose work is studied in Chapters 5 and 6 are particularly concerned with pitting rival narratives against each other in the same text.

It should therefore not be surprising that realism has often been condemned for lulling the audience into empathizing with a one-sided, thoroughly ideologized depiction of reality. But faulting the conventions of realism themselves for the abuse to which they are put (by, e.g., conservative transnational media corporations) misses the point: It is *the system of production* that is largely responsible for the absence of radical statements in popular genres, *not* the inability of the realist form to bear them. That is, it is the institutionalization of forms rather than the forms' inability to present radical thought that is the culprit.

Even in the case of Ecuador, where the fact of "our horrendous and marvelous reality" ("nuestra realidad, horrenda y maravillosa"[5]) may justify the abandonment of realist conventions as a denial of the status quo, does that automatically make deliberately difficult literature a *challenge* to the status quo? If one expects change to come from the "masses," by which I mean the 99 percent of most societies who are working- and middle class, experimentation with form *tout court* is as naively animistic in its belief in the inherent, single meaning of an act as is the condemnation of conventions for the use to which they are put. After all, nothing has prevented Eisenstein's Marxist dialectical film techniques, especially rapid intercutting and you-are-there "psychological realism," from being appropriated by such diverse groups as the Nazis in support of fascism and by Steven Spielberg, MTV, and related industries in support of wide-eyed consumer capitalism.[6]

If the imposition of a single meaning upon narratives, whether they be nineteenth-century realistic novels or the hegemonic "narratives" of national ideologies, is understood to be oppressive, then opening the cracks in those dominant, homogenizing narratives to create spaces for alternate meanings is an act of liberation, and providing texts whose very form defies the premise of a single, determinate meaning is a radical act. However, if that form is so radical that the oppressed class that is supposed to be the target audience is unable to absorb even the message that the text is defying absorption, then the project must be considered a failure in some way.

In terms of the texts themselves conveying the possibility of social change by determinate means, little has changed since 1885, when Engels wrote that the novel primarily finds readers in bourgeois circles, "and there the socialist tendentious novel can fully achieve its purpose [if it] breaks down the conventionalized illusions dominating them, shatters the optimism of the bourgeois world, causes doubt about the eternal validity of the existing order, and this without directly offering a solution or even, under some circumstances, taking an ostensible partisan stand."[7]

Not that works that are overtly radical in form are not needed, but often their role is to reinforce the popular taste for conventional forms, for which Engels's theories still are valid.

Mikhail Bakhtin has demonstrated that what are considered to be conventional forms today most often have their roots in popular forms whose original intent was that of undermining an earlier, pre-existing set of conventions. Though the danger of cooptation is ever-present (as in the astounding success of "popular" Hollywood films with fiercely reactionary agendas), because of this Bakhtinian heteroglossia, it is possible for Stuart Hall to write,

> Popular culture is one of the sites where this struggle for and against a culture of the powerful is engaged: it is also the stake to be won or lost in that struggle. It is the arena of consent and resistance. It is partly where hegemony arises, and where it is secured. . . . But it is one of the places where socialism might be constituted.[8]

This breaking up of hegemonic discourse by means of the narrative insertion of dissenting and/or popular voices is one of the key features of virtually all of Ecuadorian literature that will be examined in this book. Many of the works take the form of the group story, or at least borrow significantly from it. The group story is an "admirably democratic storytelling mode [in which] the division between tellers and listeners falls away, as does anxiety over tellability . . . all are contributing to a story that each already knows."[9] These features are particularly outstanding in José de la Cuadra's *Los Sangurimas* and in the post-1970 texts of Alicia Yánez Cossío and Eliécer Cárdenas: their novels, *Bruna, soroche y los tíos* and *Polvo y ceniza*, revolve around the possibility of reconstructing a history based on conflicting versions of what is supposed to have happened. This struggle is engaged not just in terms of a dichotomy between documentary evidence and oral statements: the Ecuadorian struggle is largely between competing oral narratives, where the authority of one oral narrative is proclaimed over others by means of political, economic, and sexual power.

One of the primary cultural conflicts that surfaces in these texts is that the group stories produced by oral cultures allow "greater fictionality."[10] So while there may be an acceptance of contradictions in the popular, oral traditions, or even a lack of recognition of what we might label contradictions, these story forms are not typically pitted against the authoritative *texts* of the oppressors, which Derrida, González Echevarría and others have discussed in such depth elsewhere. The reality of the Ecuadorian situation is that the authoritative narratives are often oral as well—so it is truly in the realm of popular appeal that the struggle for authority in narrative is waged—at least until the generals get tired of talking and call out the army.[11]

Ecuador today comprises dozens of linguistically and culturally diverse groups. Angel Rama writes that the indigenous populations of Peru, Bolivia, and Ecuador have been the most successful in Latin America at resisting cultural impositions, and that Ecuador has preserved the largest number of local and tribal languages.[12] The distinct cultures of urban and rural poverty further separate the poor from a possible common voice. Millions of indigenous Ecuadorians are bi- or even trilingual yet illiterate in the ruling language, Spanish. The majority speak Quichua, which historically was never written down. Only in the last few years have some indigenous writers been publishing short poems in Quichua (transcribed using the Spanish alphabet). How are the Spanish-language writers to address an audience such as this? In short, they do not.

The "indigenists" of the 1930s certainly wrote in a straightforward, social realist style that the working class would have been able to understand, had they been able to afford the luxury of buying a book (or find someone to read it to them if necessary). But the books were produced largely for Ecuador's left-wing intelligentsia, which in the 1930s numbered only a few hundred throughout the nation. It was thus possible to engage in radical narrative activity at the national level with press runs of four hundred. Those books never reached the masses as books. Many were serialized in magazines, however, and in this way were consumed by the working class—which is to say, the partially educated industrial working class of Ecuador's coast. The millions of mountain-dwelling indigenous people have historically had books written *about* them, but literature has not been written *for* them, except indirectly, and to date virtually none has been written *by* them. Ecuador has had no Rigoberta Menchu (an indigenous woman whose dictated memoirs were published to great acclaim) or an Arguedas (the Peruvian writer who was fluent in Quechua language and culture, but chose to write in Spanish to reach a larger audience), both of whom have reached international audiences through translation and distribution. But this will change shortly. Small but significant numbers of the Ecuadorian indigenous populations have moved in one generation from peasant status under near-feudal conditions to middle-class status under peripherally modern capitalism. Within one generation or less, indigenous authors will finally be producing literature in Ecuador. The change has revolutionary potential.

One of the fundamental problems expressed in twentieth-century Ecuadorian literature is the conflicting discourses produced by the heteroglossia present within Ecuadorian society. The central conflicts of several prominent novels revolve around the disparity between multiple speaking voices: urban, European (or Europeanized mestizo) capitalist versus rural Indian fishermen and farmers (often also mestizo) in *Los que se van*, *Don Goyo*, *Los Sangurimas*, *Huasipungo*, and *Nuestro pan* (all from the 1930s and 1940s); utilitarian, conquering capitalist Christianity versus disenfranchised, subjected, native peons in *El tigre* (1950s); and finally, the novels of Jorge Enrique Adoum, Alicia Yánez Cossío, and Eliécer Cárdenas, where even the framing of this conflict fragments, and the narrative itself is presented in a variety of different voices, further complicating the narrated conflict over whose "version" of the story will triumph.

Early in *The Dialogic Imagination*, Bakhtin contrasts the "multilanguaged consciousness" of the novel with the epic, which valorizes an "absolute" past and "knows only a single and unified world view." This absolute monoglossic unity, in which even the gods speak the same language as men, can be destroyed by laughter, which is rarely present in the majority of Ecuadorian historical novels (*Los Sangurimas* is an exception), but which finally appears as a dominant motif in recent works such as Aguilera Malta's *El secuestro del general* and Yánez Cossío's *Bruna, soroche y los tíos*.[13] But monoglossic unity can also be undermined by other forms of diglossia.[14] In Ecuador, oral, tribal forms are still very much alive, and very much in open conflict with official histories and what might be termed "narratives of identity."[15]

In terms of racial identity, Norman E. Whitten Jr. argues that the resolution of opposites found in the "doctrine of *mestizaje*, the ideology of racial mixture," is a false one.[16] Nevertheless, because of this doctrine, contemporary Ecuadorian society today has far less of the simple, binary "us:them" (i.e., native folk:foreigners) identity equation that, for example, right-wing Germans are able to use against Turkish "guest workers." In Ecuador, although a standard of beauty that raises light skin and blond hair above darker features is very much in place, the society has never had an equivalent single identity (e.g., "Aryan") against which all others can be measured and/or excluded. To the extent that it is possible to have a single identity, Ecuador's multiplicity of identities *is* its identity.

And yet exclusion is always lurking. It is precisely the struggle over the conflicting meanings assigned by two different classes *to a single word* that is the core conflict of Jorge Icaza's *Huasipungo* (see chapter 2). In the end, the power of the master language is categorically declared with the arrival of the army, and the linguistic dispute turned political dispute is silenced as all the dissenting, dialogic voices are murdered.

This path of exploration returns us to the interrelations of ideology and narrative. There *are* dominant narratives whose dominion is asserted by outright force or by the surreptitious workings of the "free market," which is unlikely to produce and distribute works critical of its own functioning. In modern society, writes Terry Eagleton, "it is not enough to occupy factories or confront the state. What must be contested is the whole area of 'culture.' "[17] But how does one do this when the means of cultural production are largely controlled by economic and socially repressive forces whose job is to pretend that they are not repressive? Ideology is in some ways a castle in the air—a very difficult place to hold a sit-down strike.

One way out of this quagmire is to combine Foucauldian ideas of discourse, in which resistant voices are always present, even under the most repressive of circumstances, with Bakhtinian dialogics.[18] This mixing of multiple voices creates what Eagleton calls "hybrid" ideology.[19]

This hybridization is very much present in Ecuador. The Ecuadorian ruling class has always bowed to what they profess are the "superior" European cultural values, and attempted to distance themselves from any trace of indigenous American influences (see especially my translation of *Bruna, soroche y los tíos* in the appendix). Yet they are also always very proud and defensive of "national" culture—whatever that may be in their minds, since at least 80 percent of the country is pure indigenous and *mestizo* in culture. The indigenous culture, of course, had European-based culture forcibly thrust upon it, and has had to incorporate it, but that incorporation has been incomplete. In many ways, indigenous-mestizo culture has already worked its way across the "border," from the margin toward the center, reappropriating and recontextualizing European images (much in the manner of Alejo Carpentier's famous "angel maraquero," one of the hybridizations that he credits with being the touchstone of new world Marvellous Realism). A great many "Catholic" traditions and festivals in Ecuador seem to owe as much to Pachacamac and Inti as they do to Santiago and Cristo Rey.

Ecuador has not had the social mobility that exists in the United States. There has always been a tremendous barrier between the castes, and so holding out the prospect of sharing a bit of the wealth in exchange for identifying with the oppressor's values has been much less a factor among Ecuadorian peasants than it has been among the underclasses in the United States, who have been taught that "In America, anyone can grow up to be president." Conformity has not typically been imposed with the promise of social mobility, but rather with the more immediate and brutal "promise" of not being murdered for inciting rebellion.

Contemporary literary production in Ecuador is mostly left-leaning, since publishing is not a multibillion dollar a year transnational operation, as it is in the United States. The problem for the left-leaning literature is that most of it is out of reach of the "masses," including much of the middle class. Literacy is still a big problem. Only canonical works are available in cheap paperback editions, while new literature is often prohibitively expensive. In 1994, a pirated edition of *Como agua para chocolate*, consisting of bound photocopies, sold for the equivalent of one week's pay at minimum wage. The "legitimate" imported edition was twice that.

Alberto Flores Galindo writes:

> El capitalismo tiende a uniformar. Edificar un mercado interno implica abolir los localismos, las tradiciones, los hábitos particulares sacrificados en beneficio de una lengua común.[20]

> [Capitalism tends towards uniformity. To build an internal market implies abolishing localisms, traditions and special customs are sacrificed for the benefit of a common language.]

Certainly the uniformity required of profitable mass production creates, or attempts to create, an equivalent uniformity of audience for mass distribution. And this has been somewhat successful. Many of the Englishisms found in the Spanish of Cuenca (Ecuador's third largest city) are the names of commercial products—"slides," "flash," "betamax," "quaker" (pronounced with a short "a," meaning "oatmeal"), etc. But this is not a blanketing hegemony; it is broken up into those pieces that the acquiring society can absorb, while other cultural products are rejected (for example, most Ecuadorians remain suspicious of canned and frozen food).[21] Although the United States still dominates the scene, a great deal of business has historically been done with Europe, especially Germany, and today with the other Andean countries and Japan. Because of Ecuador's traditional reliance on world markets, Indian women selling goods in the open market—the same women who are bilingual and nonliterate—also know both the metric and imperial measurement systems (recall the U.S. majority's near-total rejection of the proposed adoption of the metric system under President Carter).

It would certainly be a mistake to underestimate the powerful, hegemonically oriented hold U.S. interests still command over Ecuadorian import and export markets, but Ecuador has learned the difficult lessons of its "single-product" economy days to diversify its products and its markets. The area where the system still operates on a near-feudal level is, paradoxically, the "newest" product technology, oil—because, like feudalism, oil wealth is defined largely by who controls the most land.[22]

One can see in the case of Ecuadorian television a supporting situation for the critical position that absence can be preferable to misrepresentation. Indigenous popular culture, present in many day-to-day situations, is still very much underrepresented in the slick world of television narratives.[23] The *telenovelas*, the ads, strive toward a representation of Ecuador as a wealthy, European-looking country. While this is a tremendously offensive lie, ignoring 90 percent or so of the population (of course, the same is more or less true in the United States), at least the downtrodden are spared the indignity of being further belittled by stereotypical representation in popular forms. Is this good or bad? I guess the answer is, it is not particularly good, but it could be worse. Even a false presence can serve as a foot in the door of genuine presence.

Ecuadorian literature has operated very differently. One of its main goals has been to engage in the problems of the representation of the various interacting cultures, but it must be stressed, literature is not really a "popular" form in Ecuador (although economic and pedagogical changes could alter that). Thus the dominant discourse of self-representation implies a unified historical, racial, and cultural identity, while marginalized discourses address a society whose fundamental characteristic is that of *mestizaje*, even as the ruling class attempts to deny that *mestizaje* by defining it in exclusionary terms.

Ecuador's unique history suggests that the struggle between these opposing discourses will not be an armed insurrection but rather a war of words in the political and cultural spheres, hence the importance of literature, which frequently operates in the Bakhtinian realm of "parodic-ironic re-accentuation" of "high and official" speech genres.[24] Or as Jan Kott puts it, "Tragedy can be turned into comedy without one word being changed."[25] Presumably, it's all in the delivery.

Chapters 3 and 4 of the present text originally appeared in somewhat different form in *Hispanófila* and *Hispanic Journal*, respectively. Reprinted by permission.

The extract from *Bruna and her Family* that appears in Appendix 4 is reprinted by permission from Northwestern University Press. It was taken from the complete novel published under the title, *Bruna and Her Sisters in the Sleeping City.* (NWUP, 1999)

Twentieth-Century Ecuadorian Narrative

1
Anti-Realism before Realism: Pablo Palacio, the Ecuadorian Vanguard, and European Surrealism

THE ILLUSION OF CONFUSION

The complex historical situation of the Ecuadorian "vanguard," and their attitude toward surrealism in particular, must be examined in light of three interrelated issues: (1) The general movement among Latin American literati of the 1920s to resist "foreign" ideas, such as surrealism, and replace them with entirely "native" ones; (2) the apparent blindness of this same group to a number of "native" literary productions (in this case the Ecuadorian hybrid); and (3) the production in Ecuador, as early as 1922, of works that synthesized European and native voices and thus participated in the creation of a uniquely Latin American literature that finally achieved international recognition twenty-five years later, when Alejo Carpentier coined the term *marvellous realism* (lo real maravilloso) regarding his novel, *El reino de este mundo* (1948).[1] If we push the date back and accept one critic's report that Carpentier was already part of a widespread new world "consciousness" in 1923,[2] then we must also be prepared to include such non–Latin American authors as Luigi Pirandello and Massimo Bontempelli in that "consciousness."

First, one needs to problematize these highly constructed concepts of "native" and "foreign," which, in proper surrealist fashion, depend on each other for existence and yet must inevitably intermix: In the introduction to André Breton's *Mad Love*, the translator writes

> By what Breton was to call the law of objective chance, he expected the inner and the outer experiences to mingle in an ongoing, constant communion he compared to the scientific experiments of communicating vessels—in which communing opposites merge. Thus the extremes

of day and night, up and down, life and death, are held in balance, providing an extraordinary dynamism of activated images, transforming by this vital interchange the deadly dullness of "the unacceptable human condition."[3]

This is a quite acceptable definition of magic realism as well (although "dullness" has not been the problem in Latin America that it was for the European surrealists), but it also describes the debate between "native" and "foreign" that in many ways still rages in Latin America today.

There has been a considerable amount of ink spilled that, simplified, posits that European surrealism was a conscious invention, a reaction to the conditions of advanced industrial societies such as France, and was therefore an inappropriate form to import to Latin America, where a "purer" relation between the artist and nature existed. The poet Robert Bly praised Neruda's strongly surrealist-influenced *Residencia en la tierra* as

> "the greatest poems yet written in a Western language. French surrealist poems appear drab and squeaky beside them. The French poets drove themselves by force into the unconscious because they hated establishment academicism and the rationalist European culture." . . . In Bly's view, French surrealism appeals mostly to the poet's intellectual abilities, not to his entire personality. In Spanish and American surrealism, however, the poet's whole being is committed to the language of the poem.[4]

Thus the *intellect* and the *whole being* are set off as opposing terms, the former European, the latter Latin American.

An image from Carpentier's novel, *El reino de este mundo*, that of the *ángel maraquero*, a statue of an angel executed primarily in Spanish Baroque style but holding a pair of pre-Colombian maracas, is described not as

> el producto fantasioso de una imaginación individual, como la surrealista, dada a luz a fuerza de abortivos intelectuales, sino que nace de una sensibilidad colectiva que ha expresado de la manera más realista—sí, más realista—sus abruptos mestizajes, sus épicas conmociones culturales.[5]

> [the fantastic production of an individual imagination, like the surrealist images, born of abortive (i.e., forced) intellectual production, but rather born of a collective sensibility that has expressed in the most realistic manner—yes, the most realistic manner—its abrupt mixings, its epic cultural upheavals.]

Here, too, the "individual" European author is set off on the negative end of a binary opposition with the "collective" Latin American sensibility. Breton himself, visiting Mexico in 1938, declared it to be *the* surrealist country *par excellence*, and Carpentier writes that "marvellous realism" springs up "spontaneously and naturally" in Latin America.[6] Carpentier was

> contra los experimentos provocados artificialmente en favor del clima surrealista, existente en América, en estado puro.[7]

> [against artificially produced experiments in favor of the surrealist climate existing in America in a pure state.]

It is now time to complicate this binary opposition. First, it is well known that some of the most prominent names in twentieth-century Latin American literature spent several years in Paris during the 1920s and 1930s at the height of the surrealists' influence. The list includes César Vallejo, Miguel Angel Asturias, Ernesto Sábato, Alejo Carpentier, Arturo Uslar Pietri, and Ecuadorian poet Jorge Carrera Andrade, who lived in Europe from 1928 to 1933. The Chilean poet Vicente Huidobro co-edited the journal *Nord-Sud*, which was founded in 1916, with Pierre Reverdy,[8] and Carpentier, though greatly admiring Breton, as early as 1928 was already trying to open alternative spaces for deviations from "orthodox" surrealism:[9]

> "Rien n'est beau qui n'est merveilleux," decía André Breton en el trascendental *Manifiesto del surrealismo*. Pero pocas cosas tan bellas como alcanzar lo maravilloso con factores muy humanas. . . . "Digámoslo de una vez, lo maravilloso es siempre bello; todo lo maravilloso es bello; sólo lo maravilloso es bello" ¿Y dónde buscar lo maravilloso, sino en nosotros mismos . . . ?[10]

> ["Nothing is beautiful except the marvellous," wrote André Breton in his transcendental *Manifesto of Surrealism*. But few things are as beautiful as achieving the marvellous by means of very human factors. . . . "Let us say it once and for all (writes Breton), the marvellous is always beautiful; all that is marvellous is beautiful, only the marvellous is beautiful." But where should we look for the marvellous, if not within ourselves?]

Carpentier, though not disputing the spirit of Breton's words, is drawing attention to the issue of who gets to define what is marvellous. For instance, there is the famous example of Lautréamont's juxtaposition of the "distant realities" of the umbrella and the sewing machine on the dissection table.[11] According to contemporary author Isabel Allende, Carpentier's response to this image was to note that, because of the industrial and climatic conditions in Cuba, one could walk down the street in a working class neighborhood and see sewing machines with umbrellas on top of them (to keep the sun off the workers).[12]

Balakian and Stefan Baciu both use the term *para-surrealists* to describe

> writers of non-French tradition who at some point had contact with Breton's group and in retrospect found on a broad basis similarities between the general qualities espoused by surrealism and their own national literary background.[13]

Jorge Luis Borges is credited with "completely transforming" Argentine literature when he returned from Madrid in 1921 and introduced into poetry "ultraism, which can be considered as the Hispanic version of surrealism" ("el ultraísmo, que se puede considerar como la versión hispánica del surrealismo").[14] Borges followed this in 1932 with an article, "Narrative Art and Magic," in which he rejected the "mimetic presentation of reality" dominating novelistic style in favor of "non-mimetic, non-realistic fiction."[15] However, Carrera Andrade states that the "ultraist poets declared their spiritual relationship with German expressionism" and the typographical machinations of the French avant-garde.[16] Is this, then, to be taken as a "naturally occurring" phenomenon unique to the Latin American collective sensibility?

To complicate things further, in a 1931 article Carpentier cites Philippe Soupault, Robert Desnos, and Georges Bataille on why Latin America is destined to become the site of the much-sought-after quality of political and literary "liberty":

> [Soupault:] What must be forcefully affirmed is that Latin America must stop looking to the European continent, which preserves, before its very eyes, an incomprehensible prestige. Its job is to specify what will be its true destiny; today it is secure enough of itself to declare complete autonomy.

> [Desnos:] I affirm with certainty that this effervescent, virgin and fertile earth will be the theatre of formidable events . . . that "liberty" which has been crushed once again . . . will be saved next time.

> [Bataille: America is the continent that] will liberate impulses of tremendous amplitude and of prodigious human greatness.[17]

It is significant that this article was written at a time when these three authors had been expelled from Breton's inner circle.[18] Thirty-four years later (1965), Carpentier told Mario Vargas Llosa that the Peruvian novelist and his generation were lucky that they didn't have to pass through the mechanistic, futuristic, ultraistic tendency that "hurt us a great deal" ("que nos hizo mucho daño").[19] But he also wrote that same year that

> el surrealismo sí significó mucho para mí. Me enseñó a ver contexturas, aspectos de la vida americana que no había advertido, envueltos como estábamos en la ola de nativismo traída por Güiraldes, Gallegos y José Eustacio Rivera.[20]
>
> [surrealism meant a lot to me. It taught me to see contexts, aspects of American life, that hadn't been drawn attention to, surrounded as we were with the nativism of Güiraldes, Gallegos and José Eustacio Rivera (three prominent Latin American realists)].

Clearly, this was a moment of much reflection for Carpentier. Two decades earlier, he saw the Latin American continent as still being under construction. A 1945 visit to the Venezuelan jungle gave him the impression of being present at the "fourth day of Creation":

> America es el único continente donde distintas edades coexisten, donde un hombre del siglo xx puede darse la mano con otro del cuaternario o con otro de poblados sin periódicos ni comunicaciones que se asemeja al de la Edad Media.[21]
>
> [America is the only continent where distinct ages coexist, where a man from the 20th century can shake hands with another from the Stone Age or with another from villages with neither newspapers nor communications at the level of the Middle Ages.]

But here we are entering into some troublesome territory. Many would debate Latin America's "unique" condition of being a peripherally modern society in constant contact with a premodern one. There is an echo of national or racial pride in Carpentier's statement that borders on the prejudicial, and a certain blindness at work here that brings about the next point: the prominent Latin American critical discourse has largely ignored the literary situation of one of its own members, Ecuador (and presumably others, about which this study cannot comment). Why do some countries become exemplary of meta-narrative while others do not?

No less prominent a representative of this critical opinion than

Octavio Paz writes that Spain, Argentina, Chile, and Venezuela all had major surrealist movements, that Peru, Mexico, Haiti, and Martinique had major individual surrealist practitioners, although no movements, but that "no other Latin American countries had surrealist groups" ("En los otros países hispanoamericanos no hubo grupos surrealistas").[22] Perhaps the surrealists in Ecuador do not fit Paz's definition of a *movement* or *group,* but since several Ecuadorian literary journals of the 1920s continually published poems and stories by a group of writers—a significant portion of whose work has been described as surrealist—then what defines them as *not* being a group? They may not have called themselves a group, or had a single publication under their banner, but surely they deserve mention.

Stefan Baciu also gives a long list of the "most outstanding" "para-surrealist" movements—Peru, Chile, Colombia, Bolivia, Brazil, Mexico, and Argentina.[23] Again, who defines "outstanding"? The subjectivity of such lists is revealed by Venezuela's absence, since it is "outstanding" enough to make Paz's list. Ecuador is not even mentioned. And in Langowski's 200-page book, Ecuador's contribution is dismissed in a single sentence:

No ha habido mucha actividad surrealista en El Ecuador. Sin embargo, sus manifestaciones en la poesía francesa se han mencionado en: Andrada [*sic*], Jorge Carrera, *Poesía francesa contemporánea,* Quito, Casa de la Cultura Ecuatoriana, 1951.[24]

[There wasn't much surrealist activity in Ecuador. However, its manifestations in French poetry have been mentioned in Andrade, Jorge Carrera, *Contemporary French Poetry,* Quito, Casa de la Cultura Ecuatoriana, 1951.]

Perhaps Ecuador didn't have "orthodox" surrealists because they had already begun—twenty-five years before Carpentier made it an international literary concept—a synthesis of the two movements, European surrealism and Latin American "mythic" reality, as has been suggested by others. That should still qualify them for inclusion in a list of "para-surrealists." Yet they are not. Part of this is due to a lack of distribution of primary texts, which is still a problem today. International diffusion of Ecuadorian works in the 1920s was virtually nonexistent, apparently. And yet, Carrera Andrade was in Paris when all those other, more famous Latin American authors were.

Perhaps, then, the Ecuadorian situation doesn't conveniently fit

1: ANTI-REALISM BEFORE REALISM 25

the dominant episteme. But even the dominant episteme is in trouble. Rimbaud's *Illuminations* (1886) has been described as an exploration of the "otherness of this world" that resides in

> the freshness and newness of vision that allows us to discover the unknown, not in some distant *terra incognita*, but *in the very heart of material reality* dazzling to our eyes finally liberated from the leucoma [blinding eye disease] of custom and learned notions.[25]

And, prefiguring Carpentier's revelatory trip to the jungle by twenty-seven years, the Ecuadorian literary journal *Letras* printed in 1918 an interview with Guillaume Apollinaire in which he took the anti-Baudelairian stance of demanding that poets "rejuvenate their individual selves in a universal embrace" and "return to nature."[26] So this concept (expressed by Gonzalo Celorio above) of abandoning the "European individual" in favor of the "collective" may have come (in part) from a European. The point is not to belittle the very real Latin American need to get out from under centuries of foreign oppression, but to point out that in literature, national boundaries have become increasingly meaningless, at least when it comes to deciding what kind of image is "foreign" and what kind of image is "native." Each country has its own unique situation, which must be understood if its literature is to be understood, but it is impossible to erect linguistic barriers against the "foreign," or to extract its interminglings with the "native" (as the Nazis and Italian Fascists were to find out).

However, critic J. Enrique Ojeda's national literary pride may well be justified when he credits Jorge Carrera Andrade with using, as early as 1922, a "mixture of Christianity and indigenous animism" that he inherited from the native Andeans,[27] since such a mixture is one of the key concepts in Carpentier's first novel of "marvellous realism," *El reino de este mundo* (1949).

Regarding other European literary movements, another critic, Carlos Martín, positions Breton in distinct opposition to socialist realism, and Paz goes even further, claiming that the prominent groups of Latin American surrealism he has listed were, with the exception of the Chilean group, "anesthetized and corrupted by Stalinism and socialist realism" ("anestesiados y corrompidos por el stalinismo y el realismo socialista").[28] Does he say this because socialist realism is also a "foreign" importation? The major Ecuadorian writers of the late 1920s into the 1940s were all members of the Socialist or Communist Parties, and they believed that social realism was the only style in which to describe the Ecuadorian reality. Were they all "anesthetized and corrupted"? At least two of them, Demetrio Aguilera Malta and José de la Cuadra, used a brand of social realism as early as 1933 that included such magical realist elements as talking trees, axes that think and listen, and conversations with the walking dead (see chapters 2 and 3).[29] Their contributions are virtually absent from current Latin American literary discourse.

Irlemar Chiampi, who spends an entire book problematizing and qualifying the historical connections made between Latin America and marvellous realism, ultimately concludes that marvellous realism is the most appropriate form of describing the Latin American condition:

> En todas, aparece la predicación de combinatoria de elementos para América, pero la que mejor se presta para denominar ese referente semiotizado y proyectado en la modalidad narrativa del realismo maravilloso es, sin duda, real maravilloso.[30]

> [In all (the works described in which a synthesis of contradictions takes place, including Carpentier), appear a predilection for combining elements of America, but that which best lends itself to the denotation of this semiotized and projected referent in a narrative modality of marvellous realism is, without doubt, the marvellous real.]

So the question of the origins of this style becomes an important one.

Focusing on the specific situation of Ecuador, Humberto Robles notes that *Letras* published selections from *Les Chants de Maldoror* in Spanish translation as early as 1913,[31] and that, in addition to the previously mentioned interview, articles appeared in praise of Apollinaire, Max Jacob, Lautréamont, Picasso, and Dadaism in the late 1910s.[32] There were also detractors, sometimes in the same journals, but the point is that the material was known and under discussion long before the more celebrated twentieth-century Latin American authors made their well-known trips to Paris.[33] An essay by Henri Barbusse and Anatole France run in the weekly journal *Caricatura* (1918–21), "To the intellectuals and students of Latin America," was also very influential. Joaquín Gallegos Lara, a militant Communist and a writer of social realist works in the 1930s and 1940s, dedicated one of his stories to Barbusse.

By 1927 Ecuadorian writers and poets were heatedly expressing complex attitudes toward "foreign" influences. Though there were calls for creating "an autocthonous culture" with "American mud,"[34] the prominent poet and novelist Gonzalo Zaldumbide declared:

> El americanismo literario tiene algo de ridículo. Se quiere a todo trance vestirnos de plumas y taparrabos, queriendo con eso hacernos aparecer más originales. . . . Dígase lo que se quiera, nosotros tenemos más de europeos que de los indios. . . . Todo lo que somos, malo o bueno, lo hemos recibido de Europa, estamos atados a nuestros orígenes europeos por mil lazos indestructibles.[35]

> [Literary Americanism is a bit ridiculous. They want at all costs to dress us in feathers and loincloths, hoping with this to make us more original. . . . Say what you like, we have more of Europe in us than we do of Indian. . . . Everything that we are, good or bad, we have gotten from Europe, we are tied to our European origins by a thousand indestructible knots.]

This is certainly an overstatement. The novel and the poem, as practiced by members of the literary vanguards, were forms of European origin. But there is no denying that the influence of indigenous imagery and language was growing stronger at this time. At what point such influence becomes measurable may prove difficult to specify, but there should be no doubt that we are discussing a transitional period—or else there wouldn't be all this debating! According to Robles, the vanguardist project failed to take hold, and by 1930 both schools were replaced by the new generation of social realists. But with a difference: several of their majors works could be described as social *magic* realism.

María del Carmen Fernández affirms that the "Dadaist and Ultraist" poems of Ecuadorian Hugo Mayo began to appear in national publications beginning in 1921, and that the first issue of the journal *Hélice* (1926) includes a clarion call from poet Gonzalo Escudero to resist, be aware of, and yet synthesize and

> universalizar el arte de la tierra autóctona, porque la creación criolla no exhuma las creaciones extrañas, antes bien, las asimila, las agrega, las indentifica bajo el techo solariego.[36]

> [universalize the art of our autocthonous earth, because native creation doesn't exhume foreign creations, rather, it assimilates them, it adds to them, it identifies them beneath the roof of the ancestral manor.]

Yet two years later the Cuenca-based journal *Mañana* was reiterating that Apollinaire's reaction against European high art was inapplicable to the Latin American situation, because "art is still new here, because we still believe in it."[37] One must conclude that while a need for self-identification and a sense of self-creation may be essential for a national literature, the very idea of a national literature that exists separately and uncontaminated by external ideas is unrealizable.

This portion of the argument closes with two citations from Carrera Andrade alongside two from Massimo Bontempelli, who first used the term *realismo magico* referring to literature in 1926. Here is Carrera Andrade:

> Pero, mientras la imagen para los surrealistas es una creación pura del espíritu, una creación gratuita, para mí es una operación de acercamiento de dos realidades existentes, operación por la que ejerzo libremente mis facultades interpretativas.[38]

> [But, while the image for the surrealists is a pure creation of the spirit, a free creation, for me it's an operation of bringing two existing realities closer together, an operation in which I freely exercise my interpretive faculties.]

And here is Bontempelli:

> La realtà, quando è fatta arte, è pure fantasia.... l'arte consiste non nel darci il surreale pur (che non vuol dir niente) ma nello scopire e *indicare il surreale nel reale*.[39]

> [Reality, when made into art, is pure fantasy.... art consists not in giving pure surrealism (which means nothing) but rather to discover and to *indicate the surreal in the real*.]

This interplay between reality and imagination, a two-way system where both poles shape each other, Bontempelli calls "realismo magico." One wonders if the Latin American writers who were struggling so hard simultaneously to make use of and rid themselves of French surrealism were aware that a parallel struggle was being waged by other literary figures, or that the language of their manifestoes should so closely parallel that of this single figure, their contemporary in Italian literature. In any case, such manifestations as we have seen would tend to indicate that "pure" or "orthodox" surrealism from its very inception was already being diffused into a much wider discourse than even the practitioners themselves seemed to know.

Carrera Andrade concludes:

El paso del surrealismo por el campo de la poesía hispanoamericana fue como una lluvia de verano, pero dejó un saldo positivo: el ejercio de la imaginacion como fuerza suprema.[40]

[The passing of surrealism over the sphere of Spanish-American poetry was like a summer shower, but it left a positive credit balance: the exercising of the imagination as a supreme force.[41]]

The Illusion of Logic

To Alfredo Pareja Diezcanseco, one of the five Ecuadorian authors in the prominent "grupo de Guayaquil" of the 1930s, the writings of Pablo Palacio (1906–47) expressed an "unlimited interior freedom" and "a spontaneity" that was "in rigorous opposition to the black and white" characterizations of evil oppressors and good oppressed that dominated Ecuadorian social realism of the decade.[42] Another member of the *grupo*, Joaquín Gallegos Lara, a militant Communist and an orthodox socialist realist himself (in theory), reacted to Palacio's 1932 novella, *Vida de ahorcado*, as follows:

Es justo rechazar . . . el realismo naturalista o zolesco, rudimentario y superficial hasta cierto punto. . . . Pero . . . creíamos que [Palacio] llegaría a meter en su literatura la cantidad indispensable de análisis económico de la vida, para darse cuenta de contra quién debía dirigir sus tiros.[43]

[It is correct to resist . . . naturalist or Zolaesque realism, which is rudimentary and superficial up to a point. . . . But . . . we believe that (Palacio) will eventually put into his literature that indispensable quantity of economic analysis of life, in order to realize against whom he should be directing his shots.]

To which Palacio responded:

Si la literatura es un fenómeno real, reflejo fiel de las condiciones materiales de la vida, de las condiciones económicas de un momento histórico (una superestructura, en suma), es preciso que en la obra literaria se refleje fielmente lo que es y no el concepto romántico o aspirativo del autor. . . . Vivimos momentos de crisis, momentos decadentistas, que deben ser expuestos a secas, sin comentario.[44]

[If literature is a real phenomenon, a faithful reflection of the material conditions of life, and of the economic conditions of an historical moment (that is, a superstructure), it is correct that a literary work faithfully represents what is and not the author's romantic or "pipe-dream" ideas. . . . We live moments of crisis, of decadence, that should be dryly exposed, without commentary.]

Both sides seem to agree that a writer should represent reality; the argument lies in the differing perceptions of that reality. Pablo Palacio was suspicious of the transparent treatment of the nature of reality, what could be called the Western illusion of logic.

Ecuadorian critic Agustin Cueva calls Palacio "a sort of island within his generation" ("una especie de isla dentro de su generación"; this is true only for Ecuador: there are many similar figures contemporary with Palacio in other Latin American and Brazilian literature).[45] And Antonio Sacoto refers to Palacio as the "sole case of fragmented, schizophrenic narrative" of mid twentieth-century Ecuadorian literature ("de la literatura ecuatoriana es el caso insólito de una narrativa fragmentada, esquizofrénica").[46] Why should this be? Such uniqueness is indeed rare. Perhaps Palacio was not *that* unique. Cueva contextualizes Palacio, citing him as the "maximum expression" of a vanguardist movement that had been going on for most of the 1920s. The difference, according to Cueva, is that

> Palacio declara la guerra a un realismo por cierto inexistente en un Ecuador que, a diferencia de países como Chile o Brasil, no lo tuvo a finales del siglo xix ni en lo que iba del xx. . . . Como escribe Jorge E. Adoum: "Lo extraño es que Palacio se haya considerado anti-realista, y más que lo haya declarado en 1927, antes de que el realismo proliferara en América Latina y antes de que apareciera en el Ecuador."[47]

> [Palacio declared war on a realism that was certainly non-existent in Ecuador, which, unlike countries like Chile or Brazil, did not have it at the end of the 19th century or the beginning of the 20th. . . . As Jorge E. Adoum writes: "What is strange is that Palacio considered himself to be anti-realist, and he even declared himself so in 1927, before realism spread in Latin America and before it even appears in Ecuador."]

These are very provocative statements, but they must be qualified. Humberto Robles contends that Palacio was reacting against the pseudo-realism of the nineteenth century, citing Luis A. Martínez's *A la costa* (1904), and other works as examples of early twentieth-century Ecuadorian realist novels.[48] Cueva and Adoum are apparently referring only to the politically engaged social realism of the 1930s.

1: ANTI-REALISM BEFORE REALISM

When the story collection featuring "Un hombre muerto a puntapiés" appeared, avant-garde poet Gonzalo Escudero gave it a rave review. Palacio's work was described as

> cuentos amargos, acres, helados como la cocaína. Araña de doce garras. . . . Jazz band de la muerte. He ahí un nuevo libro. . . . Pablo Palacio persigue una álgebra revolucionaria en el arte burgués de hacer cuentos: el álgebra ilógica y tremenda de construir valores ecuacionales entre "un paraguas y una máquina de coser encontrado en una mesa de disección" según el descubrimiento sacrílego de Isidore Ducaesse [sic], el Conde de Lautréamont.[49]

> [bitter tales, tart, icy as cocaine. A spider with twelve claws. . . . A jazz band of death. This is a new kind of book. . . . Pablo Palacio is pursuing a revolutionary algebra in the bourgeois art of writing stories: the illogical and fearsome algebra of constructing equivalent values between "an umbrella and a sewing machine on top of a dissection table," the sacrilegious discovery of Isidore Ducasse, the Count of Lautréamont.]

This amalgam became the quintessential image for the surrealists, but is that the same as "anti-realism"? The "anti-realism" of Palacio may follow a more subtle path in "Un hombre muerto a puntapiés" than the deliberate juxtaposition of obviously unrelated elements. Fernández writes that in this story collection

> los personajes que se caracterizan por su "sabiduría," esto es, los sociólogos, los historiadores, los profesores universitarios y los alumnos que se toman en serio sus estudios, son vencidos por la plenitud de la vida: son hombres impotentes engañados por sus esposas, temerosos de la opinión pública, o víctimas reales de sus estudios. Personajes cuyas teorías, sesudamente construidas, no corresponden a la realidad ecuatoriana.[50]

> [the characters whose main quality is their "knowledge," that is, the sociologists, historians, university professors and those students who take their studies seriously, are vanquished by the fullness of life: they are impotent men fooled by their wives, afraid of public opinion, or victims of their own studies. Characters whose theses, so prudently constructed, do not correspond to the Ecuadorian reality.]

Specifically, in the title story, we have an example of an amateur sociologist/sleuth who believes his own theories too much. Of this story in particular, Fernández asserts that Palacio writes

> a negar los esquemas de pensamiento . . . tradicional . . . reniega del método deductivo y . . . reduce al ridículo a la cultura de élite que dominaba en el Ecuador de los últimos años 20.[51]

[to negate the schemas of traditional thought . . . negate the deductive method and . . . reduce to ridiculous the elitist culture that dominated Ecuador at the end of the 1920s.]

The plot of "Un hombre muerto a puntapiés" concerns a man who, significantly, is never identified by name, who reads a short, inconclusive newspaper article about an unsolved crime—a man who was apparently kicked to death in the street—and becomes obsessed with "solving," that is, reconstructing the "facts" in the case.

To be sure, the anonymous narrator convinces the reader that the deceased was the victim of a homophobic assault—fairly uncharted territory in 1927—but there is a Borgesian quality of self-reflexive/self-negating textual hermeneutics by which the narrator unravels his own textual authority (incidentally, this collection precedes Borges's first short stories by about six years). It is precisely the narrator's unlimited faith in the authority of his deductions that undermines them. Sherlock Holmes, after all, continually negates his own talents as being insufficient or sluggish, even though the reader may believe otherwise. But the cheaper imitations of the Holmes style represent a class-bound total faith in their own infallibility.

It is this latter that Palacio seems intent on unraveling in "Un hombre muerto a puntapiés." First of all, the newspaper article that serves as the narrator's *ur*-text contains the following:

> Lo único que pudo saberse, por un dato accidental, es que el difunto era vicioso.[52]

> [The only information known, by chance, was that the deceased had one or two vices.[53]]

The Spanish is ambiguous regarding the severity of the "vices." There is also no explanation of the source of this accidental piece of "data," which the nameless narrator obsessively reads and rereads and never questions. In fact, his first response is to laugh out loud:

> Lo cierto es que reí a satisfacción. ¡Un hombre muerto a puntapiés! Era lo más gracioso, lo más hilarante de cuanto para mí podía suceder. (37)

> [I laughed my head off. A man kicked to death! As far as I was concerned that was the funniest, the most hilarious thing that could possibly happen.]

1: ANTI-REALISM BEFORE REALISM 33

So he who is so concerned with motive (he keeps asking himself *why* the victim was attacked) turns out to have highly questionable morals and motives himself. This should be our first major questioning of the narrator's credibility. He waits for more news (anticipating more laughs), and only when it doesn't appear does he try to find (or invent) it. When he sets out to reconstruct the events, the narrator explains:

> Hay dos métodos: la deducción y la inducción (Véase Aristóteles y Bacon). (38)
>
> [There are two methods: Deduction and induction (See Aristotle and Bacon).]

Surely when one begins an investigation of any kind, there are more than two ways of going about it. This rigid European-based binary categorization is about to be incorrectly applied to the specifically Ecuadorian situation. The narrator admires and chooses the inductive method, but admits that he is not very good at it:

> La inducción es algo maravilloso. . . . (¿Cómo es? No lo recuerdo bien. . . . En fin, ¿quién es el que sabe de estas cosas?) Si he dicho bien, éste es el método por excelencia. (38)
>
> [Induction is something marvellous. . . . (How does it work? I don't remember. . . . Well, who knows about these things anyway?) But as I said, this is the method *par excellence*.]

This should be our second major questioning of the narrator's credibility. He now decides to make up in style what he lacks in substance:

> encendida la pipa y con la formidable arma de la inducción en la mano, me quedé irresoluto, sin saber qué hacer. (38)
>
> [I lit my pipe and with that formidable inductive weapon in my hands, I remained irresolute, not knowing what to do.]

The irony may be clear when we isolate these passages, but the continuity of the narrative works to mask this effect. The charade continues:

> dando vigorosos chupetones a mi encendida y bien culotada pipa, volví a leer la crónica roja arriba copiada. Hube de fruncir el ceño como todo

hombre de estudio. —¡una honda línea en el entrecejo es señal inequívoca de atención! (38)

[taking vigorous puffs on my fired-up, big-assed pipe, I reread the bit of sensational journalism reproduced above. I had to wrinkle my brow like all studious men—a deep line between the eyebrows is the unequivocal sign of attention!]

Surely, what we have here is a man *performing* the act of reasoning. One almost expects him to look at himself in the mirror to verify that he looks like what a man engaged in reasoning is supposed to look like. This should be at least our third major questioning of the narrator's credibility.

Our narrator then goes to the police and examines the file on the victim, whose name we learn is Ramírez (recall that we do not know the narrator's name). The police have no more information than the newspaper article. The narrator describes his bizarre "excitement" as he looks at the photo in the police file. Bizarre because this scene is devoid of tension, so the narrator's excitement is all internal: He is getting aroused by this in some way. This arousal will climax at the story's conclusion. The narrator then describes the victim, and in doing so betrays his own subjectivity once again:

esa larga y extraña nariz ¡que se parece tanto a un tapón de cristal que cubre la poma de agua de *mi* fonda!, esos bigotes largos y caídos; esa barbilla en punta; ese cabello lacio y alborotado. (40)

[that large and strange nose—it looked so much like the crystal stopper in the water carafe in *my* cheap little diner!—those large and limp whiskers, that little pointed beard; that straight, messy hair.]

The nose may be "large," but "strange" has no meaning for us unless we have a sense of the narrator's sense of normal. We do not find this out. He presumes that we know this, acting throughout as if his conclusions are so valid, his values to universal, that they require no further elaboration. The illogical reference to the similarity between Ramírez's nose and "the crystal stopper in the water carafe in *my* cheap little diner" should strike *us* as "strange," but this is merely a prologue to what occurs a few lines later: Staring at the photo, trying to figure out why the victim was killed, the narrator tells us:

Entonces confeccioné las siguientes lógicas conclusiones:
    El difunto Ramírez se llamaba Octavio Ramírez (un individuo con la nariz del difunto no puede llamarse de otra manera);

1: ANTI-REALISM BEFORE REALISM

Octavio Ramírez tenía cuarenta y dos años;
Octavio Ramírez andaba escaso de dinero;
Octavio Ramírez iba mal vestido; y, por último, nuestro difunto era extranjero.
Con estos preciosos datos, quedaba reconstruida totalmente su personalidad. (40)

[Then I concocted the following logical conclusions:
The deceased Ramírez was named Octavio Ramírez (anyone with a nose like that couldn't have had another name);
Octavio Ramírez was forty-two years old.
Octavio Ramírez had very little money.
Octavio Ramírez was poorly dressed; and, finally, our deceased was a foreigner.
With these precious data, his personality was totally reconstructed.]

Since the police have identified the victim—he was actually alive when they brought him in—his age, economic status, and the condition of his clothing may be precise empirical data, but the reader does not get this information from "reliable" sources, and this litany of knowable facts is derailed by the narrator's invention of a first name for Ramírez because "anyone with a nose like that couldn't have had another name," which is certainly not a very "logical" conclusion.

The victim's "vice" seems to be deduced in a more justifiable way. If the assault had been over a woman, a matter of honor, or even a simple fight, reasons the narrator, surely some witnesses would have corroborated this, or the victim would have been able to name his attackers. But since neither of these occurs, the narrator deduces that the victim was doing something shameful and therefore deliberately hidden. That done, however, the narrator proceeds to reconstruct an account of the event that is impossibly filled with the minutest details (e.g., the exact time at which certain events occurred). The best detectives always try to embellish the known in order to arrive at the unknown, but any reconstruction of events based on incomplete evidence is usually accompanied by some qualifiers, even if it is as simple as, "Here's what I think happened," or "He went out at *about* 8:00." The narrator in Palacio's story is not so modest. He says, without qualification, "He went out at 8:00" (41). Then:

Anduvo casi desesperado, durante dos horas, por las calles céntricas, fijando anhelosamente sus ojos brillantes sobre las espaldas de los hombres que encontraba. (42)

[He wandered almost desperately, for two hours, through the central streets, anxiously fixing his sparkling eyes on the backs of the men he encountered.]

Why are the victim's eyes "sparkling"? With what quality is the narrator infusing them? As the expression of desire or as the object of the narrator's desire? One curious aspect of this story is how difficult it is to specify at what point the "logical" or even "brilliant" Holmesian deductions blend into the arbitrary narrative embellishments of an obsessed storyteller—or further, the deranged visions of a lunatic—since the narrator continually betrays total confidence in his invention. There is no suggestion that the dialogue in the fateful encounter may have been "something like" what he presents us with, rather, the dialogue is reproduced *as dialogue*, as if this *is* what happened:

-¡Pst! ¡Pst!
  El muchacho se detuvo.
  -Hola rico. . . . ¿Qué haces por aquí a estas horas?
  -Me voy a mi casa. . . . ¿Qué quiere?
  -Nada, nada. . . . Pero no te vayas tan pronto, hermoso . . .
  Y lo cogió del brazo. (42)

Psst! Psst!
  The boy stopped.
  "Hey, cutie. What are you doing out this late?"
  "I'm going home. What do you want?"
  "Nothing, nothing. . . . But don't go so soon, pretty one . . .
  And he took the boy's arm.

And the final deluge of violence, containing an impossible exactness of unsubstantiated detail, is perhaps the place where, in spite of its furious cascade of brutal images, the text shows that it is merely confronting a void—the unknown—which the narrator is filling with his story, his own invention, and perhaps, very likely, his own vice and desire. So we may indeed have reconstructed an entire personality out of unknowns, but the question to ask then must be, Whose personality? The "vice-ridden" Ramírez? Or our hopelessly confused narrator, attempting to mask his own ridiculous emptiness with blind faith in European inductive methods, or, beyond that, revealing the "weakness" within himself as he attempts to expose it elsewhere? The final passage runs as follows:

Epaminondas, así debió llamarse el obrero, al ver en tierra a aquel pícaro, consideró que era muy poco castigo un puntapié, y le propinó

1: ANTI-REALISM BEFORE REALISM 37

dos más, espléndidos y maravillosos en el género, sobre la larga nariz que le provocaba como una salchicha.
 ¡Como debieron sonar esos maravillosos puntapiés!
 Como el aplastarse de una naranja, arrojada vigorosamente sobre un muro; como el caer de un paraguas cuya varillas chocan estremeciéndose; como el romperse de una nuez entre los dedos; ¡o mejor como el encuentro de otra recia suela de zapato contra otra nariz!
 Así:
 ¡Chaj! con un gran espacio sabroso
 ¡Chaj! [. . .]
 ¡Chaj!
 ¡Chaj! vertiginosamente,
 ¡Chaj!
 en tanto que mil lucesitas, como agujas, cosían las tinieblas. (43)

Epaminondas, which must be the worker's name, seeing the prick on the ground, considered that one kick was too little punishment, and gave him two more, splendid and marvellous ones, in that large nose that provoked him like a sausage.
 How those marvellous kicks must have sounded!
 Like the splattering of an orange, vigorously thrown against a wall; like the collapse of an umbrella whose ribs smack and shiver; like a nut cracked between two fingers; or better like the encounter of another firm soul of a shoe against another nose!
 Like this:
 Whack!
  with a delicious space between.
 Whack! [. . .]
 Whack!
 Whack! Dizzyingly,
 Whack!
 until a thousand points of light like needles pierced the darkness.

The apparently untroublesome creation of the worker's name (and a rather unusual one, too) is another example of the narrator's almost psychotic self-assurance, though he would call it "inductive logic," and the "sausage" simile, like that of the "big-assed" ("culotado") pipe, is one that the Freudians could surely exploit. There is also a highly questionable involvement, or empathy, perhaps a desire to be partaking, either as attacker or as victim, in this vertiginous, near-orgasmic display of violence. Thus the identity of the true "pervert" in this tale becomes highly problematized. Palacio's story simultaneously contains both a sociological tract *and* a tale of madness and horror after the style of Poe. If the juxtaposition of seemingly unrelated elements produces surrealism, this simultaneity produces an anti-realism, because in order to label the narrative as categorically one or the other, we must claim the authority to label one of the characters as "perverse"—either Ramirez, his attacker(s), or the narrator. After reading this tale, such an assertion of authority is not so easily made.

Many of the writers discussed in this study challenge authoritative narratives by juxtaposing them with the diverse, opposing voices of the marginalized victims of that authority. Palacio deconstructs authority by presenting the reader with a single authoritative voice that ultimately self-destructs, splitting in two and revealing itself to be unreliable, yet that nevertheless seems to come close to a plausible reconstruction of the events. Perhaps, in spite of our knowledge, narrative authority and credibility is scarcely more than an intangible act of faith on the part of the reader. And those faiths prosper that best absorb (and obscure) their contradictions.

2
Social Realism and Early Magic Realism: "Stone-faced Indians and Trees that Scream" Language and Nature as Historical Self-Image in Three Ecuadorian Novels (1933–1942)

Three events have been singled out by writers and critics as having propelled "modern" Ecuadorian literature into the twentieth century:[1] A general strike that ended on November 15, 1922, when government troops massacred approximately fifteen hundred people in Guayaquil, the U.S. stock-market crash of 1929, and the 1932 civil war, which was an unsuccessful attempt by the sierran landowners to reclaim power.[2] From colonial times the traditional power base had been the oligarchy of sierran landowners. But during the 1870s, foreign markets grew for coastal products—cocoa, coffee, and tagua nuts. There was a definitive shift from domestic consumption to export agriculture.[3] Between the 1860s and 1925, coastal banks replaced individual landowners as the major source of government revenue.[4] Eloy Alfaro's "Liberal Revolution," the 1895–96 civil war, represented the triumph of the mercantile coast over the feudal sierra.

But the Liberal policies were successful only while cocoa prices were high. World War I switched Ecuador's dependency on European and American markets to American markets alone, and during the postwar depression the price of cocoa on the New York market dropped from 26.75 cents per pound in 1920 to 5.75 cents per pound in 1921. A blight destroyed several crops. Between 1928 and 1931, export prices fell nearly 60 percent, and they continue to govern the general state of the economy to this day.[5] Despite the exploitation of Amazonian oil reserves in the 1970s, public finances are "at the mercy of fluctuations" in world markets, and exports still determine the level of government income.[6]

Natural disasters still devastate the economy, and Ecuador remains little more than one bad harvest away from famine—a condition that most of Europe threw off in the 1780s.[7] Topography has shaped Ecuador's political, economic, and social structure—its national consciousness. That consciousness is of course reflected in the literature.

Most of the major Ecuadorian writers of the 1930s came from Guayaquil. Growing up in this hot, tropical climate molded their consciousnesses accordingly. Anthony Burgess writes (about equatorial Africa):

> Tropical jungles could never have produced a poet like [Wordsworth], and, often, when we read him in the tropics, we find it hard to accept his belief in a kindly, gentle power brooding over nature—it does not fit in with snakes and elephants and tigers and torrential rain.[8]

It is equally difficult for North Americans in an industrialized society to appreciate the intimate and frightful relationship many Latin American authors have with their silvan climates:

> El habitante de estas regiones ha tenido siempre el hechizo del paisaje que es al mismo tiempo su madre, su nodriza, su amante y su verdugo.[9]

> [The inhabitant of these (jungle) regions has always been bewitched by this landscape that is at the same time one's mother, wet-nurse, lover and executioner.]

In the feudal sierra, the mountains are so steep that the distances between cities is rendered great: In the 1920s, it took five days to cover the 134 miles (223 kilometers) from Quito to Tulcán,[10] and Cuenca (the third largest city, which did not have a paved road connecting it to the rest of the country until the 1970s) lies only 120 miles (200 km) from Loja, yet the bus ride can take up to eighteen hours if it's the rainy season and the roads are muddy. The coast and the sierra engendered two completely different cultures that remain worlds apart. Political regionalism is still a powerful factor in the life of the nation.

Ecuador's love/hate relationship with nature continues even in the age of its OPEC membership. Oil prices are not markedly more stable than cacao prices, and the March 1987 earthquake severed the single oil pipeline from the Amazonian oilfields to the port of Esmeraldas, dropping oil revenue by 60 percent and tripling food prices (which never came back down). Twenty-five years after the "discovery" of oil deposits, more than half the population is still below the poverty level and as many as fifty children per day die of malnutrition and otherwise preventable diseases.[11]

Thus, while U.S. mythology looks back nostalgically to a West that was "won," Ecuador is still wrestling with one of its major antagonists: its own topography. Unlike Lukács's description of history as the "concrete precondition of the present,"[12] in Ecuador, in many ways, history *is* the present. Until the 1950s, 0.2 percent of landowners in the highlands controlled nearly half of the agricultural lands, and these figures have not changed much.[13] The dominant feature was the *huasipungo*: a system under which the Indians[14] living in a region were bought and sold with the land, which they worked in exchange for a small plot—the *huasipungo*—that was theirs to cultivate for themselves. Today, Indians may not be bought and sold, but they are still paying rent for land that they feel is rightfully theirs.

In terms of literary output, the modern era in Ecuadorian prose is securely in place with the publication *Los que se van* in 1930. This collaborative compilation of short stories by three *guayaquileños*, Demetrio Aguilera Malta, Enrique Gil Gilbert, and Joaquín Gallegos Lara, definitively severed Ecuadorian narrative style from the colonial pretensions that had characterized it since the Conquest. The dialogue was naturalistic and the plots were full of violence—verbal violence, slang and dirty words, and physical violence, reflecting the reality of Ecuador's history.[15]

In two novels of the coast and one of the sierra—Aguilera Malta's *Don Goyo* (1933), Gil Gilbert's *Nuestro Pan* (1942), and Jorge Icaza's *Huasipungo* (1934)[16]—ownership and control over land and people is established via the manipulation of language, particularly writing. In all three novels, the poor are robbed with fountain pens. In *Don Goyo*, two *cholos* (mountain Indians) travel to the coast looking for work and, in one scene, buy some food:

El dependiente les hizo cuentas en un papel de despacho. Puso todo como le dió la gana. Cuando terminó, les dijo: —Aqui está. Son quince sucres. Los cholos, sin desconfiar, pagaron. (57)

[The clerk put it all down on a piece of paper. In fact, he put down anything he wanted to. When he finished, he told them: —Here it is. It comes to fifteen sucres (a price inflated roughly ten times). The *cholos* paid without questioning.] (63)

This is not unique to Ecuador; there are similar scenes in North American novels of the 1930s, such as Erskine Caldwell's *Tobacco Road* (1932) and John Steinbeck's *The Grapes of Wrath* (1939), which will be discussed below. But the most significant example is when a *cholo* tells Don Goyo that the rich, white businessman, Don Carlos

> me empezó a sonsacar . . . Que si yo lo conocía a usted, que cuantos años tenía usted de vivir por estos lados, que quién era el dueño del Cerrito y que si tenía papeles . . . (151)

> [started pumping me . . . About whether I knew you or not, about how many years you've lived in these parts, about *who was the owner* of Cerrito (the island in the Guayas archipelago where the novel takes place) *and whether he had any papers to prove it.*] (173, emphasis mine)

We have seen this scene played out countless times in the North American "struggle" to "win" the West: pieces of paper that "prove" that newly arrived Europeans own land that the Native Americans have been cultivating for thousands of years.

In *Nuestro Pan*, another Indian worker experiences the mysteries of the white man's writing:

> El lápiz llenaba la blanca cuartilla de arabescos negros. Saltaba ágil, dejando la línea, recta, curva. mixta. (2:90)

> [The pencil filled a sheet of white paper with black arabesques. It bounded along nimbly, making straight lines, curved lines, and a mixture of both.] (232)

The issue is developed further when Captain Sandoval, the fictionalized essence of the Ecuadorian myth of the "good dictator," is fighting for the *Alfaristas* in the civil war of 1912 (although no year is given). He and his men are so deep in the coastal jungle that they find out that the war they have been fighting has been over for several weeks. Thus, taking part in history has removed him from history, and so he chooses to remain outside of history by staying in the jungle to work on Don Bartolomé's *hacienda*. But the jungle *is* Ecuador's history, and so the former cannot be escaped in the latter. Don Bartolomé puts Captain Sandoval's jungle fighting experience to work. Aragundi Indians are grazing cattle on a nearby plain:

> ¿Y? ¿Quién va a pagar el alquiler?
>   ¿Alquiler? ¡Si éste es sitio comunero, so vivo! (1:123–24)

> ["And who's going to pay the rent for it?" (asks the landowner's hired hand)

2: SOCIAL REALISM AND EARLY MAGIC REALISM 43

"Rent? This is communal land, and you know it!" (answer the Indians)] (107)

Somewhat more moderate than their North American counterparts, the landowners kill only the minimum number of Indians that allows them to begin clearance for cultivation of rice, the export that most interests the rich, white, foreign businessmen.

The meaning of language, specifically the disparity between two drastically different signifieds assigned to the same signifier, is the core conflict in *Huasipungo*. As described above, a *huasipungo* is the small piece of land the peasant Indians get to cultivate for themselves. The Indians believe the *huasipungos* to be theirs permanently. The landowners—or in this case a single landowner, Don Alfonso—believes the *huasipungos* to be his gift, to be revoked or shifted at his whim. There is a brief stumbling over the gap between rhetoric and reality when Don Alfonso discusses buying a piece of land "with the Indians" because "the lands without the Indians are worth nothing," and the corrupt, lecherous priest tells him:

Son más de quinientos . . . a los cuales, gracias a mi paciencia, a mi fe, a mis consejos y a mis amenazas, he logrado hacerles entrar por el camino del Señor. Ahora se hallan listos a . . . —iba a decir: "a la venta", pero le pareció muy duro el término, y, luego de una pequeña vacilación, continuó— . . . al trabajo. (93)

[There are more than five hundred (Indians) . . . who, thanks to my patience, my faith, my counsel, and my threats, I have made follow the way of the Lord. Now they are ready for . . ." He was going to say, "for sale," but the word seemed too harsh, and, so after a slight hesitation, he continued, "For work."] (30)

And in one remarkable exchange, Don Alfonso's foreman expresses doubt over his master's ability to neutralize the Indians' interpretation of the sign *huasipungo*:

—Y estos indios puercos que se han agarrado para sus huasipungos los terrenos más fértiles de las orillas del río.
—Eso desde siempre mismo.
—Carajo. Para el otro año que me desocupen todo y se vayan a levantar las chozas en los cerros. . . . No es la primera vez que ordeno.
—¿Y quién les quita, pes?
—¡Yo, carajo!
—Uuu. (139)

["And these Indian pigs have seized the most fertile lands on both river banks for their huasipungos."
"That's how it has always really been."
"Goddam. By next year they'll have to clear out of that whole area. . . . This isn't the first time I've ordered them to move."
"And who is going to take their lands away, (then)?"
"I am, goddamit!"
"Yeah?"] (85)

Don Alfonso invalidates the Indians' claim to ownership by labeling the land as "seized." The foreman inadvertently reinforces the Indians' claim with the word "always." Don Alfonso then attempts to undo the power of this "always" by noting that "this isn't the first time" he has moved them. But when asked who is going to remove the Indians—or "seize their lands," the Spanish is ambiguous—that is, who is going to transform this debate over language into concrete actions, the foreman expresses his own doubt that Don Alfonso can accomplish this.[17]

Instead of moving the Indians, the landlord chooses not to go ahead with the annual dredging of the river bed, knowing that this will soon cause the river to flood and wash away all the *huasipungos*. But unleashing nature is not effective enough. In this novel, the Indians *are* nature, and in the end the army has to be called out to squash the inevitable rebellion. (This anthropomorphism recurs throughout these works.) The final scene, after the massacre, redoubles this association:

Al amanecer, entre los chozas deshechas, entre los escombrios, entre las cenizas, entre los cadáveres tibios aún, surgieron, como en los sueños, sementeras de brazos flacos como espigas de cebada que, al dejarse acariciar por los vientos helados de los páramos de América, murmuraron en voz ululante de taladro:
—¡Ñucanchic huasipungo! (245)

[At dawn, up from the demolished huts, from the rubble, from the ashes, from the still warm corpses, as if in a dream, a crop of thin arms sprouted like spikes of barley. Strummed by the icy winds off the paramos of all the Americas they emitted a piercing screeching cry:
"Ñucanchic huasipungo!" (The huasipungos are ours!")] (216)

Some expansion of the discussion of this lexical conflict over the meaning of the word *huasipungo* is required, since it is centered on a significant but seemingly simple difference in the denotative definition of a single term.

For many critics, the novel *Huasipungo* represents the peak of the indigenist, social realist novel.[18] For Irlemar Chiampi, *Huasipungo* is more of a trough. To Chiampi, the classic works of Latin American regionalist realism are as old, mechanical, empty, and monotonous as worn-out political pamphlets, endlessly describing the relationship of "exploiters vs. exploited" and little else.[19]

While a number of the social realist novels of the 1930s can indeed be criticized in this way, Bakhtinian thought opens up the possibility of recovering *Huasipungo* from this undesirable location. Although Icaza's novel has been criticized for being "about" Indians and not "of" or "by" Indians, its central conflict foregrounds a cultural and linguistic presentation of two wor(l)ds that oppose one another. In the end, the indigenous community is decimated, but their words remain, metamorphosed and joining the "icy winds of all the Americas."

By contrast, there is no communication at all between whites/*mestizos* and Indians in the work of Peruvian writer José María Arguedas, only violence, according to Alberto Flores Galindo ("Entre mistis e indios no hay comunicación . . . La única mediación que existe es la violencia").[20] Although this may be true in general, Arguedas's *Yawar Fiesta* (1941) complicates this model considerably: there are sympathetic bourgeois *mestizos* and unsympathetic Indians who have left their land, gone to the capital (Lima), and been "converted" to the dominant ideology. Of the utmost significantce, this complex dialogue has taught the indigenous population how to use the dominant language to their own advantage: unlike the miserable Indians in *Huasipungo*, feminized in terms of their conflict with the phallic, monosexual ruling language, the Indians in *Yawar Fiesta* have learned how to use texts and methods that had previously been used to oppress them:

> From so much going into offices, from so much running to and fro about the documents with which their lands were being taken away, the Puquios learned to defend themselves in lawsuits, buying judges, court clerks, and notaries.[21]

There is no comparable reversal in *Huasipungo*. A reversal occurs, but, as always in the Ecuadorian indigenist novels, to the Indians' disadvantage. Indigenous Andean cultures have repeatedly demonstrated a lively capacity to absorb Western/European ideas and imagery, infusing them with a multiplicity of meanings absent from or deeply submerged within their more or less monologic original, intended meanings. Reproductions of *mestizo* paintings of the

"Poor-Christ" and "Indian Christ" ("Cristo-pobre" and "Cristo-indio") are still visible on the streets of Cuenca, Ecuador, and even the image of Christ on the cross can acquire "obscure" traces of the earthquake-making Incan god, Pachacamac.[22]

In *Huasipungo* we have the opposite situation: *huasipungo*, after all, is a Quichua word, not a Spanish word, so the intended meaning in Quichua should dominate—which of course does not happen. As Raymond Williams points out, signs are not "arbitrary." Power determines the " 'correct' or 'proper' meaning of those signs."[23] Even the authority of "timeless" tradition is undone by a surgically precise application of the dominant ideology that equates history with civilization, and myth, or "timeless" religious history, with barbarism.[24] Thus the Indians' claim that "That's the way it's always been," regarding the meaning of *huasipungo*, is turned into a liability that works against them in the dominant language and ideological system that has been imposed upon them. All they can do is repeat, "The huasipungos are ours!" but this does not make it true.[25]

Unlike the diffuse, bureaucratic oppression that is present in *Yawar Fiesta* and such works of North American social realism as *The Grapes of Wrath*—in which shotgun-wielding Oakies threaten a tractor driver who is about to destroy their home, only to find that he is just another working man with a family to feed, leading them to ask in frustration, "But where does it stop? Who can we shoot?"[26]—in *Huasipungo*, there *is* someone the Indians can "shoot": the landowner, Don Alfonso. His near-total control of the region is continually stressed in the novel, although he is helped along by a corrupt bishop and ultimately by the army, it is his word that brings the army, and his command that they follow. Thus the Indians are so disenfranchised and downtrodden that even though they are in the rare situation of having a single human target on whom to put most of the blame for their wretched situation, they are (apparently) incapable of realizing the simplest solution, namely killing him, because they persist in their belief that the conflict is a misunderstanding over the meaning of a word.

Bakhtin might term this a "realistic emblematic," in which "an enormous event [is] portrayed on a small scale."[27] The Ecuadorian social realists made exhaustive use of this tactic, but typically in the context of a physical conflict, not a linguistic one. Certainly Steinbeck makes liberal use of it in *The Grapes of Wrath*, with Preacher Casy and Rose of Sharon being sometimes obvious symbolic stand-ins for Jesus and The Virgin Mary, but here, too, the usage is mythological, archetypal, not linguistic.

Bakhtin writes that "unitary language" operates "in the midst of heteroglossia," and at "at any given moment of its evolution, language is stratified."[28] Thus the dominant definition of *huasipungo* can never be the only one, and so force is required to impose the dominant definition on the heteroglossic physical world. The Indians recognize the incompatability of the two definitions, and the conflict between them, but seem to feel that the age of their tradition and their strength in numbers as they all chant, "The huasipungos are ours!" should be sufficient to secure the "dominance" of their definition of the term.

Each side is aware of the existence of the other definition, but neither engages in a dialogue with the other definition. Both sides are fixed in their views, and in the end, guns decide whose definition triumphs. The author, Jorge Icaza, is the one who presents the dialogue. According to Bakhtin,

> the novelistic hybrid is an artistically organized system for bringing different languages in contact with one another, a system having as its goal the illumination of one language by means of another, the carving-out of a living image of another language.[29]

Although Icaza's representation of indigenous culture is troublesome for today's critics because of its plainness, its neutrality, its peripheral understanding of the culture depicted, neutrality was perhaps a necessary step in the move from picturesque and stereotypical representations toward novels written from indigenous perspectives by indigenous writers, which, some critics contend, have yet to be written in Ecuador. And rather than the simple oppressor-oppressed model of much Ecuadorian social realism, the two cultures exist in some ways on equal terms in this novel—novels being perhaps the only place in some societies where this can happen.

One more quote from Bakhtin, who writes:

> Every discourse has its own selfish and biased proprietor; there are no words with meanings shared by all, no words 'belonging to no one.' . . . All direct meanings and direct expressions are false.[30]

Thus there must be a "radical scepticism toward any unmediated discourse" (perhaps because there is no such thing as unmediated discourse). The Indians seem to learn this, but in the end, have nothing left but the "dignity" of knowing who is crushing them.[31]

As discussed above, in many Ecuadorian novels of this period, humans and nature have a two-way anthropormorphous relationship that is unlike dominant European models. In an oft-cited article, Sherry Ortner notes that in many societies female goddesses are worshipped while human females are demeaned.[32] In *Nuestro Pan*, the jungle is a woman, and woman as jungle is respected while woman as woman is not. But the fearsome jungle river, so near the ocean that it swarms with crocodiles *and* sharks, is an estuary, so its current continually reverses direction. Further textures await. A worker named Moreira, haunted by a murder he committed years before, thinks:

> Si se pudiese coger al tiempo como a veces se coge la corriente de los ríos y se lleva por donde es la voluntad del hombre. (1:49)

> [If only a man could catch hold of time, as sometimes he catches the current of a river and is carried by it wherever he wishes to go.] (21)

So feminized nature is also time that flows both ways. Only Moreira is stuck in linear time. His corporeality is too real (despite frequent visions of the ghost of the woman he murdered). By contrast, Don Goyo enters cyclical, eternal time by becoming one with the ocean after his bodily death. This is a key element in magic realist texts.

In *Nuestro Pan*, nature is often highly anthropomorphic, but not necessarily magic. The wind snarls "like a mad dog," trees have "bony arm[s]," the earth holds back its fertility, "just like a woman" that needs to be "tamed," rice doesn't grow four feet high, the "ripe ears" come up to "the women's breasts," land grows fertile "like a girl of fourteen," and repeatedly the characters' sweat and blood mingle with the earth and mud (5, 9, 38, 72, 149).[33] It is particularly interesting that once Sandoval's son goes off to the big city to learn engineering and returns with heavy machinery to replace the workers, their blood now mingles with gasoline in the fertile earth (237). Thus a connection is forged between the vital fluids of humans, plants, earth, and machines (cf. also *The Grapes of Wrath*: when Tom Joad cuts his hand while fixing the truck, his blood flows down and mixes with the crank-case oil [188]).[34]

There is also a strikingly emblematic passage in the novel:

> Del este venía, por un aire claro y luminoso, el azul andino de las montañas. Y casi confundido con las nubes indendiaba apenas su cabeza densa de nieve el Chimborazo remoto. Mientras el río Guayas pasabe ancho, fuerte, espeso, forcejando entre la margen de yerba y la áspera margen de cemento. (2:51)

2: SOCIAL REALISM AND EARLY MAGIC REALISM 49

[In the east, through the clear luminous air, the Andean blue of the highest ranges was faintly showing. Almost indistinguishable from the clouds, the snow-capped head of Chimborazo glowed with remote fire. Meanwhile the Guayas flowed wide, powerful and turbid, thrusting its current against grassy banks and harsh levees of concrete.] (193)

This mythopoetic passage is a description of the National Seal of Ecuador, displayed in all public offices and on the currency. This is the Ecuadorian construct of nature as self-image *par excellence* and would be as instantly recognizable to the Ecuadorian reader as if I were to describe a scene for U.S. readers in which figured, say, purple mountain majesties above a fruited plain.

In *Don Goyo*, nature is more protean, alternating between masculine and feminine, between plant and animal species. The *cholos'* bodies smell of fish, some say "their souls too" (55), and the mangrove trees they cut down to sell to the Guayaquil businessman become their bodies as well, first by empathy:

—Hoy me ha dolido cada hachazo para tumbar mangle, como si me le pegara yo mismo. (84)

[Every time I swung the axe today to fell a *mangle*, I felt as if I were cutting myself down.] (97)

Then the trees, whose "seamed knots looked like entrails torn out" (89) actually speak to Don Goyo and tell him they they are leaving unless the *cholos* stop cutting *mangle*. When Don Goyo switches to catching shellfish instead, the islands surrender "like lascivious women" to him (149). But the other *cholos* cannot make a living shellfishing and go back to cutting *mangle*, at which point, "A kind of scream emerged from every slashed *mangle*" (180). The *cholos'* way of life is doomed for not listening to the trees and for selling their bodies—tree trunks and human trunks—to the city-based capitalists.

Ortner suggests that the male/female division in society places woman in secondary roles because man creates "lasting, eternal, transcendent objects, while the woman creates only perishables—human beings."[35] In the Ecuadorian novels studied here, *all* is perishable. Again, the contrast is between a North American/European mythology of nature as Other and as conquered, and the Ecuadorian reality-*cum*-mythology of nature as self and perpetual adversary. *Nuestro Pan* ends with the fertile, life-giving/life-taking river flooding and reclaiming all of the land the Sandoval dynasty has worked for (and murdered for). It flows both ways.

The Seal of Ecuador. Compare the central image to the scene depicted in Gil Gilbert's *Nuestro Pan*.

Huasipungo has a similarly destructive flood and a landowner who believes he is taming the region and bringing civilization.[36]

"Soy la cabeza de la gran muchedumbre. La antorcha encendida. Sin mí no habría nada en esta tierra miserable." (122)

["I am the chief of a mass of workers. The flaming torch. Without me, there would be nothing in this whole damned region."] (64)

Don Alfonso labels the road he is building through a swamp that regularly sucks Indian laborers down into it as an artery, "the very life of towns" (73), projecting the standard European image of man conquering nature, in marked contrast to the capricious, anthropomorphous two-way "life" of the jungle. And in a typical passage, the Indians are described as "immobile as ageless stone" (99). This has dual significance. The Cañari Indians of the high sierra were animists. They worshiped stones with unusual markings (marble is native to the region), particularly if they bore or could be altered to bear a resemblance to human features. Ecuador's most important pre-Incan Cañari cultural remnant is a seventy-five-foot high face carved out of the mountainside approximately ten thousand feet above sea level. Clearly, Icaza is addressing an audience that would immediately associate "ageless stone" Indian features with this enormous sculpture that is not a sculpture but is in fact part of the very earth, the mountains that have shaped Ecuadorian history from the beginning.

The other association would be with Rumiñahui, the last native Ecuadorian general who resisted the Spanish until the end, then burned the northern Incan capital to the ground (the present site of Quito) and retreated—legend has it—into the eastern mountains with a fortune in treasure that no one has ever recovered. "Rumiñahui" means "Stone-face," and he now grimaces defiantly from the thousand-sucre note, which is a bit like the United States putting Sitting Bull on the $20 bill.

Certain elements of magic realism function as nonchronological history in these works. Two theorists are of particular use in examining how the native South American Indians' worldview was filtered through the European-style literature of the *mestizo* authors to create a third, thoroughly new form that resembles other European "modernisms" only in the end result, but not in the formation process.

Don Goyo is a proto-magic realist text.[37] Cueva also considers it Social Realism, but realism of "another reality."[38] To Cueva, the

La Cara del Inca. The misleadingly named "Face of the Inca" at Ingapirca (Province of Cañar, Ecuador).

political shock of the "progressive" capitalists turning their guns on working men and women in 1922 propelled Ecuador from feudalism to modernism in one decade, creating a group of "indigenist" socialist realists whose originality, verve, and stylistic cohesiveness is unmatched by any other literary movement in Ecuador's history. While Cueva's orthodox Marxist approach stretches some cases quite far to make them fit his framework, he makes the point that the "magical" or "mythic" elements in these authors are still more "realistic" than the false baroque style of their colonial predecessors.[39] Like Carpentier before him, Cueva suggests that while European authors such as Mann and Joyce had to turn their literary sights inward to bring *The Magic Mountain* and *Ulysses* to the discourses of modernism, Ecuadorian authors after 1922 merely had to look at their world "as it really was" to produce works that Europeans and Americans would label "magical":

Nuestro mundo es de todos modos otra cosa, tal como aparece en *Los Sangurimas*, en *Don Goyo*, en *La isla virgen*: sus personajes son los árboles y los ríos antropomórficos, los patriarcas de prole más numeros que los granos de una mazorca de maíz, los héroes visiblemente no problemáticos que se ufanan de que "por cada hijo que han hecho han deshecho el hijo de otro"; dentro de una temporalided dilatada y gelatinosa que, al igual que los demás elementos, presagia ya *Cien años de soledad* y, con su violencia torrencial, también *Crónica de una muerte anunciada*.[40]

[Our world is completely another world, just as it appears in *Los Sangurimas* (José de la Cuadra, 1934), *Don Goyo* and *La isla virgen* (Aguilera Malta, 1933, 1942): their characters are trees and the rivers are anthropomorphic, the family patriarchs more numerous than the kernels in an ear of corn, heroes visibly unpurturbed and proud that "for every child they have made, they have unmade someone else's child"; within a dilated and gelatinous time scheme that, along with other elements, firmly presages *One Hundred Years of Solitude* and, with its torrential violence, *Chronicle of a Death Foretold*.]

The literature of any country is inextricably bound up with its history. In Ecuador, part of this is simple demographics: The country is roughly 40 percent "pure" Indian and 40 percent *mestizo* (literally, "mixed"). The remainder are Europeans, Afro-Ecuadorians, and Asians. By far the majority of Ecuadorian industrial and commercial workers, doctors, lawyers, bureaucrats, politicians, professors, and literati are *mestizos*. This historically tangible physical synthesis of European and Native American culture has produced a comparable intellectual synthesis as well, at least in literature. (*Mestizo* bankers are not especially sympathetic to Indian causes.) According to C. Michael Waag, European-style literature tends toward mortal characters in linear, sequential narrative. By contrast:

> Las vidas de los Amautas y su lucha contra la opresión se repitan inevitablemente en los ciclos de un tiempo que se repite eternamente. Este concepto es el que predomina en la cosmovisión indígena de América.[41]

> [The lives of the Amauta (Indians) and their struggle against oppression are inevitably repeated in temporal cycles that repeat eternally. This concept predominates the indigenous American cosmovision.]

Waag cites a later work by Aguilera Malta, *El secuestro del general* (1973), in which characters devoured by pirañas come back to life and a General tells a priest, "But you don't exist. You're only a legend" ("Pero usted no existe. Sólo es una leyenda"). The priest explains,

> A veces, la leyenda es más verdadera que la verdad que captan los sentidos. La verdad—mi verdad—es que vivo, muero, y vuelvo a vivir, y vuelvo a morir, y vuelvo a vivir en una rotación constante.[42]

> [Sometimes, legend is more truthful than truth as perceived by the senses. The truth—my truth—is that I live, die, and live again, and die again and live again in constant rotation.]

We see this reality "of another reality" operating in *Don Goyo*, when a wise old man, Don Encarna (whose name means "incarnate," to make living flesh out of), tells stories that *he* is convinced are absolutely true:

> Si, por casualidad—cuando hacía hablar a un caimán o bailar a un difunto en una de sus charlas—alguien se reía, don Encarna enmudecía, cogía su sombrero, se terciaba el poncho a la espalda y se marchaba, para no volver hasta después de algunos días:
> —¡Todos son unos desgraciados . . . ! (18–19)

> [If by chance someone laughed—when he was making a crocodile speak or a dead man dance in one of his tales—Don Encarna would stop talking, pick up his hat, throw his poncho over his shoulder and leave, not to return for at least a week:
> —Bunch of fools . . . (18)

The nonbelieving audience of *cholos* and *mestizos* are becoming like the "white" man by insisting on mortal characters and linear time in the old man's tales. Having warned the reader against this response, Aguilera Malta appropriates Don Encarna's narrative techniques:

> Voces aguardentosas coreaban al cantor. La casa temblaba. Afuera, la noche prendía sus dientes negros sobre el vientre fecundo de la tierra. (29)

> [Voices raucous with liquor joined the singer in the chorus. The house trembled. Outside, night sank its black teeth into the fertile belly of the earth.] (28)

There are many other instances of such "incarnating" in *Don Goyo*. Axes "listen," trees think and act, and after his death,

> Allá, en el centro del río, estaba don Goyo. Parecía abofetear la negrura de la noche. Se deslizaba sobre el agua como sobre la tierra firme. Tenía un aspecto de fortaleza que nunca se le viera. Iba rodeado de tiburones y catanudos, que parecían seguirlo sumisamente, hilvanando alfombras de espuma a su pase. Estaba completamente desnudo. Reía con una extraña rise triunfal. (168–69)

> [There, in the middle of the river, was Don Goyo. He seemed to be slapping at the blackness of the night. He was sliding over the water as if he were on solid ground. His strength seemed greater than ever before. All around him were hammerheads and tiger sharks that appeared to follow him submissively, weaving carpets of foam as he moved. He was absolutely naked. He was laughing a strange, triumphant laugh.] (192)

But one of the main curiosities is that the author has actually inserted an object lesson in how *not* to react to his text.

Aside from anthropomorphic trees and a woman's ghost, *Nuestro Pan* has other ghosts as well:

> Cuando la luna viene, los fantasmas del río salen a caminar. Pasan manos de ahogados, tiesas, chorreando agua, magras, enverdecidas, luminosas. (2:95)

> [When the moon rises the river ghosts come out to walk. Stiffly, from the passing current, rise the hands of dead men, thin dripping hands, hands that glimmer with a greenish light.] (239)[43]

In reality, the river *has* swallowed up the lives and bodies of the rice paddy workers. But if this is "social realism," as Cueva labels it, it is truly "realism of another reality,"[44] hence my provocational coinage, social magic realism.

Even *Huasipungo*, a work so enthusiastically realist that it has been compared to Steinbeck's *The Pearl* (see Cruz), is full of images that amplify or explode the real. Two examples: The wealthy landowner Don Alfonso and his family are traveling by horse along a precipitous mountain trail to examine the site for the new road. They get to a quagmire so deep and slippery that to attempt to continue on horseback would be deadly. So the family dismounts, their delicate feet never touching the ground, and *climb on the backs* of their Indian guides, who then carry their "precious cargos" the rest of the way (13), their feet sinking deeper into the fetid mud under the weight of the load: About as precise and potent an image of capital riding on the back of labor as one could ask for. Although the scene implies quite bitterly that the Indians are worth less than the horses, it could also be read as silhouetting the fragility, the almost ridiculous precariousness of the grip on power the wealthy have over the oppressed masses.

Don Alfonso's daughter is portrayed as a lascivious oppressor of the fertile, faithful Indians. After she gives birth out of wedlock, her upper-class breasts are found to be *dry*. The solution is to find an Indian wet-nurse. To the Indian women who haven't enough to feed their starving children, the job of wet-nurse would literally be a life-saver. In their exhuberance to prove how full of milk they are, the Indian women beg the landowner's mayordomo to look at their breasts; the most desperately motivated

> sin ningún rubor, sacáronse los senos y exprimiéronles para enredar hilos de leche frente a la cara impasible de la mula que jineteaba el mayordomo.
> —¡No se ordeñen en los ojos del animal carajo! (100)

> unblushingly took out their breasts and squeezed them to weave threads of milk in the impassive face of the mule which the mayordomo was riding.
> "Don't squirt your milk in the animal's eyes, goddamit!" (38)

This may indeed qualify as social realism—surely the desperation of starving people is no laughing matter—but it seems unlikely that Stalin's censors would have tolerated the possible humor generated by such an otherwise gray passage. Although the miserly infertility of the bourgeoisie is marvellously contrasted with the bountiful fertility of the peasants, it also provides a moment of absurd comic relief that brings to mind a scene from Buñuel rather than Pudovkin.

At the same time, the scene also clearly accomplishes its mission of symbolically condemning how Ecuador's plentiful resources are being wasted on uncaring, unworthy consumers. The powerful, even divine, symbolism of breast milk is exploited in the closing scene of Steinbeck's *The Grapes of Wrath*, in which the mother who has just lost her baby instead nurses a starving man of "about fifty" to keep him alive. Such a scene, written in plain documentary prose, nevertheless deliberately strikes a vibratory chord within the Western reader, who reflexively conjures up an illuminated image of a madonna and child and/or the *pietà*. Such mythic associations lead the reader slightly beyond reality—call it the extra-real (since few would call Steinbeck a surrealist), throwing a numinous template over the reality described. Is that "magic realism"? This is the same effect we see working in these Ecuadorian novels. But what are the "mythic associations" for the Latin American audience? The national seal? Labor supporting capital? Ninety-nine percent of Ecuadorians are Roman Catholic, and so could be expected to respond "mythically" to the nursing mother in the barn. *Huasipungo* predates *The Grapes of Wrath* by five years and *The Pearl* (to which it has been compared)[45] by thirteen. It therefore seems reasonable to suggest that the literary styles U.S. readers are trained to associate with authors such as Faulkner, Hemingway, and Steinbeck were part of a much broader discourse than is typically acknowledged.

Pareja Diezcanseco writes that he and "el grupo de Guayaquil" were visited during the 1930s by such prominent American writers as John Dos Passos and Thornton Wilder.[46] Did literary influence travel primarily from the North Atlantic to the South Atlantic, as is commonly professed in the U.S. literary media?[47] Or did it travel from South to North? (a case can be made for this: *Huasipungo* was Ecuador's first international best-seller.) Of course, it probably traveled both ways—but, as in all discourse, power determines whose version dominates.

This leads to the concluding discussion of *The Grapes of Wrath*. Although there are many reasons to question and perhaps undermine the form of comparison that, for example, labels Toshiro Mifune as "the Japanese John Wayne," such a method is sometimes a necessary shorthand for attempting to bridge a cultural gap, even if at a possibly contrived common point. For many historical reasons, a U.S. citizen could be told that *Huasipungo* is "the Ecuadorian *The*

Grapes of Wrath" (just as an Ecuadorian could be told that *The Grapes of Wrath* is "the American *Huasipungo*"): both are socially conscious realist novels of the 1930s; both depict the sufferings of a few named and a great many unnamed, anonymous masses of people on whose backs the oppressive socioeconomic structure rests; and both happened to sell extremely well (*Huasipungo* sold more copies during the decade than any other Ecuadorian novel, although most of them were printed in other countries in pirated editions for which the author, of course, was not paid).

This brief description, of course, fits a great many novels. But the common point has been formulated, and the most convenient place to begin to stretch that point to fit my argument is the realm of lexical dispute and Bakhtinian dialogics, where the signifier's meaning begins to float. Both novels put a great deal of emphasis on the representation of stratified speech communities. In the worlds of these novels, poor folk generally tell the truth and some representatives of the "upper" working class and the middle class, such as truck drivers, storekeepers, and small farmers, can be sympathetic (while many are not) and can be spoken to on more equal terms; any higher on the socioeconomic scale and their words turn into lies.

Some of the workings of the power behind the system are explored in *Huasipungo*. The capital behind Don Alfonso is revealed in the person of his more powerful and phallic uncle, who is himself backed by thoroughly abstract U.S. business interests. The priest as well is shown to be quite corrupt as he charges Andres Chiliquinga, the central Indian character, more money for a grave closer to the church so that his wife Cunshi will get into heaven faster (183ff).[48] In *The Grapes of Wrath*, the upper-class owners and bankers are never shown, only their lower representatives: men in cars wearing suits, cops, guards, foremen, vigilantes—all of whom lie. This contradiction is continually stressed; Steinbeck repeatedly points out that the migrants and the vigilantes are the "same folk," which is to say that they are all white.

The absence of racial difference in *The Grapes of Wrath* (except for a few Native American characters who seem naturally to accept and fit in with "authentic, honest" [i.e., poor] white culture) differs considerably from *Huasipungo*'s famous indigenism. Racial hegemony is assumed in *The Grapes of Wrath*, and the class conflict is played out almost entirely between the lowest representatives of capital stepping on the lowest level of labor. Just how similar the two groups are is exemplified by the passage in which the vigilantes are described as follows:

the clerks who drilled at night owned nothing, and the little storekeepers possessed only a drawerful of debts. But even a debt is something (312).

Once the poor laborers are labeled "migrants," towns turn hostile and "clerks and storekeepers with shotguns" guard the world "against their own people" (312). These "people" are the plain, honest folks who up until the Dust Bowl have apparently lived in a world where differences are overcome naturally (by the men getting drunk together), where the sexual union between a "Texas boy" and a "Cherokee girl" is presented as natural and inevitable; trying to stop it would be like trying to stop "the fall from comin' " and "the sap from movin' in the trees," where mistakenly stolen property is returned, where they make their own laws that are understood without so much as a single word being spoken, where a self-governing, utopic "government camp" can be created where the *oppressors* need valid texts to enter (arrest warrants; 29, 45, 214, 326, 364).

Like the word *huasipungo*, characters in *The Grapes of Wrath* must learn to fight over the competing meanings of the word "Okie." A fellow dust bowl refugee tells Tom Joad:

> Okie use' ta mean you was from Oklahoma. Now it means you're a dirty son-of-a-bitch. Okie means you're scum. Don't mean nothing itself, it's the way they say it. (225)

Very soon after, a representative of California's police authority calls Ma Joad a "goddamn" Okie, and Tom confirms that it's "how they say it" that makes them feel bad (235, 237). There is also a report of a boy's fight in school over the locals' use of the term (374).

This questioning of authoritative labeling occurs in many other locations in *The Grapes of Wrath*. When Tom would rather spend the night sleeping in the dirt by the side of the road than spend fifty cents to sleep in a different patch of dirt twenty yards away that has been designated by the authorities as a lawful place to spend the night, he is told that California has "Got a law against sleepin' out in this State. Got a law about vagrants." Tom replies, "If I pay you half a dollar I ain't a vagrant, huh?" (205). He receives an oral report about the existence of a written text that labels him as something negative, and he responds with an acknowledgment that if he performs the act of recognizing the economics behind the text that would label him, then the label will not be applied to him. The conversation continues:

"the time ain't come when us local folks got to take no talk from you goddamn bums, neither."

"It don't trouble you none to take our four bits. An' when'd we get to be bums? We ain't asked ya for nothin.' " (205)

Later on in the novel, the men have learned that "a vagrant is anybody a cop don't like" (369).

But "honest" speech is still worth something. Later in the scene above, a "ragged man" approaches to tell his own horrible tale of starvation and death in California. The proprietor attempts to undo the man's words with his own, more authoritative words: "Prob'ly shif'less. They's so goddamn many shif'less fellas on the road now" (210). But Casy is the proprietor's equal, at least in this speech community, and declares,

"He's tellin' the truth, awright. The truth for him. He wasn't makin' nothin' up."

"How about us?" Tom demanded. "Is that the truth for us?"

"I don' know," said Casy. (210–211)

Casy's willingness to acknowledge the limitations of his verbal authority is not shared by most of the authoritative figures in this text. Casy even gets arrested, not for kicking a cop in the head and knocking him unconscious, which is the obvious crime, but, according to his own verbal reshaping of the event, for talking back (294).

Similar to the floating signifiers *Okie* and *vagrant*, the term *red* is used so indiscriminately by the representatives of oppressive authority that its meaning becomes so diluted as to cover everybody— that is, as one boss explains, "any son-of-a-bitch that wants thirty cents an hour when we're payin' twenty-five!" To which the seemingly bewildered fruitpicker replies, "Why, I want thirty cents an hour. Ever'body does. Hell, Mr. Hines, we're all reds" (329).

Authority did not initially manifest its power through texts. In chapter 19 of *The Grapes of Wrath*, we are told that California once belonged to Mexico, but squatters invaded and soon, after a few harvests, possession became ownership (254; this is remarkably similar to the establishment of a matriarchal domain in *Los Sangurimas*: see chapter 3). The crucial point is that this is exactly the "Okies" claim to the land that they have been sharecropping: that living and working and dying on the land makes that land *theirs*. But as always, power decides whose definition of the same concept triumphs. There is even fear of new squatters in California, because the system still apparently recognizes planting and harvesting as signifying ownership. We are then informed that the big California land owners "imported slaves, *although they did not call them slaves*: Chinese, Japanese, Mexicans, Filipinos" (255; emphasis mine).

It is significant to note how the authority of texts is constantly undermined, then reestablished, in this novel. The Joads have lived virtually all their lives in the oral world of Bakhtinian innocents.[49] Tom is knowledgable enough and experienced enough to know what speech acts will cross local class boundaries, namely, setting them in opposition to larger ones. A truck driver from whom Tom is trying to hitch a ride points to an authoritative text that declares No Riders. Tom replies, "Sure—I seen it. But sometimes a guy'll be a good guy even if some rich bastard makes him carry a sticker" (7). But he is also able to play the part of a Bakhtinian naïf since he is returning to his parched, dry homeland after a four-year absence in prison, knowing nothing of the disasters that have befallen the Oklahoma farmers and thus rendering the familiar as strange. Similarly, later on in the novel, the Joad family inadvertently takes on a job as strikebreakers before they realize what they have done (406). But they are not alone. Masses of people from the Midwest and Southwest "had not grown up in the paradoxes of industry" (311).

These paradoxes are mulled over in minds that struggle to comprehend them but become quite concrete when the abuse of power manifests itself in the medium of print. At first, orality is prized out of habit: Pa Joad "always says what he couldn' tell a fella with his mouth wasn't worth leanin' on no pencil about"; Muley's rambling oral digression is understood to be completely true in terms of the meanings Tom is seeking in it, and Grandma Joad even comically interjects inappropriate, formulaic "Amens" into the pauses in Casy's very untypical "grace" (26, 48, 88). But the rules have now been changed. The ruling classes, who gained their wealth by squatting-turned-"ownership," have now declared that what the tenant farmers are doing—the same thing—does *not* constitute possession, "a paper with numbers on it" does (35). Then Tom confides that his Pa "don't even like word writin'. Kinda scares 'im I guess. Ever' time Pa seen writin', somebody took somepin away from 'im" (58).

The printed handbills promise plentiful, high-paying jobs in California. Repeatedly, the Joads are given verbal warnings by experienced migrants that the handbills are lying, but the arrival of print contaminates their world without them knowing it yet. Still the

Bakhtinian innocents, they claim, "They wouldn't go to that trouble if they wasn't plenty work. Costs 'em good money to get them han-'bills out. What's they want ta lie for, an' costin' 'em money to lie?" (99; cf. also 208–11; they finally figure it out on page 269). Then there's that other bit of authoritative print, the blacklist, which one gets on for causing trouble (271), and newspapers, where one ends up for causing *more* trouble:

> They'll find you in a ditch, with the blood dried on your mouth and nose. Be one little line in the paper—know what it'll say? "Vagrant foun' dead." An' that's all. You'll see a lot of them little lines, "Vagrant foun' dead." (272)

The authorized texts that the migrants have procured are no help, as policemen tear up valid drivers' licenses to make a crime out of driving without one (130). As discussed above, the authority of the dominant discourse can be undone by speech, but only at the local level: when the newspaper reports that a squatter's camp was burned to the ground due to community outrage over "agitators," Tom replies, "Well, I was there. They wasn't no agitators," and his word is understood and accepted to be truthful by the members of his speech community (325, 328).

There are many references to Oklahoma's Pretty Boy Floyd, who, like Naún Briones in *Polvo y ceniza* (see chapter 5), is labeled a crook by the authorities, yet the people—his "people"—refuse to give him up. His violent alternative to subjugation is fully validated by the community but is seen as a dead-end option, quite literally, as far as challenges to the system go. But that system is changing, a new paradigm is arising:

> Uncle John broke in, "We never did have no paupers."
> Tom said, "Maybe we got to learn. We never got booted off no land before, neither." (152)

It is repeatedly emphasized that common law is natural and superior to the oppressor's written laws, however, this is usually expressed in the politely veiled language permitted the Bakhtinian innocents: "They's lots a things 'gainst the law that we can't he'p doin' " (493). Tom knows about the law. Half a dozen times, prison life is depicted as being better than a "free" life of poverty (e.g., "You eat regular, an' get clean clothes, and there's places to take a bath," 27; see also 98, 190, 327, 407), and some of the work camps are quite clearly compared to prisons, with armed guards patrolling the streets and restricting the fruit pickers' movements (419, 423).

Preacher Casy recognizes that a new paradigm is forming, although he continually states that he cannot figure out what it is, precisely. Nevertheless, he is aware of the breakdown of traditional signifiers:

> The hell with it! There ain't no sin and there ain't no virtue. There's just stuff people do. It's all part of the same thing. And some of the things folks do is nice, and some ain't nice, but that's as far as any man got a right to say. (24)

Far be it for Casy to engage in the hateful practice of authoritatively labeling things. Even as they kill him, he does not pronounce his enemies to be in the wrong, merely that they "don' know what [they]'re a-doin'" (426). This, of course, is a paraphrasing of Jesus Christ's famous plea, "Father, forgive them, for they know not what they do" (Luke 23:34), relocated to a lower social register than the high language of the familiar King James translation.

Steinbeck's mythification of his characters reaches an intertextual climax with Tom's parting speech:

> I'll be ever'where—wherever you look. Wherever they's a fight so hungry people can eat, I'll be there. Wherever they's a cop beatin' up a guy, I'll be there.... I'll be in the way guys yell when they're mad an'—I'll be in the way kids laugh when they're hungry an' they know supper's ready. An' when our folks eat the stuff they raise an' live in the houses they build—why, I'll be there. See? God, I'm talkin' like Casy. Comes of thinkin' about him so much. Seems like I can see him sometimes. (463)

Such mythic transformation from the individual to the universal is present in such diverse works of roughly the same period as the Soviet film *Arsenal* (1929), at the climax of which the heroic protagonist turns out to be immune to bullets because he represents the unkillable "Ukrainian people," and in "La mala hora" (1927), which has been called one of the first social realist short stories published in Ecuador.

In this story by Leopoldo Benítez Vinueza, a poor peasant, Nicasio Ronquillo, commits what is clearly supposed to be justifiable homicide to prevent his wife's (and possibly his mother's) rape by corrupt rural police ("bandits with uniforms," "bandidos con uniforme"[50]), representatives of a government that is described as a "despotic phantom that collects taxes" ("fantasma despótico que cobra impuestos," 44). One can see that oppressed Ecuadorians should be able to relate to a novel, such as *The Grapes of Wrath*, that defines business as "ritualized thievery" (169). Nicasio hides in the jungle, where this once-peaceful man finds the strength to kill a jaguar.

Surely it is time to question the "realist" label that has been applied to this and other Ecuadorian works of this period (see further discussion in the conclusion). Robin Hood–like, he spends an unknown number of years in the jungle before returning to see his mother in the final scene, covered with fresh blood from having just dispatched the murderous local landowner. Demonstrating that rebellion runs in the family, *she* curses all those who want to "take the shirt off a poor person's back" ("descamisar ar pobre," in *costeño* dialect, 48). In the final paragraph of this story, as in Tom Joad's parting speech, the local hero goes forth to become part of a much larger struggle, to join with the powerful, unstoppable forces of nature:

—No se preocupe, mamá. Yo mandaré por usté —dijo—, y cogiendo su alforja, su poncho y su machete, salió hacia la selva brava, hacia la libertad, hacia la vida, en medio de la tempestad que hacía crujir los árboles con su música plutónica y magnífica. (48)

["Don't worry ma. I'll send for you," he said, and, grabbing his saddlebag, his poncho and his machete, went out towards the untamed jungle, towards freedom, towards life, in the middle of a storm that twisted the trees into X's with its earth-shaking and magnificent music.]

3

Early Magic Realism 2: Sterile Fertility/Fertile Sterility—Identity, Negation, and Narrative in José de la Cuadra's *Los Sangurimas* (1934) in a Comparative Context with Gabriel García Márquez's *One Hundred Years of Solitude* (1967)

Much of dominant discourse ignores previous generations of Latin American writers, privileging Western European and American literature as the sole fountain from which the contemporary Latin American "Boom" literature has sprung.

Yet, when I suggest, as others have, that Ecuadorian writer José de la Cuadra's 1934 novel *Los Sangurimas* is an "undeniable" precursor to *One Hundred Years of Solitude*[1] I am certainly not claiming to have found the "source" of García Márquez's 1967 novel. There is no shortage of "patriarch" novels in Latin American literature. It may therefore be coincidental that both works tell the history of a pioneering patriarch (Nicasio Sangurima and José Arcadio Buendía) and the subsequent generations (and degeneration) of a landowning dynasty in the tropical coastal regions of Ecuador and Colombia, respectively. The Sangurimas' *hacienda*, appropriately called "La Hondura" ("The Depths"), like the town of Macondo, is a world unto itself, isolated from the rest of society, where children inherit their parents' sins and where incest and deadly sibling rivalry flourish. But the list of similarities goes on: In both works, a hasty, passionate murder prompts the flight from justice into the jungle and the founding of the patriarchal domain.[2] Both patriarchs converse at length with the dead, who are bodily present;[3] both patriarchs end up having to be tied down, impotent and insane; and both works cover a span of four to five generations *without ever citing a single date* or event that allows for absolute fixity of time.[4]

Both authors seem preoccupied with the tension between spoken and written words, and the reader is continually presented with simultaneous and contradictory information.[5]

This simultaneous self-identification and self-negation begins with the title. Who are the Sangurimas? Although the members of the family obsessively identify themselves by name, in the first two-thirds of the novel we gather much of our information about them from dialogue between unidentified characters.

"Nicasio Sangurima, el abuelo, era de raza blanca, casi pura" ("Nicasio Sangurima, the grandfather, was of the white race, almost pure," 9). The first line of the novel identifies the patriarch by name, family position, and bloodline. Or does it? Don Nicasio repeatedly identifies himself proudly as the "son of a *gringo*" ("hijo de gringo," 10), which is supposed to make him superior to the local *montuvios* (coastal campesinos), and as a Sangurima, which was his mother's name. But these two identities contradict and cancel out each other.[6] The unnamed *gringo* father merely passed through the region *in illo tempore*, supplied the seed, and got killed by the mother's uncle; she retaliated by killing her uncle, literally cutting all family ties, thus negating both elements from which Don Nicasio persistently constructs his identity.[7]

In both novels, the patriarchs' attempts at self-replication through their names ultimately result in self-annihilation. The seventeen Aurelianos of *One Hundred Years* are paralleled by sixteen "legitimate" Sangurimas (29) and an illegitimate progeny as numerous as the grains "in an ear of corn" (22). Not surprisingly, Nicasio reduces the various mothers to fallow objects when speaking of his "multitude" of children:

> Son cocinados en hornos diferentes, pero están hechos con la misma masa. (54)

> [They're baked in different ovens, but they're made from the same dough.]

And later:

> Hasta en Guayaquil tengo hijos. Es pa que no se acaben los Sangurimas. ¡Buena sangre, amigo! (22)

> [I've got kids as far as Guayaquil. So there'll be no end to the Sangurimas. Strong blood, friend!]

But this fertility is illusory and sterile. In both texts the subsequent generations gradually grow weaker and more depraved, and both family bloodlines end with extreme cases of incestuous self-creation breeding self-negation. It is this very pride in the family name that leads to love-matches with first cousins. With respect to naming, however, García Márquez goes de la Cuadra one further by introducing an additional element of lexical self-replication. There are not seventeen children, but seventeen *Aurelianos*, and so many José Arcadios that the reader loses track of them. Thus the Buendías' attempt at lexical self-replication results in a lexical confusion of identities that *erases* their identities in the mind of the reader.

An interesting alternative to the same problem occurs in *Los Sangurimas*. In order *not* to get lost in the shuffle of identity, many of the Sangurima children adopt elaborate self-generated nicknames, like "Raspabalsa," "Chancho Rengo" and "Los Rugeles." But here too the effort backfires. Los Rugeles have lexically removed themselves so far from identification as Sangurimas that they begin to believe this removal and deny the family relationship that condemns their love of their first cousins as "incest," and in so doing bring about the physical annihilation of the family name through violent conflict. The progeny in both works take slightly different routes to the same destination: self-negation.

The ear of corn that Don Nicasio uses to describe the fertility of his line is an attempt to equate his dynasty with such biblical images as God's promise to Abraham (the patriarch) that his progeny will be as innumerable as grains of sand on a beach or stars in the heavens.[8] Although numerous, the grains in an ear of corn are finite, short-lived, and consumable. So the very image Nicasio uses to express the plenitude of his progeny is in fact an image of a finite, organic transience. Elsewhere the same effect occurs: Nicasio, bragging about his youthful sexual prowess, refers to himself as having gotten around as fast as the "monilla del cacao" (9). This refers to a disease that struck the Ecuadorian banana crops in 1915 and was, by all accounts, a natural and economic disaster,[9] certainly an exceedingly negative image of fertility.

But the negation in de la Cuadra's work is not merely a function of plot elements. The narrative, too, self-consciously explores the strengths and limits of the textual. The first two-thirds of the novel do not really have a conventional "plot," but instead reproduce fragmentary dialogues from the rise (and fall) of a family, introduced with such phrases as "se refería," "se aseguraba," "se susurraba," "se decía," "relatan," "comentaban," "se había murmurado," "dizque," "decíase," "contaba alguna vez," and "había muchas anécdotas"[10] ("it was referred that," "it was assured that," "it was rumored that," "it was said that," "they related," "they commented," "they had whispered," "they say that," "they said," "one time it was told," and "there were lots of anecdotes").

These were followed or furthered by "así es," "claro," "ah," "así ha de ser," "y qué pasó," "qué hizo," "como fue."[11] ("That's how it is," "sure," "aha," "that's how it must be," "what happened," "what did he do," "how did it happen.")

And when an unnamed speaker tells about "the terrible fables and more terrible truths of the tropical coastland" ("las fábulas terribles y las más terribles verdades del campo montuvio," 33), one hears echoes of Aureliano's "hallucinated version" of reality that "was radically opposed to the false one that historians had created and consecrated in the schoolbooks" (García Márquez, 322).

One of the most interesting ways in which storytelling can be seen as going contrary to all historical fact yet producing a "truth" for the listeners is illustrated in the case of one of Nicasio's "legitimate" sons, Terencio, who has become a priest at his father's command (just as other sons have become doctors, lawyers, etc. at Don Nicasio's command). For this reason, he is less than the ideal priest: He drinks, curses, fornicates, listens to dirty songs, and reads dirty books (45) and—significantly—rewrites the Bible for local consumption. When his brother, Ventura, asks Terencio about his "method," he explains:

> Si yo les digo a los montuvios que cuando el judío Malco le dio una bofetada en la mejilla a Jesucristo, éste volvió la otra, se escandalizarán, y pensarían que Jesucristo era un cobardón que no vale la pena tomarlo en cuenta. . . .—Yo les digo, más o menos: "Iba Nuestro Señor con esa cruz grandota que le habían cargado los verdugos, cuando en eso sale el judío malamansado de Malco y le suelta una bofetada. . . . ¿Saben lo que hizo el santo varón? En vez de haberle rajado el alma, que era lo que provocaba, como él era tan buen corazón apenas se contentó, con decirle al judío: "Anda a golpear a tu madre" . . . Así. (45)

> [If I tell the folks that when Malcolm the Jew socked Jesus on the cheek, he turned the other one, they'd be shocked, and they'd think that Jesus was a weakling who isn't worth listening to. . . .—So I tell them, more or less: Our Lord was hauling this huge cross that the bastards made him carry, when that damn Jew Malcolm socked him. You know what the holy guy did? Instead of busting his skull, which is what he wanted to do, because he was such a good-hearted guy, he was content to tell the Jew: "Go sock your mother" . . . Like that.]

It is fair to suggest that de la Cuadra's Jesus parable is a veiled description of his own narrative technique (Aguilera Malta also makes use of this technique in *Don Goyo*: see chapter 2). One Ecuadorian "modernist" project that was so shocking to followers of traditional nineteenth-century literary practices was the deliberate use of the idioms, curses, and speech patterns of the lower classes.[12] (It is important in this regard to note that Ecuador is considered to have been the most conservatively "Catholic" of the Latin American countries in the nineteenth century.)

A "plot" develops in the final third of the book. The patriarchal gluttony for self-replication is directed initially outward at others, and an "other"-ized nature. Ventura understands this, and proudly declares:

> Yo soy de la carne misma de mi papás, que por cada hijo que ha hecho ha desecho un hijo de otro. (41)
>
> [I'm of the same flesh as my old man, who for every kid he's made he's unmade someone else's kid.]

Soon after, the patriarch says:

> Yo no me jodo por naidien. Yo hice este abogado: Yo mismo lo deshago. (48)
>
> [I don't let myself get screwed by nobody. I made that lawyer: And I'll un-make him.]

This is a crucial concept that returns to undo the undoers. While Don Nicasio is questionably referred to as the strong and ageless "trunk" of the family tree and his sons as somewhat weaker "branches," the third generation—the "leaves"—are utterly uncontrollable. As mentioned above, three troublesome Sangurima grandsons, who, significantly, call themselves by another name, "Los Rugeles," show an incestuous interest in three Sangurima granddaughters, their own first cousins.

Don Nicasio commands his son Ventura (father of the three women) to "take care of the girls" ("Cuida a esas muchachas," 65). The constant textual interplay between the meaning and power of words (particularly names) that operates throughout this novel now assumes tragic proportions. Ventura takes the command to mean "protect the girls (from Los Rugeles)." When Los Rugeles come calling to propose marriage, Ventura stalls for time, agreeing with the boys that it is *better* to marry your own blood, but his putting them off is understood (correctly) by the boys as a rejection (68–69). At this point Ventura could be seen as the decent son trying (and failing) to effect some change for the better in his world, much in the manner of Col. Aureliano Buendía fighting thirty-two wars and still being unable to bring about decent government. The daughters vacillate between accepting and rejecting Los Rugeles, which is to say between negation and affirmation of their identities as Sangurimas as opposed to their identities within larger society. But the Sangurimas reaffirm that they are a world and a law unto themselves, and it brings about their downfall. Later that same night Los Rugeles return and the first daughter, María Victoria, goes off with them. Don Nicasio is furious with Ventura: To Nicasio, his command to "take care of the girls" meant to "do what is best for the girls" (i.e., "Let them marry Los Rugeles").[13] Soon after, María Victoria is found dead and cruelly mutilated so as to be *unidentifiable* except by her clothing.[14] Don Nicasio blames Ventura:

—Ya ves. Vos tienes la culpa. Por no cuidar a tus hijas. Yo te manoseaba el consejo. Vos no lo has oído. (75)

[—You see. It's your fault. For not taking care of your daughters. I hand-delivered the advice. You didn't hear it.]

But Ventura did hear the words; he just assigned them a completely different meaning from the one his father intended. In a typical *machista* valuing of grandsons over granddaughters, Don Nicasio is sure that Los Rugeles are innocent of the crime (Ventura, significantly, is no longer sure of anything [75]). Los Rugeles have previously stated:

La mujer no es de naidien, sino del primero que la jala. Mismamente como la vaca alzada. Hay que cogerla como sea. A las buenas o a las málas. (64)

[A woman belongs to nobody, but to the first who jumps her. Just like a mature cow. You gotta grab them the way they are. The good ones or the bad ones.]

That their actions simultaneously uphold and contradict the statement should not come as a surprise at this point (that is, while they seem to state that all women are the same, their rigid *machista* insistence on matches with three particular women contradicts this, and brings death).

The news of a murder brings in state authorities—a challenge to Don Nicasio's hitherto total authority. The illusory unity of the Sangurimas now fragments, finalized by the armed assault and establishment of outside police power in Nicasio Sangurima's house, but that is only the culmination of an assault on the monolithic patriarchal power of Don Nicasio that began when the news of the murder made it into the media. (This will be discussed further below.)

Broken in mind and spirit, Don Nicasio explodes in an "impotent rage" (81) and curses his son, Ventura, whose challenge of Los Rugeles's authority is perceived as an attack on the family: Even though the challenge comes from his own son, a Sangurima, it is directed at three grandsons who are, after all, also Sangurimas. Unable to bridge the gap between these self-annihilating contradictions (and the collapse of his patriarchy), Nicasio succumbs to a deranged lexical impotence that leaves him using an excess of the *condicional perfecto* and *pretérito pluscuamperfecto* forms (e.g., "hubiera dicho," "would have told") that he has rarely used up until this point (he is used to giving commands):

> Don Nicasio explicó largamente el plan que no pudo poner en práctica; lo que habría sido el epílogo verdadero y era ahora no más que el epílogo imaginario, viviente sólo en su cabeza afiebrada. . . . Don Nicasio hubiera dicho a los policiales, "Más mejor es que nos vayamos con los presos por agua" . . . Los policiales habrían aceptado sin desconfianza. Y al llegar a la revesa de los Ahogados, habría mandado sacar la tabla falsa del fondo de la canoa, y éste se habría hundido en dos minutos. De tierra los peones habrían dado balo a los rurales, que estarían en el agua. Dios habría querido que nos hubiéramos salvado a "los Rugeles" . . . Los rurales, con el peso del fusil, se habrían ido a pique. . . . (82)

> [Don Nicasio explained at length the plan that he was unable to put into practice; what should have been the true epilogue and which was now no more than the imaginary epilogue, living only in his feverish head. . . . Don Nicasio would have told the police, "Why don't we take the prisoners by boat" . . . The police would have accepted without distrust. And once past the rapids he would have pulled up the canoe's false bottom and it would have sunk in two minutes. From the riverbanks, the peons would have shot the rangers, who would have been in the water. God would have wanted us to have saved Los Rugeles . . . The rangers, under the weight of our guns, would have all drowned like rats. . . .]

Note particularly how even God's actions follow Don Nicasio's wishes in the "imaginary epilogue" that exists only in the "feverish head" of a fictional character. Does this not resemble Aureliano Babilona reading his own life (and death) in the final pages of *One Hundred Years of Solitude*? Or to José Arcadio Buendía's lexical "madness" when he begins speaking only in Latin to uncomprehending ears? Don Nicasio spent his life creating his own laws, and in turn he created sons who make their own laws, which destroy him, and each other.

Let us now return to the earlier point about the textual assault on Nicasio Sangurima's patriarchal power. De la Cuadra's novel describes more than one attempt to chip away at Nicasio's power by legal means. But lawsuits are only paper attacks that can be deflected with paper defenses, or bought off with paper money. (Nicasio made one of his sons become a lawyer for precisely this purpose.) But something very different happens when there is a murder on the family property: The Guayaquil newspapers get ahold of the story, and they print it. And suddenly the outside world discovers that the Sangurimas are "a dynasty of savages" ("una dinastía de salvajes," 76). *Now* the Guayaquil police are obliged to do something about it.

What happened? Since the Sangurimas have never been anything other than what has been said about them by themselves and outsiders, what has changed? I suggest that it is when the stories about the fearsome deeds of the Sangurimas told by outsiders *switch from oral to written texts* that their authoritative system begins to break down. De la Cuadra appears to be privileging the power of *text* as the only weapon capable of initiating the downfall of the feudal patriarchy that was still being condemned as obsolete thirty-three years later, when García Márquez wrote *One Hundred Years of Solitude*—and curiously enough, using many of the same devices: if twentieth-century governments have learned how to manipulate history through texts, then the only recourse is to reclaim—or remanipulate—that history through other texts (García Márquez, 285–86). Benedict Anderson declares that print united the bourgeoisie "on an essentially imagined basis."[15] Perhaps one could say that orality united the feudal patriarchy on an imagined basis. The threat to the patriarchy from print seems real enough: Until the "media circus" of the Guayaquil newspapers prompts an invasion from "outside," the Sangurimas' hacienda is truly a world unto itself: There is complete "solitude."

The main difference between *One Hundred Years* and *Los Sangurimas* from this textual-historical perspective is that de la Cuadra blames Ecuador's sorry state entirely on internal contradictions. There is no banana company to share the blame, unless one considers the absent *gringo* sperm-donor as a symbolically absent precursor of García Márquez's banana company. And why not? When he was writing in the 1930s, the *gringos*, their banana companies, and the brutal squashing of resistance were still very much a presence in Ecuador's economic life. So perhaps the only way to write about them at the time was to silently suggest their absence and move on to the results of their presence. Perhaps this explains in part why Don Nicasio so frequently insists that he is the son of an *absent* "*gringo.*"[16]

Thanks to García Márquez's novel, numerous critics have discussed the impact of the labor unrest, the violently suppressed strike in Aracataca, Colombia's banana-producing region, in 1928, and the subsequent economic depression, on a generation of Colombian authors.[17]

But outside of Ecuador, few have noted the impact of the labor unrest, the violently suppressed strike in Guayaquil, Ecuador's banana-producing region, in 1922, and the subsequent economic depression, on a generation of Ecuadorian authors. According to Agustín Cueva, the political shock of the "progressive" capitalists turning their guns on working men and women in 1922 propelled Ecuador from feudalism to modernism in one decade, and a group of "indigenist" writers created a "new language" to depict "a savage capitalism . . . advancing by blood and fire through all previous economic, social, and cultural forms."[18]

De la Cuadra's effort was to discredit or make a clean slate of "the Ecuadorian myths of reality."[19] One of the many ways in which García Márquez approaches the same problem in *One Hundred Years* is the use of a narrator who shuttles

> almost imperceptibly from one perspective to another, now imitating the naiveté of his characters, now commenting ironically on that naiveté.[20]

I hope that this discussion has done something to show that these much admired literary qualities of free-floating, self-reflexive narrative, with contradictory mythologies—all focused on a patriarchy that falls from virtual omnipotence into decadence, corruption, and self-annihilation (which found such fertile territory in *One Hundred Years of Solitude*)—were planted by others a generation earlier, in territory that might have been every bit as fertile, if the territory had only belonged to them and been theirs to cultivate.

4

The "Transitional Period" (1950s-1960s) Myth, Nonlinear Time and Self-Negation: Demetrio Aguilera Malta's *El tigre* (1955) and Eugene O'Neill's *The Emperor Jones* (1920)

> It is myth which gives the visions, both of the transcendent world and of historical time, their structure—myth which is intrinsically neither eternity and intelligibility after the Greek fashion, nor history and time of the Christian type. Myth is articulated atemporality.
> —Henri-Charles Puech, "Gnosis and Time"

> Myth tears man away from his own time, from his individual, chronological, "historical" time—and projects him, symbolically at least, into the Great Time, into a paradoxical moment that cannot be measured because it has no duration. . . . myth implies a breach in time and the surrounding world, it opens up a passage to the sacred Great Time.
> —Mircea Eliade, "Time and Eternity in Indian Thought"

There is a mode of examining and discussing myth that sees myth in terms of a three-dimensional space that exists somewhere, separate from the banal 3-D space of everyday life, yet somehow obtainable through the telling of myth, in which "narrator and audience are projected into a sacred, mythical time," or by some other means.[1] Ecuadorian author Demetrio Aguilera Malta's "expressionistic," Magical Realist one-act play, *El tigre*, complicates this dichotomy. In this work, Aguilera Malta presents a clash of two irreconcilable realities, one mythic and atemporal, one banal, materialistic, and chronological, inhabiting the *same* 3-D space. Although these self-negating elements simultaneously share the same physical space, there is little or no communication possible between them because the separation is unperceived by either party.[2]

In *El tigre*, this clash of opposing spaces produces a victor who problematizes some of these cosmic but straightforward ideas about the superior, transcendent qualities of myth. The old superstitions lead to self-destruction, not enlightenment (for death is the ultimate atemporality), but the modern "victor" is empty and soulless.

In his book on the plays of Aguilera Malta, Gerardo Luzuriaga describes both *El tigre* and *The Emperor Jones* as "expressionistic," despite the thirty-five-year gap between their moments of production;[3] although *El tigre* should certainly be seen as part of a general surfacing of "expressionistic" elements in Latin American drama of the 1950s, the central action is based on an incident from Aguilera Malta's 1942 novel, *La isla virgen*. This comparison is tantalizing in part because it is restricted to a few lines, but also because elements of what is called magic realism are present in Aguilera Malta's work as early as 1930 in the short stories in *Los que se van*, and quite prominently so in his 1933 novel *Don Goyo* (see chapter 2 and conclusion). Thus the development of these two authors' styles is not as temporally separate as an examination of these two plays in isolation might indicate.

There are a number of significant similarities between these two works. Briefly, *El tigre* is set in a tiny clearing in the dense jungle of an island off Ecuador's coast. Two *lumpenproletariat* cane-cutters, Mite and El Tejon, tend the campfire, the only respite from the jungle darkness, while the foreman Don Guayamabe incessantly puffs a cigar. A third worker, Zambo Aguayo, stumbles in terrified.[4] A tiger is after him.[5] In three short scenes, the foreman continually dismisses Zambo Aguayo's fear of a tiger as an irrational weakness, while the marked man's two comrades vacillate between Don Guayamabe's "practical" interpretation of the events and Zambo Aguayo's "mythic" one. For Zambo Aguayo, however, there is no escape, and in the end he is fatally mauled by the tiger, who is then killed by Don Guayamabe. *The Emperor Jones* of course is much more familiar to U.S. audiences. The main action involves Brutus Jones's fruitless attempt to escape his native pursuers through a Caribbean island's jungle. Significantly, all of his "ha'nts" and fears are individualized at first—that is, they involve recreations of his evil actions—but they become progressively more anonymous and ancient (the crocodile god, etc.). *El tigre* and *The Emperor Jones* both depict isolated human victims struggling in vain against the dark, mysterious forces of the jungle.

In his multivolume history of contemporary theater, Juan Guerrero Zamora describes *El tigre* (with a brief comparison to *The Emperor Jones*):

La obra, que transcurre linealmente y en lenguaje popular, apenas urde una anécdota sobre su hueso mondo: el miedo que el tigre inflige a Zambo Aguayo y que, progresivo hasta la obsesión, se torna algo consustancial con él, momento en que incapaz de huir—no tanto del tigre de fuera como del otro que lleva dentro—se somete fatalistamente a su destino de ser devorado. . . . El tigre se convierte en algo más que una fiera: es la potencia maléfica, el imán hipnótico equivalente al tan-tan en el oneilliano *Emperor Jones*, el signo mágico y hostil del trópico.[6]

[The work, which proceeds linearly and in simple, common language, merits an anecdote about its central image (lit. "bare bone"): The fear that the tiger instills in Zambo Aguayo, and that, progressing towards obsession, becomes something tangible for him, until he is incapable of flight—not so much from the external tiger as from the other tiger he carries inside him—he submits himself fatalistically to his destiny of being devoured. . . . The tiger is converted into something more than a wild beast: It is evil power, the hypnotic attractor equivalent to the drumming in O'Neill's *Emperor Jones*, the magical and hostile sign of the tropics.

Luzuriaga also assigns the tiger this relatively straightforward role as the as "personification of evil."[7] But is it really that simple? True, Zambo Aguayo's "fatalistic acceptance of his destiny" implies the kind of cyclical, eternal repetition of world events that Mircea Eliade posits as the antithesis of the linear Christian time that the boss, Don Guayamabe, represents. But not without complications.

Both plays feature characters who are pitted against the jungle-as-entity, god-like, older, and more powerful than mere mortals, that will outlive them under all circumstances. Both main characters are thus destined to die from the moment we meet them. But there are some important differences. Brutus Jones is attempting to escape from *two* pasts—his past as the Pullman porter who fled the United States after killing a man in a card game and his immediate past as the Emperor who must be sacrificed—both of which are inescapable. This is what results in his death. By contrast, Zambo Aguayo hasn't harmed anyone, nor does his position as a peon place him in the same league with the Emperor who must be sacrificed.

Brutus Jones, out of his "true" element, has more of an accidental encounter with the mythic realm that brings about his poetically justified death, whereas Zambo Aguayo and the other peons live surrounded by the mythic realm at all times, described in *El tigre* as if it were a contagious disease that any one of them could be felled by *arbitrarily* at any time, for no real poetic "reason." Because of the separateness of the jungle experience for Smithers, the only white character in O'Neill's play, the work, though expressionistic, fits more snugly into First World tradition: The power of the jungle is real, but only for those who have dared to enter and challenge it in some way. Because the peon and the boss in *El tigre* inhabit two utterly different times, mythic and nonmythic, sacred and profane, *in the same space*, with neither party fully understanding their situations (although Don Guayamabe *thinks* he commands his realm), because neither recognize that there are two separate realms, Aguilera Malta's drama belongs to a thoroughly different, more contemporary Third World point of view. That is, unlike the "center" and "other" binary opposition in *The Emperor Jones, El tigre* presents simultaneously the contradictory viewpoints of conqueror and conquered, without privileging either one. They are both simply there.

More or less. Aguayo has apparently "caught" myth (in the same way one "catches" a disease) and the master, Don Guayamabe, who is responsible for establishing order amid the chaos of the jungle, who quantifies existence and therefore time, is utterly safe from myth because he lives entirely in the profane. But the two other peons, Mite and El Tejon, seem able to inhabit both. What for Don Guayamabe is a mere nuisance—a troublesome tiger—is an inescapable death force for Aguayo. The other two peons, however, seem to vacillate between one and the other. Though they never enter Aguayo's realm of myth, for that would be the death of them too, they do understand what has happened to him, and suggest various remedies, while all Don Guayamabe can do is belittle his underling's fear and wait for the chance to kill the tiger.

Doesn't this contradict the above statement about the nonrecognition of the two "irreconcilable realities"? Doesn't that mean these two characters bridge the gap between the two realms? The answer may be that they recognize the existence of the other realm (in a way that the boss never will), but they are not of it. Do they then function in a Levi-Straussian way and "mediate between contradictions"? In a way, yes, but theirs is *not* the mythic position. They stay clear of the myth because they know it is true. Again, one must stress the arbitrariness of myth's hold on its victim. Myth in *El tigre* is not something one chooses to enter, either to transcend time or to set some transgression right and reestablish order. The openings into myth are not known, and, once entered, there is no return.

According to Puech, the Christian adoption of Jewish mythology served to authorize and extend their predetermined revelations that much further back in time.[8] In *El tigre,* we confront the failure of Western Christianity to supersede previously existing forces, at least in myth's stronghold, the heart of the jungle. This is not a reflection on the weakness of the Christian God against the pagan ones, but rather an indication that the Western, Christian, capitalist exploiter of the land triumphs not because of the strength of his faith, but because of his lack of faith of any kind. He commodifies everything, and thus for him the tiger is just a tiger, a threat to his capital interests (it eats farm animals) that must be destroyed for that reason alone. The cynical outcome is that he triumphs—the conquest of Latin America by Western Christian capitalists is a reality, after all. It is an empty victory, but a victory nonetheless. Thus this clash between the modern and the mythic is in some ways more complex and problematical in Aguilera Malta than in O'Neill.

In *El tigre,* the two central characters' names, (Zambo) A*guayo* and (Don) *Guaya*mabe are reflections of each other, two sides of the same river (the Guayas River is historically Ecuador's most important river). While Aguayo's name more closely resembles "aguado" (watery, weak, limp), Guayamabe's name is closer to "guayaba" (fraud, trick), which might be a further equation of Zambo Aguayo with nature (and myth) and Don Guayamabe with cultivation and capital. Unlike Eliade's triumphant cultivation of chaos,[9] however, Don Guayamabe has only one machete with which to clear a path through the jungle, illustrating the inadequacy of the conqueror before the conquered and the reality of Latin American underdevelopment.

That the jungle is in fact finite—they are on an island—does not lessen the infinitude of its terrors. For example, none of the workers can provide a satisfactory explanation of how the tiger got to the island in the first place.[10] And with only a campfire between them and the jungle night, the men are part of the darkness they are trying to keep at bay. They are surrounded by the chaotic forces of nature, like the mosquitoes they try in vain to brush away (169).

But this fire is not their weapon alone. The tiger who is stalking Aguayo has fire in his eyes, too ("ojos como dos candiles," 170). Mite recognizes Aguayo's problem and ventures a diagnosis: The only way to deal with a (mythical) tiger

> es desafiarlo. Donde te siga el rastro y se orine en tus pisadas.... ¡Ahí sí que te fregaste! (170)

> [is to face him down. (Otherwise) he'll follow your tracks and piss on your footprints.... Then you're really screwed!]

Throughout this, Don Guayamabe smokes his cigar as if he weren't there ("como ausente"), which of course, he isn't. He is physically present in the same space, but is inhabiting a completely different world.

In the world of myth, belief is stronger than external—or separate—"reality."

> AGUAYO: ¡Yo creo que a mí me va a comer el tigre! . . .
> MITE: La contra, la única contra es no tenerles miedo. (172)

> [AGUAYO: I think the tiger's going to eat me! . . .
> MITE: The defense, the only defense is not to be afraid of them.]

The only solution is not to believe. (The use of the plural *them* is also interesting: Mite understands quite well that there is more than one "tiger.") Curiously, it is Brutus Jones's failure to believe that causes his destruction—at first. That is, he makes insufficient preparations to escape through the jungle because he underestimates the powers of its magic. However, when these magical powers begin to manifest themselves—as the Little Formless Fears and the other intangible manifestations of his past transgressions—now it is *his belief* in these manifestations as physically real (rather than mythical projections of his own transgressions) that bring about his "timely" (fatalistically appropriate) end. The tragedy is that Brutus Jones knows the power of the performative: "Ain't a man's talkin' big what makes him big—long as he makes folks believe it?"[11] But only when *he* uses it.[12]

In *El tigre*, this gap between realms is heightened when even the other peons show how impossible it is for them to know what Aguayo is experiencing, even though they try to help him get off the island:

> AGUAYO: Ya todo es en vano . . .
> EL TEJON: Hablas por hablar, Zambo. (180)

> [AGUAYO: It's all in vain . . .
> EL TEJON: That's just talk, Zambo.]

Don Guayamabe, however, never willingly acknowledges that Aguayo is inhabiting a separate reality, though his statement "Maybe you're carrying the tiger's eyes inside your head" ("A lo mejor, llevas ya los ojos del tigre dentro de tu cabeza," 173) is unintentionally meaningful. Guayamabe merely means "It's all in your head," in the sense of it not being real, whereas, it may all be in

Aguayo's head, but in the mythic realm that is precisely what makes it real. If Aguayo is being stalked by something within himself, then there is truly no escape for him. Thus the tiger is much more than the "evil personified" that others have labeled it. The evil is personified in the sense that it seems to permeate the island's atmosphere, yet only attains destructive force when it successfully inhabits someone's mind—this is, quite literally, personification.

When the second scene begins (several days later), the two peons discuss the tiger:

> MITE: Y dicen que está retobadísimo.
> EL TEJON: ¿Será el mismo? (174)
>
> [MITE: They say he's as tricky as can be.
> EL TEJON: Could it be the same one?]

One is reminded of the white whale in *Moby Dick*, known to all the harpooners as an existing reality, yet never isolated as a single target by them, only by the obsessed "master" of the ship.

Brutus Jones knows his day will come, although he hopes to avoid it. Still, he recognizes that from the moment he became Emperor, the end of his reign was already predetermined. It was just a matter of time.

> I has de silver bullet moulded and I tells 'em when de time comes I kills myself wid it. I tells 'em dat's 'cause I'm de on'y man in de world big enuff to git me. (9)

In *El tigre*, the characters are all good at reading the signs of the inevitable. The tiger can be heard roaring and creeping through the underbrush, his tracks and the remains of his meals are frequently found. In other words, the others only experience *indexes* of his presence. No one but Aguayo ever "sees" the tiger until the very end, when Guayamabe kills one—but the tiger that can be killed is not the tiger that threatens the mythic character from within. Frequently entreated to have a look for themselves, the others can say little more than "I see nothing" ("No veo nada," 171, 173).

How, then, does one transcend this fatalistic cycle? Brutus Jones attempts to do so first by stripping away at his assumed identity of Emperor and trying to become anonymous.

> Damn dis heah coat! Like a straitjacket! [He tears off his coat and flings it away from him . . .] . . . And to hell wid dese high fangled spurs. Dey're what's been a-trippin' me up an' breakin' my neck. [He unstraps

4: THE "TRANSITIONAL PERIOD" 81

them and flings them away disgustedly] Dere! I gits rid o' dem frippety Emperor trappin's an' I travels lighter. (23)

O'Neill's use of the term "trappings" is not likely to be accidental. But Jones's attempt to drive away the fears—by firing his revolver at them point blank—only gets him in deeper by giving away his position to his pursuers. Later on Jones also strips off his shoes and comments, "Look at you now. Emperor, you'se gittin' mighty low!" (27).

Eliade suggests that transcendence might be achievable if one metaphysically depreciates one's individual "human history":

One is devoured by time, *not* because one lives in time, but because one believes in the *reality* of time and hence forgets or despises eternity. . . . to be delivered from illusion it is sufficient to achieve consciousness of the ontological unreality of time and to "realize" the rhythms of Great Cosmic Time.[13]

The interesting thing is that in *El tigre* we find the opposite: The one who believes in the reality of time remains alive in triumph at the end, and the one who has fallen into the rhythms of Great Cosmic Time gets swallowed alive. But Eliade goes on to posit an intermediate situation of

him who, while continuing to live in his own time (historic time), preserves an opening toward Great Time, never losing his awareness of the unreality of historic time.[14]

This would appear to characterize Mite and El Tejon quite well. They are aware of the two different times, but do not transcend the one they live in, namely historic time. By contrast, Puech feels that "Salvation places us outside of time. . . . It releases us from time in order to carry us back to our original, atemporal condition."[15] This optimism is completely absent from *El tigre*, where the only solution the other two peons can propose is that Zambo Aguayo should leave the island (177). But again, you can't escape what is inside of you.

For Eliade, the breaks in time are our best hope. New Year's ceremonies, so essential to rebirth and revitalization, are mythical moments

in which the world is destroyed and re-created. The dead can come back now, for all barriers between the dead and the living are broken.[16]

Elsewhere he writes, "The periodic recitation of myths breaks through the walls erected by the illusions of profane existence," in fact, any "passage from ignorance to illumination [suggests] a cutting across the planes."[17] Still, the *physical* separation of these two realms appears to be a given, and the trip between them as generally a necessary, rejuvenating experience.

This is not the case in Aguilera Malta's play. It is precisely the irreconcilability of the two realms that is the Latin Americans' tragedy. How can the modern world accept the old mythological dichotomies?[18] How do we posit the jungle as mythical, omnipotent force when today the jungles need to be protected from the threat of advancing commodification? One cannot isolate a work of art from political reality.[19]

While Zambo Aguayo's involuntary encounter with timelessness is ultimately self-destructive, for Eliade, a willful seeking of the timeless leads to positive transcendence. The present does not exist, because of time's "immediate destruction, there is no (real) motion."[20] In *The Secret of Dr. Honigberger*, the title character's ventures into transcendence result in his bodily disappearance from this reality, although his mind and body are presumed to be existing in some other reality, "For although my spirit remained active, my body was no longer participating in the passage of time."[21] Eliade presents this as a worthy project to pursue.[22] What accounts for this desire to escape profane time, aside from a recognition of its banality?[23] Eliade writes:

> Modern man's boasted freedom to make history is illusory for nearly the whole of the human race. At most, man is left free to choose between two positions: (1) to oppose the history that is being made by the very small minority (and, in this case, he is free to choose between suicide and deportation); (2) to take refuge in a subhuman existence or in flight.[24]

How relevant is this to our discussion of *The Emperor Jones* and *El tigre*? Clearly, Brutus Jones chooses (2), but what of Zambo Aguayo? He attempts flight, fails, and ultimately chooses a sort of suicide—but this is the result of his resignation to the inevitable triumph of timelessness, not a willful *opposition* to history. Neither Brutus Jones's deliberate attempts to strip himself of the "trappings" of sovereignty nor Zambo Aguayo's passive acceptance of his "fate" lead to a positive, transcendent experience. Indeed, Zambo Aguayo abandons this world and embraces nothingness.

In *The Will to Power*, Nietzsche writes, "The Dionysus cut to pieces is a *promise* of life! He will be eternally reborn and come home from destruction."[25] In *El tigre*, we have perhaps Nietzsche's Dionysian suffering, but *without* the rebirth. In Paul Ricoeur's interpretation of Aristotelian poetics, "Reversal is essential to every story or history where meaningless threatens the meaningful."[26] But how can this be seen operating in *El tigre*? Both worlds threaten each other, but which one is which? Who are we to label one of them "meaningless" and the other one "meaningful"? A solution may lie in the *connection* rather than the separation between these two elements. Ricoeur describes a "Hidden affinity between the secret of where the story emerges from and the secret to which it returns."[27] Perhaps all narratives pass through a deceptively linear arc, but they all begin and end in the same ineffable *nothing*. Thus there is no "reversal," but a *continuity* between opposing states that endlessly create and annihilate each other.

What, in the end, transpires in *El tigre*? Aguayo returns, having failed to leave the island. The two peons stare at him "as if they were seeing an otherworldly being" ("como si vieran un ser de otro mundo," 179). He has "an empty look" ("una mirada vacía"), looks back at them "as if he doesn't see them" ("como si no los viera," ibid.) and wanders off into the jungle, leaving El Tejon to describe him in his absence:

Parecía un muerto parado. ¡Quién sabe si él mismo ya no siente en este mundo! . . . ya olía a muerto. Quién sabe si ya está muerto por dentro. (182)

[He was like the walking dead. Who knows if he still feels he's in this world! . . . He already smelled of death. Who knows if he isn't already dead inside.]

At this point we hear Aguayo's "ultrahuman scream" ("un grito ultrahumano de Aguayo," ibid.) and the offstage voice of Don Guayamabe shouting as he apparently shoots the tiger and cuts open its belly with a machete, shouting the curtain line, "Now you won't screw anybody anymore! Damn you!" ("¡ . . . ya no fregarás a nadie más! ¡Maldecida!", 183). Don Guayamabe kills a tiger—the tiger that was real for him. Perhaps there are "two" tigers, a mythic and a material one, but they, too, inhabit the same space. This "same" tiger is a real, ordinary animal for Guayamabe and is unreal, an unstoppable force, his "fate," for Aguayo. Don Guayamabe has killed a tiger, but not the fear of tigers that will soon manifest itself in someone else, because, as is said several times, this fear is "contagious":

> Mite: ¿No se habrá contagiado la Domitila? (179)
>
> [Mite: Do you think Domitila (Aguayo's wife) could have caught it?]

Don Guayamabe can kill it because for him it is only a tiger, while Zambo Aguayo is paralyzed with fear and lets himself be killed in a seemingly predetermined self-destruction. What is the difference between these two men? Who triumphs? Is Aguayo a scapegoat (à la Girard)[28] whose mythic destruction allows the others to continue their profane existence? Either way, unlike *The Emperor Jones*, where the *means* of Jones's downfall may remain mysterious but the *reasons* for it do not, the conflicting myths of the Western Christian cultivation of chaos and the pagan self-sacrifice to the hungry, capricious gods of the jungle stand on equal terms in Aguilera Malta's play precisely because they do not directly confront one another; the two times merely coexist in the same space and the loser, unfortunately, is the poor soul whose homeland must play unwilling host to the two of them.

5
Between Ethnicity and Internationalism: Jorge Enrique Adoum and *Entre Marx y una mujer desnuda* (1976)

> Los escritores de hoy [tienen] una conciencia lúcida de toda su desgarradura, lo que equivale a otra desgarradura. Tal vez allí comienza esa tenacidad con que el personaje de la novela latinoamericana de ahora—el autor—se busca su identidad, su definición entre dos momentos historicos o más, entre dos mundos o más, entre dos o más civilizaciones.
>
> [Today's writers have a keen awareness of their being torn between things, which amounts to a further tearing apart. Perhaps this is where it begins, that tenacity with which the main character in the current Latin American novel—the author—searches for his identity, his definition between two or more historical moments, between two or more worlds, between two or more civilizations.]
> —Jorge Enrique Adoum, "El realismo de la otra realidad"

In the above essay, published four years before his landmark novel, *Entre Marx y una mujer desnuda* (*Between Marx and a Naked Woman*), Jorge Enrique Adoum elaborates on the theme of "betweenness." According to Adoum, contemporary Latin American writers are torn between historical junctures, trapped between culture and underdevelopment, between nearly identical governments perpetually announcing cosmetic "structural transformations" and the millennial violence of *guerrilla* warriors, between withdrawal and engagement, between alienation from consumer-oriented societies and the fight for economic justice, between hating the social class that they supposedly belong to and the barriers that keep them from fully entering it.[1] But he doesn't openly discuss the "between" of ethnicity in a multiethnic society, which is a major part of the "betweenness" felt by many Latin American writers who do not belong to the dominant European Christian ethnicities.

In current U.S.-style terminology, Adoum would be considered a Lebanese-Ecuadorian writer, but he rejects that label:

> Soy hijo de inmigrantes por ambos lados, pero jamás sentí formar parte de su cultura. Digamos, retomando la vieja oposición entre los lazos de la sangre y los lazos de la tierra, que jamás sentí los primeros. Desde la infancia asumí una nacionalidad ecuatoriana, casi indígena y, en la edad adulta, latinoamericana.[2]

> [I am the son of immigrants on both sides, but I never felt that I was part of their culture. That is, taking up the old opposition between being bound by blood or bound to the land, I never felt the former. Since childhood I assumed an Ecuadorian nationality, almost indigenous, and, as an adult, Latin American.]

Adoum was born in Ambato, Ecuador, so there was no legal need to "assume" a native Ecuadorian nationality, unless it was a deliberate decision to eliminate at least one of the multiple "betweens" of the writer's identity. He specifies, however, that he was probably about six years old when he "decided to become Ecuadorian,"[3] so the mature, intellectual entanglements described above would have been considerably minimalized. What appears to be operating, then, is a conscious choice, at a very early age, to mask or abandon all traces of "ethnicity." This is a common second-generation immigrant writer's response to the dilemma of ethnic "betweenness," and a reasonable one, given the historical conditions at that moment (the early 1930s), when univocal nationalism was heavily favored over diversity.

But such ethnic masking is no longer required today. Adoum's rejection of "ethnicity" may therefore be primarily an attempt on the part of a left-wing intellectual to reject class, particularly as embodied in the bourgeois, assimilationist identity of the "successful" Lebanese immigrants (first by embracing an "almost indigenous" identity, then an international one).

As with other Mediterranean (and Eastern European) groups, the great wave of Lebanese immigration to the new world took place between the 1880s and the 1930s, peaking during the First World War and into the early 1920s. Hundreds of thousands of Lebanese emigrated, two-thirds of them moving to the United States, and the majority of the remainder to South America. Besides the ravages of war, during which as much as one-eighth of the population died (more than 500,000 people), the social factors favoring Lebanese immigration included a larger urban, educated middle class than most of the surrounding Middle Eastern countries.[4] The Lebanese emigrants were also overwhelmingly Christian, which must have made the generic local Spanish term for them, "turcos" ("Turks"), especially irritating: many of them were in fact fleeing persecution by the Ottoman Turks.

Often arriving with limited funds or knowledge of the local languages, many Lebanese immigrants got their start in the new society the same way that members of American immigrant groups of this same period (such as the Jews) did: as traveling salesmen and peddlars. While this generated negative stereotypes (in both societies), U.S. Jews and Lebanese Ecuadorians also share the fascinating characteristic of having had considerable impact on their adopted national cultures in spite of the relatively small size of their populations within those cultures. In the late 1920s, the Lebanese population of Ecuador was less than the Lebanese population of Flint, Michigan (1,066 to 1,500, respectively),[5] yet the community has produced prominent businessmen, writers, politicians (including congressional deputies and senators), and two presidents of the republic, Abdala Bucaram, who served from 1996–97, and Jamil Mahuad, who was elected in 1998. (Colombia's president from 1978–82, Julio César Turbay Ayala, and Argentina's President Carlos Saúl Menem, are also of Lebanese descent.)

Did they need to exchange "ethnicity for nationality" in order to accomplish this, as Adoum seems to have done?[6] How does such successful assimilation in a previous generation inform and interrelate with the current (re-)emergence of "ethnicity" in Ecuador (and other societies)? Because there is a myth, and a downside, to *mestizaje* as well. The myth, as expressed in Ecuadorian high school history books, is that *mestizaje* was part of the future Ecuadorian national identity "thousands of years before the Spaniards landed on American shores," and that the Conquistadors were themselves *mestizos*, coming from a land that had been previously occupied by Romans, Vandals, Arabs, and Christians, among others, and that "for this reason the union of these two groups [Conquistadors and native Americans] met no resistance."[7]

This is the *mestizaje* of magical realism, in which we experience "the closeness or near-merging of two realms, two worlds."[8] But not all mixings are like water for chocolate. Adoum's poem "*Mestizaje*" appeared in his collection, *Los cuadernos de la tierra* (1962), the year before he left Ecuador for a fifteen-year period of political exile. In it, Adoum clearly equates *mestizaje* with rape:

Mestizaje

Quién conoce a su padre, quién
le ha visto fatigarse el riñón
o palpó por el revés la piel
entre el viento y el alma. ¿Las viudas,
tinajas aburridas, las fértiles descuidadas
por asalto?
    Yo sé que fui una mancha
de la noche en un cuerpo, la no lavada,
la que no preguntó por mí. ¿Cómo pregunto:
Pasajeros de apuro, cuál de ustedes
me llenó de odio desde el útero, como
desde una pieza de hotel para parejas,
quién alisó la funda de violencia
donde gritó mi madre (oigo en mi hueso
el grito, más bien un eco de su hueso),
puede ella reconocer la barba, probar
—el regimiento en formación—la lengua
con la lengua y decir: este fue el hombre?
¿Tuvo una palabra de varón, rota
en silabas por el beso, o sólo pelo
y líquido? ¿Y el resto, es mío el resto
de vivir cada día todo el día, toda
la oscuridad de la frente y el comienzo?

Ahora bien: existo de repente, recién
inaugurado. Y no hay cedazos en la sangre,
no hay visitante que la conserve sola,
el nombre a veces: oh apellido del vientre,
estirpe que averigua quién mismo es, qué
diablos quiere, para juntar como aguas
dos memorias y el rencor que resulta
entra las dos costillas.
        (Pero es grave
lo demás: ser porque sí, ilícito, de urgencia,
este empezar con un soldado y acabar
con un soldado, como un cuento de guerra.)[9]

[Who knows their father, who
has seen him tire out his kidneys
or touched the other side of the skin
between the wind and the soul? Widows,
bored earthen vessels, fertile women untouched
by assaults?
    I know that I was a stain
of the night on a body, unwashed,

that doesn't ask about me. How do I ask:
Rushing passengers, which one of you
filled me with hate from the uterus, as
from a hotel room for couples,
who smoothed out the wrapper of violence
where my mother screamed (I hear the scream
in my bones, or rather an echo of her bones),
could she recognize the beard, try
—the regiment in formation—his tongue
with her tongue and say: this was the man?
Was a man's word given, broken
into syllables by the kiss, or just hair
and liquid? And the rest, the rest is mine
to live all day every day, all
the darkness of my face and the beginning?

All right then: I suddenly exist, brand
new. And there are no filters in the blood,
no visitor who keeps it separate,
the sometime name: Oh name from the belly,
race that seeks to find out what it is, whatever
the hell it is, to unite like waters
two memories and the enmity that comes
between two ribs.
      (But the rest
is serious: to exist because yes, illicitly, urgently,
this begins with a soldier and ends
with a soldier, like a war story.)]

While the dominant practices within literary and cultural studies, the present volume included, tend to perceive *mestizaje* as the fascinating mixture of indigenous perspectives, cosmologies and worldviews with those of Western culture, within Ecuador attempts have been made to present ethnic and cultural diversity as a "burdensome residue of the republic's colonial past and as an impediment to its future progress," and to resolve the problems connected with such diversity by claiming that all Ecuadorians are *mestizos* and therefore equal.[10] Furthermore, this particular, politically useful definition of *mestizaje* means, "becoming more urban, more Christian, more civilized; less rural, less black, less Indian," in other words, more *white*; this form of mestizaje is even called *blanqueamiento* ("whitening")[11] by both supporters and detractors. The hegemonic viewpoint thus begrudgingly acknowledges that the "Ecuadorian man" ("el hombre ecuatoriano") is a mixture of Spanish-European, African, and indigenous DNA, but so far has done very little to incorporate the Lebanese, Chinese, and other immigrant populations into that identity.

In *Entre Marx y una mujer desnuda, mestizaje* is not the wondrous mix, the unification of opposites, the mediation between contradictions of the magical realists; it is a vertiginous, unsettling, terrifying betweenness. Perhaps that is why Adoum so urgently sought, at first, the solid, individual identity of an Ecuadorian, and later, the broadly encompassing plenitude of a "Latin American" identity.

As the title indicates, in this novel, Adoum posits as diametric opposites the sites of Marxist intellectual and collective political struggle and the individual sensual pleasures of (the implied male) enjoying a woman's body. While one may perhaps agree that engaged, selfless political struggle and self-absorbed hedonism are near opposite ends of the human scale of activities, today's feminists would have little trouble arguing that a woman's body can be (and often is) just as much a site of intellectual and political struggle as Adoum's writing desk seems to be.[12]

As Adoum put it, in a 1977 interview:

Entre Marx y una mujer desnuda corresponde a los dos extremos de lo que constituye la vasta gama de las preocupaciones del hombre contemporáneo: los problemas sociales y colectivos, y los problemas íntimos y privados, que no siempre se complementan pero que tampoco se oponen siempre.[13]

[*Between Marx and a Naked Woman* corresponds to the two extremes of what constitutes the vast scale of contemporary man's preoccupations: social and collective problems, and intimate and private problems, which don't always complement each other, but which don't always oppose each other either.]

But there are far more than "two worlds" in this novel. *Entre Marx* is obsessed with multiplicity. There are three principal narrative perspectives—an author who addresses the reader in the second person, a first person narrator, and a third person narrator—plus a fourth voice ("Bichito," who appears sporadically in the physical margins of the text). Numerous recurring images, themes, and even whole scenes continually disappear and reappear. Other items are torn from newspapers, creating a collage that defies the hegemonic in favor of the multiform, patchwork "betweenness" of modern identity.[14]

As a text that "invites—and incites—multiple readings,"[15] *Entre Marx* is a challenge to the hegemonic projects of those who believe that there is only one way of doing things, one way of thinking and being. This challenge is of central concern to other ethnic Latin American writers, although their specific historical and political situations often require them to employ less direct "challenges."

Writing in Argentina in the early 1970s, Alicia Steimberg uses the indirection of exaggerated, even zany (yet bitter) humor to skewer her targets. In *La loca 101* (*Crazy Woman #101*), Steimberg describes one variety of crazy people ("locos") who understand each other

> perfectamente en el único idioma entendible que existe, que es el español, variedad rioplatense, subvariedad porteña, actualizado a junio de 1971, en el sector de la clase media con pretensiones de intelectual, y los que no lo entiendan que revienten.[16]

> [perfectly in the only understandable language that exists, which is Spanish, the River Plate variety, Buenos Aires subvariety, dated June 1971, in the sector of the middle class with intellectual pretensions, and whoever doesn't understand it can drop dead.]

Other examples of condemnation by indirect association in *La loca 101* include a description of a group of Argentines who are studying English, to whom it must be explained "a thousand times" that things are done *differently* in English, who laugh at the fact that adjectives come before nouns, as if nothing but the Spanish word order could possibly be correct (89). Although the people who think there is only one way of doing things are, in this case, language students, when you are holding up one type of fool for ridicule, do not related fools get dragged in as well? Fools who think there is only one race, or one correct political point of view? In 1972, Ecuador's leader General Rodríguez Lara declared, "There is no more Indian problem, we all become white when we accept the goals of national culture,"[17] as if there were *one* national culture.

In *Entre Marx*, Adoum depicts the use of outdated, traditional pedagogy to criticize the meaningless of the rote memorization of pat answers to profound religious questions: "Tell me, my son, is there a God?" "Yes, father, there is a God" ("¿Decidme, hijo, hay Dios?" "Sí, padre, Dios hay," 7), but is able to make obscene fun of it as well: one of his friends is expelled from Catholic school "because during Mass he said (and we only learned Latin by ear) 'Agnus Dei clitoris pecata mundi"—instead of "quitolis pecata mundi" ("porque en misa dijo [y nunca aprendimos latín sino de oídas] 'Agnus Dei clitoris pecata mundi,'" 42).

The hegemonic goals of neighboring educational systems are ridiculed when the young protagonist in Goldemberg's *Jacobo Lerner* describes his inability to absorb the foundational myths of Peruvian society as they are taught in secondary school ("It's a story all about a man called Manco Capac, who is the father of all Peruvians, and comes out of Lake Titicaca with his wife, and that's all I remember. I think he might have something to do with the god of the sun," 15), and a similar central character in Gerardo Mario Goloboff's "The Passion According to San Martín" is taught a version of Argentine history so insular and self-contained that it is without proper names, only glorious epithets: he learns about the "Great Captain," the "Condor of the Andes," and a general called the "Saint of the Sword."[18] One is reminded of the native Indochinese under French colonialism who were given primary textbooks that "educated" them about their "Gallic ancestors," and perhaps the textbook accounts of the *Mayflower* in the United States as well.

One of the goals of magical realism is to invalidate the colonial enterprise through an expression of difference,[19] but such expressions of difference can be deadly. In Goldemberg's *Play by Play*, the narrator describes the beating of a soldier who has the nerve (or perhaps the ignorance) to insist that he is both Jewish *and* Peruvian, when it is clear that in the other soldiers' minds one is not allowed to be more than one thing.[20] In *The Strange Nation of Rafael Mendes*, Scliar mocks the figures of Torquemada, who refuses to believe that the world is round and that new sea routes can be found, plotted and explored, and King Manuel of Portugal, who declared in 1497, "All Jews must convert to Christianity," and even the idea that "The period at the end of this sentence marks the end of the story" (115, 122). Adoum's solution to the latter issue is to have *Entre Marx* begin and end in the middle of two different sentences. In between, Adoum lashes out at the Chilean military of 1973, which executed people for "obeying a foreign doctrine" (meaning communism), and then poses the question about Christianity: "Did the aborigines invent it?" ("¿inventado lo han los aborígenes?" 234).

Against this context of exclusion, even annihilation, of the "foreign," Lois Parkinson Zamora has written, "to write universalizing fictions is a revolutionary act."[21] But what if the "universal" is achieved through ethnic masking, or perhaps complete denial, a flight from ethnicity into hyper-assimilation? Can a writer be both local and universal, ethnic and international? The problem of cultural specificity versus international acceptance resonates throughout the history of Ecuadorian literature and is still operative today.

Neither the encyclopedic *Indice de la narrativa ecuatoriana*, nor the majority of articles and biographical sketches in his books specifically mention Adoum's Lebanese heritage. Perhaps, in Ecuador, his last name is understood to represent his ancestry, as if no further word on the subject were needed, but this ethnicity is foregrounded, for example, in the Mexican press: In a tribute published in *Nivel* (1972), the poet Mahfud Massís is referred to as "A poet of our time, of our continent, whose name, with such clearly Arabic resonances, enriches Spanish poetry" ("Poeta de este tiempo, de este Continente, con cuyo nombre de claras resonancias arábigas se enriquece la poesía de lengua castellana").[22] Massís was born in Chile in 1916, and he is repeatedly referred to in the *Nivel* article as being Chilean, Latin American, as well as a "brother" of the Arabic "race." The only prominent article on Adoum that contains an extended discussion of his Lebanese origins was published in Mexico.[23]

On the one hand, there is little doubt that, except for some childhood discrimination while he was still in elementary school, Adoum is completely accepted as an Ecuadorian within his society.[24] And this security can be seen as he claims the uniquely Ecuadorian smells of "cumin, machica and earth" as his own, as well as the national foods, "the cooked corn of Alausí [in the *sierra*], the plaintain-balls of Bucay, the pineapples of Naranjito [both on the coast]" ("los choclos cocidos de Alausí, los bollos de plátano en Bucay, las piñas de Naranjito," *Entre Marx*, 37, 110–11).

But what is the cost of this acceptance? What has been suppressed? According to Adoum, his father was a hard, indifferent man who insisted on maintaining elements of the traditional Lebanese culture that Adoum felt were out of place in the new society, such as a prohibiton against talking during meals. When the young Jorge Enrique protested that he couldn't take it anymore, his father answered evenly, "If you can't take it anymore, leave" ("Si no aguantas más, vete").[25] Adoum left for Chile at age 18, where he met Mahfud Massís and became Pablo Neruda's personal assistant. This broadening of experience began to put Adoum on the international literary map, but something had to be left behind. Adoum exchanged ethnicity for nationality.

It is a common theme in ethnic literature of the Americas: the native-born child becomes increasingly uncomfortable with his or her parents' embarrassing accents, table manners, attempts to fit in or, conversely, their ignorance of the local language and customs and occasionally spirit-crushing adherence to obsolete cultural codes, so that as they grow up the children change their names, fix their "accents" (or their noses), and try to get as far away from the "ghetto" as possible, whether in geographic distance or social ascendance.

If the images of the parents in immigrant and ethnic literature can often be understood as stand-ins for the central character's genetic cultural origins, what Werner Sollors refers to as "descent,"[26] then Adoum's numerous interweaving narratives in *Entre Marx* present us with equally numerous and problematic relations with his "parents." At one point, the first-person narrator describes his sensations while contemplating a 4,000-year-old skull unearthed near the coastal town of Punín, clearly identifying himself as the child of one of the oldest known Ecuadorians:[27]

> De modo que esto es mi padre . . . esta calavera no tiene personalidad, se parece a otras, a todas. . . . los antropólogos pueden reconstruir, a partir del cráneo y del tegumento blando, el retrato del difunto. . . . Pero yo no soy antropólogo [y] nunca vi su retrato. (16)

> [In some way this is my father . . . [yet] this skull has no personality, it looks like any other, like all others. . . . Anthropologists can reconstruct, from just the skull and the soft tissue, a portrait of the deceased. But I'm not an anthropologist and I never saw his portrait.]

The narrator then slides into childhood memories of the priest telling everyone that he is "the child of a drunk" and his shouting in response that that was a lie, that his father was a smuggler: "Too bad he wasn't a bandit, a highway robber, a dynamiter, because . . . I was left without a hero" ("Lástima que no hubiera sido bandolero, salteador de caminos, dinamitero, porque . . . me quedé sin héroe"). What is publicly understood to be his heritage is such a source of discomfort that he attempts to alter it, but he remembers his mother commanding him, "You have to love him because he's your father" ("Tienes que quererlo porque es tu padre"). And when his revisionist aunts try to "change his father" by "cleaning" up his image, the narrator quotes a popular joke about ethnicity suggesting that such changes are impossible, even absurd: "I tell you I was a blond-haired, blue-eyed baby, but they switched me at the clinic" ("De bien chiquito yo dizque era rubio y ojizarco, pero me cambiaron en la clínica"; all quotes 17). Finally he returns to the skull, profaning it with his thoughts: "What connects me to this bone? A few drops of semen: He made me, thanks a lot old man, and took off" ("¿Qué me une a este hueso? Algunas gotas de semen: Me hizo, muchas gracias papá, y se mandó a cambiar," 19).

Later, Adoum returns to this image of "el Hombre de Punín,"

where "the whole story" of Ecuadorian identity begins: "I didn't choose the social class I was born into and which is held against me, and which I have tried to get out of for reasons of aesthetics and hygiene" ("No escogí la clase social de la que vengo y que me reprochan, y de la que he tratado de salir por razones de estética e higiene," 224).

The reflections upon this skull are fictional inventions that are not directly autobiographical in any way. Adoum even ridicules the "idiots" who think that all first-person narratives are necessarily autobiographical (22). Yet parts of *Entre Marx* clearly are autobiographical, for example, the description of a portrait of General Franco hanging in the physics lab in a Jesuit High School, next to a portrait of "la Dolorosa," Our Lady of Sorrows (229). Adoum attended a Jesuit High School during the 1930s, and he testifies that it had a portrait of Franco hanging in the chemistry lab.[28]

Perhaps, for Adoum, this skull, this ancestral "father" refers to the past, to the weight of history upon us, what he calls "excrement from some prehistoric asshole that's still falling on us in this century" ("excrementos de qué ano prehistórico que sigen cayendo en nuestro siglo," 234); Franco seems to fulfill a similar role in Scliar's *The Strange Nation of Rafael Mendes*, representing through his perpetual comatose condition a past that simply refuses to die. Even the Marxism of Adoum's title appears in the form of Marx's mother complaining that her son should have spent his time amassing capital rather than writing about it. This is followed by the narrator's rejection of his matrilineal heritage as he confesses that all of his schoolmates had pretty mothers (or so they said), while his was short, mean, and vulgar (24). No wonder there is an identity crisis in *Entre Marx*: one cannot escape from or change the "parent" of human history, no matter how far one travels.

One of the more effective defensive weapons in this desperate situation is a brand of humor that borders on the blasphemous, as in the "prehistoric asshole" image above. Humor is iconoclastic (especially scatological humor)[29]; it is a great leveler, bringing the mighty and the pretentious down to the same level as the clown, who has always enjoyed the fool's prerogative of indirect criticism through humor. Adoum writes:

> esa gran aventura de lo imaginario que es *Cien años de soledad*, es al mismo tiempo la burlona epopeya de ciertas luchas frecuentes en América Latina. Burlona, porque el humor es una de las formas del cuestionamiento, de la impugnación, del rechazo de esta realidad.[30]

[that great adventure of the imaginary, *One Hundred Years of Solitude*, is also an epic mockery of some frequent Latin American struggles. A mockery because humor is one of the forms of questioning, of opposing, of denying this reality.]

In *Entre Marx*, Adoum applies this mockery to twisting the original words of sacred texts, as in the "clitoris pecata mundi" example above, or calling the "Testigos de Jehová" (Jehova's Witnesses) the "Testículos de Jehová" (Jehova's Testicles, 41), or near-sacred texts, in the case of Ecuador's national anthem, whose opening chorus runs:

> ¡Salve oh Patria, mil veces! ¡Oh Patria!
> ¡gloria a ti! Ya tu pecho rebosa
> gozo y paz, y tu frente radiosa
> más que el sol contemplamos lucir.
>
> Hail, oh country, a thousand times! Oh country!
> Glory to you! With your heart overflowing
> with good cheer and peace, and your radiant brow
> brighter than the sun that shines before us
>   —words by Juan León Mera

Here is Adoum's version:

> la patria salve oh patria mil veces oh patria
> ya tu pecho rebosa gozo y paz—sí mucho gozo y mucha paz cojudos—
> y otras ñoñerías del señor juan león mera y otros señores.
>   25
>
> the country hail oh country a thousand times oh country
> with your heart overflowing with good cheer and peace—Yeah, so much good cheer and peace, you jerks—
> and other shittiness of Mr. Juan León Mera and other gentlemen.

Mahfud Massís employs this technique as one of the driving concepts of his most popular work, *Leyendas del cristo negro* (*Legends of the Black Christ*), a "social poem" that went through six editions within ten years (the title itself is a direct challenge to some firmly held beliefs). Massís imitates the language and formulae of the New Testament, but turns out nearly blasphemous variations on the original theme: the biblical Jesus miraculously cures a blind man by throwing water in his eyes; Massís has him spitting in a drunkard's face before explaining to the man that he should try to mend his ways;[31] where Jesus defies the crowd who would stone a prostitute to death with the admonition, "Let he among you who is without sin cast the first stone," Massís's Jesus says, "Who among you, sons of the massing crowd, did not enter her and snuggle between her breasts?" ("¿Quién de vosotros, hijos de la turba, no entró en ella y se holgó en sus pechos?" 32). Another "miracle" involves turning a dark-skinned child into a light-skinned one (23), which bears some intertextual relation to Adoum's joke above about being born blond, but having been switched at birth.[32]

The function of such a "blasphemous" re-visioning of Jesus is not merely to shock the bourgeois reader (who no longer shocks that easily), but to remove the figure of Christ from an untouchably distant and sacred representation to the present reality, just as in need of reform as Roman Jerusalem, using the language of our time. Massís's Jesus is thus quite similar to the "santo varón" of José de la Cuadra. The comments one Chilean critic made in 1964 are worth quoting at length:

Mahfud Massís, poeta nuestro, mano a mano con el peligro, retoma y reelabora la figura de Cristo, trasladándolo a nuestro siglo traspasado de cambios profundos y dramáticas contradicciones. [Massís] recoge la figura de Cristo en su condición verdadera: la de un luchador contra la injusticia social, la de un genuino revolucionario. Lo despojó de su halo divino, humanizándolo, convirtiéndolo en un hombre de hechura total. [Massís utiliza] la verdad quemante, la ironía, la burla . . . la más efectiva y terrible prédica contra los fariseos, contra los explotadores de la miseria, contra las más arraigadas hipocresias . . . Es el aporte de Massís a esa literatura para llegar al corazón mismo de los pueblos. . . . Todo en un lenguaje universal. . . . Si alguna vez alguien pretendió negar la poesia de Massís porque no fue capaz de comprenderla, ahora sus objeciones serán barridas.[33]

[Our poet, Mahfud Massís, hand-in-hand with danger, reexamines and remakes the figure of Christ, translating him to our century, which is full of profound changes and dramatic contradictions. (Massís) puts Christ in his true condition: that of a fighter against social injustice, that of a genuine revolutionary. He removes his divine halo, humanizing him, turning him into a man of pure action. [Massís uses] the burning truth, irony, mockery . . . the most effective and devastating attack against pharisees, against exploiters of misery, against the most deeply-rooted hypocrisies. . . . Massís's contribution with this literature is to deliver it right to the heart of the people (because it is) written in a universal language. . . . If someone has ever ignored Massís's poetry because they couldn't understand it, their objections will now be swept away.]

This issue of writing works that challenge the status quo, but that "the people" can understand, is a particularly complex one for Adoum. Humor may be the people's weapon for temporarily or symbolically bringing down authority figures, or for indirect political criticism, and Adoum uses humor in this fashion (just as Steimberg gets away with depicting unnamed, disembodied authoritative voices who admit to eating human flesh, because these accusations are dismissable as the ramblings of "la loca" of the title). But one of Adoum's frequently stated desires in *Entre Marx* is to challenge the status quo by writing a work that "the people" *can't* understand. He repeatedly "ridicules the passive and conformist reader, seeking instead the reader as accomplice, as critic, and as participant."[34]

Because Adoum's "people" are not Massís's "people." In 1972, Adoum wrote,

en América Latina no se puede por ahora escribir para el pueblo; en muchos casos no llegan a él ni siquiera los medios de información (de dominación, decía alguien) de masas. Para los campesinos analfabetos casi en su totalidad y para los obreros alfabetizados que prácticamente no leen por falta de costumbre o de apetencia de lectura o porque no pueden pagar el precio de los libros, resultan exactamente iguales una novela policial o un volumen de cuentos fantásticos: porque no existen.[35]

[In Latin America today you can't write for the people: in most cases the media of mass communication (domination, someone once said) don't reach them. For peasants, who are almost all illiterate, and for literate workers who practically never read because they're not accustomed to it or have no desire to read or because that can't afford to buy a book, a police novel or a volume of fantastic tales turn out to be exactly the same: because they don't exist.]

Because of the small, mostly urban, middle class audience for Ecuadorian books, a self-reflexive essay in the middle of *Entre Marx* complains that a book "almost always ends up precisely in the hands of those readers for whom it has not been written" ("casi siempre va a parar precisamente en manos de esos lectores para quienes no a sido escrito," 95)—presumably meaning that the people who need to read it are the bourgeoisie and imperialists he attacks, as well as the great masses of educationally marginalized people who need to be "brought into the conversation" (although this level of precision is never spelled out). Perhaps that is why Adoum has stated that "getting published in Ecuador is the same as remaining unpublished" ("publicar en Ecuador quivale a seguir inédito").[36]

It should not be surprising, then, that throughout *Entre Marx*, Adoum's narrative voices struggle with the question of the function of literature in society. Critic María Dolores Aguilera prefaces an interview with Adoum with the thought, "Words are conventional by definition, but taken to their limit by poets" ("Convencionales por definición, las palabras son arrastradas hasta el filo de sí por el poeta").[37] Adoum revels in neologisms, inventing words, "demujerado," "verdaderabsurda" ("dewomaned," "veritabsurd"), and turning nouns into adverbs: "indiamente," "febreramente," "parasiempremente," etc. (Indianly, Februarily, foreverly).[38]

This reduction of the magical realist technique of melding disparate worlds, plotlines, scenes, and images to the smallest unit available in the novel form, individual words, continues the magical realist project of producing new knowledge, which suggests an appropriation of power from the traditional sources of knowledge. According to Lois Parkinson Zamora and Wendy B. Faris, "magical realist works remind us that the novel began as a popular form, with communal imperatives that continue to operate in many parts of the world."[39] Many canonical national authors (e.g., Shakespeare) are credited with having invented words and phrases, which in some cases may in fact have been the first textual recording of existing popular expressions. Much twentieth-century immigrant literature, often written for tightly knit ethnic-American communities, focuses on the mingling of languages: new words must be brought into the old language to facilitate survival in the new society, while "foreign" words insinuate themselves into ethnic works written in English. This fluidity of language and concepts, located at the basic level of individual words, suggests a society in which identities are still being invented, in which all things are not necessarily fixed.[40]

In *The Strange Nation of Rafael Mendes*, Scliar writes how the Christians, once a marginalized, oppressed group, "transformed the language of their former torturers into a weapon of victory," in other words, the Latin spoken by their Roman persecutors becomes the language of the Church (and then of the Holy Office of the Inquisition, 137). Ethnic-Americans and other hyphenated groups often use the language and imagery of the "outsiders" so effectively that the dominant group may not be aware that a transnationalization is taking place. Scliar uses the example of the Jews rising "like the phoenix . . . from our own ashes." The character, Rafael Mendes, then notes, "The phoenix was an invention of the Greeks, the same Greeks who had kept the Jewish people subjugated until the advent of the Maccabees" (138). Alicia Steimberg's veiled attack on the Argentine legacy of the *desaparecidos*, "Cecilia's Last Will and Testament," bears a resemblance, through extremely black humor, to the Christian New Year's tradition of reciting a comical *testimonio*.[41] And as noted in the Introduction, Engels supported the tactic of using existing tools (i.e., the "bourgeois" novel) for one's own purposes.

Adoum struggles with the issue of getting answers from art. In 1972, this produced the identity crisis of the practicing artist who feels that

> al fin y al cabo el arte no es tan, tan importante; no da soluciones—eso se sabe—sino que plantea preguntas; no da explicaciones, las exige. Las grandes interrogaciones humanas inmediatas no piden respuestas artísticas, sino una fractura de la historia, dolorosa, violenta, que no puede ser realizada por la literatura.[42]

> [in the end art is not so very important; it doesn't provide solutions— that is well-known—it asks questions; it doesn't give explanations, it demands them. The great contemporary human questions don't require artistic answers, but rather a painful and violent fracture from history, which cannot be accomplished by literature.]

We are certainly no longer in the era of *Uncle Tom's Cabin*, in which a work of fiction can allegedly start a civil war (while outselling nonfiction books on the same topic by a factor of thirty to one).[43] But what is so unimportant about asking questions, with demanding explanations? In the semi-autobiographical "Prologue" to *Entre Marx* (which appears nearly four-fifths of the way into the book), Adoum confesses that

> en fin de cuentas, todos tenemos las piernas más o menos rotas por la comodidad, atadas por la costumbre, deformadas por el temor, inválidas por la complicidad con un sistema que rechazamos en nuestros momentos de lucidez pero al que nos sometemos cada día. (189)

> [in the end, all of us have had our legs more or less broken by our comfortable tendencies, tied down by customs, deformed by fear, crippled by complicity with a system that we reject in moments of lucidity but to which we submit ourselves every day.]

5: BETWEEN ETHNICITY AND INTERNATIONALISM 101

Adoum appears to be arguing (confessing?) that class-conscious—but middle-class—writers and intellectuals are not really capable of breaking any real-world molds. However, this passage suggests another possibility, that the stability of the continental identity of a Latin American that he sought in response to the ethnic (and other) betweenness that was thrust upon him has in some way been stifling his voice. Is the multivocal primal scream of this (literally) endless novel a desire to contain the disparities of difference within some kind of all-encompassing wholeness? Just after the novel was published, Adoum stated that "reality is much broader than that which [literary] realism can contain" ("la realidad es mucho más amplia que la que el realismo puede contener"),[44] suggesting that the "new" Latin American novel is even more totalizing in some ways than traditional narrative realism.

Etienne Decroux, who turned traditional white-face pantomime into "modern mime" during the 1930s–60s, used to say, "Art begins with a taking away."[45] Thus, Plato's charge that art fails to fully represent reality is in fact the primary starting point of art. Ethnic Latin American authors such as Moacyr Scliar and Clarice Lispector, both Brazilian Jews, have approached the multiple possibilities of betweenness as a liberation from closed-mindedness. Lispector writes in the dedication to *The Hour of the Star* that the novel is "an unfinished book because it offers no answer."[46] Rather than being a lament, this provides her with a reason to keep moving forward: "So long as I have questions to which there are no answers, I shall go on writing" (11). The multiplicity of *The Hour of the Star* begins even before it "begins," with thirteen possible subtitles or alternative titles offered, suggesting that one fixed meaning simply cannot be applied to this tale. A short work, Lispector's "The Fifth Story," begins:

> This story could be called "The Statues." Another possible title would be "The Killing." Or even "How to Kill Cockroaches." So I shall tell at least three stories, all of them true. . . . Although they constitute one story, they could become a thousand and one, were I to be granted a thousand and one nights.[47]

One of the traditional Jewish approaches to textual analysis, Talmudic study, contains the essential, driving concept that final answers are not possible, but that, rather than producing a crisis, the lack of final answers shall be the impetus for further questions and further searching. "Final" answers can only result from hubris, and lead to prejudice, narrow-mindedness, intolerance, death. Scliar's Rafael

Mendes profits from this legacy of ongoing, unfinishable thought to escape from a painful life into a dream-world that awaits his construction: "Instead of solutions, fantasies; instead of answers, imaginary possibilities. The perfect message from a perplexed individual" (306). Even Lenin believed that fictional (fantastical, utopian) thinking could eventually lead to real-world action, for a better world must first be imagined before it can be realized.[48]

By 1988, Adoum had come to believe that art *can* bring about real-world change, "if we understand cultural action as the vehicle of the social change to which it aspires" ("entendiendo la acción cultural como el vehículo del cambio social a que aspira").[49] One wonders what the results might be if Adoum, who is clearly a world-class man of letters, were to return to the wellspring of Lebanese culture that he apparently abandoned as a child and examine with new eyes this alternative source of inspiration to the Western-style idiosyncratic thought patterns that have plagued him, and Ecuadorian society as well.

6
Two Contemporary Novelists: Dialogic Cycles of History in Eliécer Cárdenas's *Polvo y ceniza* (*Dust and Ashes*) and Alicia Yánez Cossío's *Bruna, soroche y los tíos* (*Bruna and Her Family*)

At first glance, these two novels appear to be quite different. *Bruna, soroche y los tíos* features the daughter of a wealthy, urban family with a centuries-old, privileged life in the capital city in Ecuador's northern *sierra*, while *Polvo y ceniza* features the son of a poor, rural family in the south. However, both of these Ecuadorian novels, published in the 1970s, attempt to re-vision Ecuadorian history and society. Bruna is in the process of discovering (and thereby re-making) her family's complete history, and *Polvo y ceniza*'s Naún Briones makes his own marginal forms of history. This re-visioning based in part on two concepts that have been put forth by Josefina Ludmer (in the context of the Argentine "gaucho" genre).

First, Ludmer contends that there is often a "double system" of justice operating in Latin American societies—urban and rural—characterized by the written codes of state law and the traditional, oral codes of common law, respectively ("un doble sistema de justicia que diferencia ciudad y campo . . . una ley estatal, escrita, que enfrenta en el campo al código consuetudinario, oral y tradicional").[1]

Second, Ludmer introduces the critical concept that popular culture "can be considered as conservative," especially when it idealizes the past, but that it is also by its very nature rebellious because it always depicts the struggle against a situation in which the people are subjected to unjust domination ("La cultura popular puede ser considerada conservadora—en sus formas y en los modos en que idealiza el pasado—pero es constitutivamente rebelde: manifiesta siempre . . . una situación de dominación-sujeción y la rebeldía frente a ella").[2]

Dominant discourse typically classifies the oral tale as a traditional form, in contrast to the written word, which is considered to be a conveyor of modernity. Dominant discursive practice likewise frequently links the traditional with repression, while the modern signifies liberation. Under certain circumstances, this is a valid equation. But the reader will not be astonished by the proposition that the written word can also serve as an instrument of oppression. In the case of documented history, the written word holds the dominant position, marginalizing oral (hi)stories. When the written word is used to further concretize repressive hegemony, does the oral tale serve a counter-hegemonic function?[3]

Possibly, but *which* oral tale? Who speaks in this tale? Many marginalized discourses reproduce on a smaller scale the oppressive role played by traditionally dominant discourse systems, for example, the case of the feminine literary voice, which has been frequently suppressed by both dominant and marginalized discourses.[4] How is one to determine how many voices have been silenced? How do we converse with silence? Alicia Yánez Cossío, who has been called Ecuador's foremost woman writer ("la primera voz literaria femenina del Ecuador"),[5] said in a 1990 interview:

[¿]cuántas mujeres habrá que escriben y no lo sabemos, cuántas mujeres que todavía tienen que escribir a escondidas[?] Hace algún tiempo hablé con una mujer muy mayor que me contó que ella escribía poesía, y que cada poema lo escondía en una caja de zapatos, un buen día el marido los descubrió y los quemó.[6]

[how many women have written without our knowing it, how many women are there who still have to keep their writing hidden(?) A while back I spoke with an elderly woman who told me that she used to write poetry, and that she hid each poem in a shoebox, and one fine day her husband found them and burned them.]

The totalizing power of official narrative—which could be characterized as masculine—has often been used historically to suppress other narratives, namely the popular and marginal—and therefore feminine (following this model)—in the broad sociopolitical and cultural arena. The novels *Bruna, soroche y los tíos* and *Polvo y ceniza* examine the possibility of reconstructing a history based on conflicting versions of that history, pitting rival narratives against each other in the same texts. This breaking up of hegemonic discourse by means of the narrative insertion of dissenting and/or popular voices is engaged not just in terms of a dichotomy between documentary evidence and oral statements. Yánez Cossío employs specifically female voices and points of view in order to challenge the dominant, masculine codification of historical events. She also uses humor in a Bakhtinian sense to move these codes "from the official sphere into the sphere of familiar communication . . . with parodic-ironic re-accentuation."[7] This is why the dialogue, especially in the early historical portion of *Bruna, soroche y los tíos*, frequently contradicts the rest of the text, and when Bruna questions the thoughts and words of her traditional family members, it is often in a tone that makes them appear hypocritical and even ridiculous.

Orality by nature is more open-ended than the written text. But even written texts, though "in one sense, explicit and finished forms" are not made "present" without "specifically active 'readings.' "[8] This is what the reader of *Polvo y ceniza* is asked to do. It is this presence, this opening of the apparently "finished" that is sought by these two writers, who do not merely construct an implied reader but also an implied *listener* in their desire to reproduce this quality of openness. Within this theoretical framework, we will discuss *Polvo y ceniza*, which presents the forty-year aftermath of the Liberal Revolution (1895) by means of competing tales of action and re-action in a nonchronological presentation of history that is broken up by the multiplicity of narrative voices relating the events, and *Bruna, soroche y los tíos*, which takes a similar approach to all of Ecuadorian history since the Conquest.[9]

Both *Polvo y ceniza* and *Bruna, soroche y los tíos*, make use of the technique of oppositional narratives "as a means of correcting the fictions of history."[10] This technique also serves to highlight "Ecuador's pluricultural heritage, a reality frequently unknown to or denied by families like the Catovils," the name of Bruna's family in Yánez Cossío's novel ("la herencia pluricultural del Ecuador, una realidad frecuentemente ignorada o negada por familias como los Catovil").[11] This heritage is the product of "the brutal union of a Spanish [Conquistador] with the daughter of an Indian chief" ("la unión brutal de un español y la hija de un cacique," ibid.), a violent encounter that results in the absolute silencing of the native Ecuadorian princess, María Illacatu.

This silence lasts from the Conquest to the present, until the arrival of Bruna, by means of whose investigations into *both* areas of national culture—the written documents that have been poorly hidden in dusty archives *and* the oral tales of the family's hitherto silenced Indian maid, Mama Chana—María Illacatu recovers her voice, and speaks through Bruna.

Eliécer Cárdenas's novel, *Polvo y ceniza*, begins seventeen years after the Liberal Revolution, with the restoration of traditional authority in the form of a reactionary bishop returning from exile after "the brutal death of the liberal *caudillo* Eloy Alfaro" in 1912. Mercedes Robles explains that this novel constitutes a questioning of official history by illustrating "the struggle for power from multiple perspectives."[12]

It can be argued that this is not a terribly revolutionary project, questioning official history when one is separated from the events in question by a safe cushion of more than sixty-five years. But if one accepts the idea that canonization, whether of ideas or of a hero, can serve paradoxically to silence those ideas (or, conversely, any ideas that might "tarnish" the hero's legendary nature), then to destabilize that canonization would indeed be a progressive project. As Raymond Williams writes, "Many positions can be tolerated when they are dead," even the most revolutionary ideas can be appropriated by the guardians of dominant culture, provided that nobody is left fighting for them.[13] Thus, one can imply that Alfaro's image is fixed in the inaccessible and untouchable pantheon of national symbols expressly to silence his ideas.[14]

Agustín Cueva follows another line of thinking: "Ecuador entered the modern age beginning with the Liberal Revolution of 1895." Even though the Revolution "did not succeed in radically transforming Ecuador's social and economic structure," the liberals instituted public, lay education, which permitted the development of an educated middle class, which resulted (among other things) in the country's first literary "explosion," a generation of Ecuadorian writers during the period 1925–1950 ("la edad moderna del Ecuador empieza con la Revolución Liberal de 1895. . . . no logró transformar radicalmente la estructura social y económica del Ecuador"). With the intent of creating a new speech-based, genuinely American, artistic language ("crear un nuevo lenguaje artístico, genuinamente americano, a partir del habla popular"),[15] these authors used dialogue that may be labeled Bakhtinian for its use of "jeering, satire, sarcasm, insults, cursing, more cursing, blasphemy, words shot like flaming arrows into the lies men tell" ("escarnio, sátira, sarcasmo, improperio, imprecación, maldición, blasfemia, palabras como dardos quemantes contra la mentira de los hombres").[16]

All of these authors dedicated themselves to exploring the possibilities of Ecuador's various *mestizo* identities. Cueva writes:

Como solía decir Jorge Icaza, en el "alma mestiza" no se desarrolla en realidad un monólogo interior, sino un permanente diálogo entre dos mundos irreconciliables.[17]

[As Jorge Icaza used to say, the "*mestizo* soul" does not really resonate with an interior monologue, but rather with a permanent dialogue between two irreconcilable worlds.[18]]

In *Polvo y ceniza*, Eliécer Cárdenas gives the readers a cyclical presentation of history that is deconstructed by the multiplicity of narrative voices. The novel opens with a scene that apparently uses a purely epic convention, beginning *in medias res* with the above-mentioned restoration of a previously exiled monarchist bishop. Very soon after the narrator presents us with the scene of the bishop's exile, in the form of what might be termed a modern, cinematic flashback (although it is important to note that Homer uses essentially the same technique in *The Iliad*). Cárdenas admits that he chooses historical themes for many of his novels in order to make the works "more epic" ("más épica").[19] Dialogic criticism considers the epic to be a closed form—that is, the action of the epic is so distant from the present, historic realm that the meaning of those actions is supposedly indisputable, and the language is so monologic that even the gods speak the same language as human beings.[20] Cárdenas undoes this definition of "epic," presenting us instead with an epic work that is fragmented and dialogic. This ironic imitation of epic style continues when Naún Briones's father, always referred to as "the muleteer" ("el arriero") rather than by his name, speaks with the bishop about the identity of the novel's "hero," who has yet to appear in the narrative. The hero's reputation, transmitted orally, always precedes his appearance in the epic narrative. But in traditional, monologic epic, this reputation is equally indisputable. The narrative has one voice only. By contrast, in *Polvo y ceniza*, while we learn a great deal about Naún Briones' reputation, there is little or no agreement between the various narrative voices.

To the father, his son is someone who sees injustice and inequality everywhere he looks, whereas to the bishop, Naún Briones' is a "lost" soul, who "would be better off if he had never been born" ("está perdido, que más le valiera no haber nacido").[21] To Major Deifilio, Briones "was nothing but a killer, a highway robber," but he also knows that many people say that he was "a good man, they describe him like a hero, they paint him as an unforgettable man" ("fue sólo un asesino, un salteador de caminos," "un buen hombre, lo describen cómo héroe, lo pintan como macho inolvidable," 72). That is why the Major tells one of the many invisible listeners in this novel,

> No permití que fotografiaran su cadáver cuando, atado a una mula, lo llevábamos para la ciudad de Loja. No. Hubieran querido hacer de él un héroe y sus reproducciones fotográficas andarían vendiéndose como relicarios en las fiestas, los mercados, las romerías. (72)

> [I didn't let them take photos of his body when we took it to Loja tied to a mule. They would have wanted to make a hero out of him, and reproductions of his photo would have been sold like reliquaries at *fiestas*, in the markets, and at shrines.]

Ironically, it is precisely the absence of documentary evidence of Briones's death that results in his mythification: "It's not true, they couldn't kill him in Piedra Lisa [Bald Rock]. He lived a long time after and died an old man, quietly, in his bed, surrounded by his children and his grandchildren," says one of many unidentified narrators ("No es verdad, en Piedra Lisa no pudieron matarlo. El vivió hasta muchos años después y se murió de viejo, tranquilo, en su cama, rodeado por sus hijos y sus nietos," 201).

But neither does the presence of documentation inhibit the production of mythical narratives. In the chapter, "Pajarito," the old bandit of the same name talks about how it is impossible to reproduce someone's life "between the dry pages of a book. . . . The man who wrote about me would be a liar, because if one's own memories are lies, someone else's memories would be even bigger lies" ("dentro de las hojas secas de un libro. . . . El hombre que escribiera sobre mí sería un mentiroso, porque si el recuerdo propio es una mentira cómo de engañador será el recuerdo ajeno," 99). But none of us are anything more than the sum of our memories, even false memories, narrativized by ourselves, others, and the narrative conventions of our society. So that in the chapter, "Victor Pardo," the poet, "with mere words" ("con sólo palabras"), tells the story of Briones's gang so effectively that he fills them with nostalgia, grief, and rage (121).

In one of the novel's many episodes the authorities attempt to dissipate the power of oral myth by means of the written word:

> la voz resfriada del viejo le estaba pidiendo el nombre, aquel nombre que al pronunciarlo allí, en esa oficina, no produjo temor, ni siquiera simple curiosidad. Ese nombre que el viejo transforma en letras con el chirrido de su pluma entintada sobre el papel. (239)

[the old man's voice was coldly asking for his name, the name that, spoken there, in that office, did not produce fear, not even simple curiosity. The name that the old man transforms into letters with his ink-dipped pen scraping across the paper.]

The municipal office tries to demythify the figure of Naún Briones, to reduce him to just another document, but in the next instant a character who "asks if he is really Naún Briones," ("le pregunta si de verdad es Naún Briones") turns out to be

> un pobre lojanito extraviado como él y que anda en esta oficina puerca averiguando el caso de un hombre muerto a puntapiés, en plena calle, hace unas semanas, unos meses, unos años. (239)

[a poor man like him, far from (his native province of) Loja, who was hanging around this goddamn office investigating the case of a man who was kicked to death in the street just a few weeks ago, a few months ago, a few years ago.]

This authoritative project of demythifying oral myth by means of written text is derailed by the insertion of an intertextual reference to the supreme representative within Ecuadorian literature of the impossibility of reproducing reality in prose: Pablo Palacio. As discussed in chapter 1, the Palacio story mentioned, "The Man Who Was Kicked to Death" ("Un hombre muerto a puntapiés"), has as one of its primary goals the total dispersion of all confidence in the authority of narrative and/or the narrator.

In "the many stories that circulated about Naún Briones," including the episodes where he apparently reproduces himself into numerous false Naúns ("las múltiples historias que corren por Naún Briones"),[22] Cárdenas offers us the paradox of a rebel hero who, by virtue of being a hero, even a popular hero, becomes a somewhat semi-official figure, who therefore is ready to be appropriated by the dominant powers. Part of Cárdenas's narrative project is to reappropriate the images of Briones from its opposite but fixed places within the official and the popular domains in order to give us unstable images and thus, in the author's own words, "rescue those of our characters who have been hidden by history and official literature" ("rescatar nuestros personajes escamoteados por la historia, la literatura oficial").[23]

In *Bruna, soroche y los tíos*, we have the same struggle to reconstruct a past as in *Polvo y ceniza*, but this time the struggles are perhaps even more difficult, because in the exceedingly unstable female space represented in this novel, not even the family name remains fixed: it continually transforms, from García—and Illacatu—to Villacatu to Villa-Cató to Catovil.[24] The dialogue is presented separately from its context, without identified speakers or listeners. In this novel, we are not dealing with several (hi)stories fighting on more or less equal terms for a bit of recognition as "truthful." In *Bruna, soroche y los tíos*, generations of lies dominate both the oral and written worlds. These lies are "recorded in the pages of a book, or even worse, in the minds of a whole generation" ("registradas en las páginas de un libro, o lo que es peor, en las mentes de toda una generación," 73). Thus, *all* sites of expression and thought are controlled by the hegemonic forces of the dominant powers. Poor Bruna seems to have no way out, until she finds the written documentation of her real name in the archives. Then she discovers that "there was another truth" in her family's house, a house in which even the door is "false" ("había otra verdad," "la puertecilla falsa," 90, 92).

But even though the first drops in this eventual flood of self-discovery come from the written word, understanding also springs forth from several intangible sources: Bruna seems to learn her more or less true history from the same object that we, the readers, do—from the narrative of the novel, *Bruna, soroche y los tíos*. This novel investigates the potential power of the feminine narrative voice and explores of the question: from *what* source can we learn our true history?

Where *Polvo y ceniza* presents us with multiple historical moments fragmented by multiple points of view in a style reminiscent of the cinematic *montage* technique of Sergei M. Eisenstein or the cubist painters, *Bruna, soroche y los tíos* seems to present each (hi)story at least twice through its technique of alternating long paragraphs of poetic prose with short, decontextualized fragments of dialogue.

Both novels play with unclearly marked alternations between multiple narrative points of view, in which the barriers that traditionally separate distinct narrative voices become more fluid. But in *Polvo y ceniza*, time is considerably fragmented (the episodes are not described in chronological order), although the pieces fit together in a somewhat unified mosaic, whereas in *Bruna, soroche y los tíos*, time appears to be more elastic: it is not possible for María Illacatu to be both Bruna's great-great-grandmother and for her to have lived more than three hundred years earlier, since six generations do not normally span the period of time that the novel covers. Thus even time works against Bruna in her struggle to recuperate and reconstruct her identity.

Official history claims to construct national identity. Concrete facts, such as dates (for example, 24 May 1822, the decisive Battle of Pichincha effectively ending Ecuador's war for independence from Spain, or 15 November 1922, discussed in chapter 2), are more or less indisputable. But the *meaning* of those historical facts is the polysemic battleground in the fight to construct an identity. This is why the struggles in *Bruna, soroche y los tíos* to re-appropriate one's identity from the family's (and the country's) "official history" become so important.

Bruna's Aunt Camelia, who is a widow, married and single all at the same time, drives the men mad as they try to figure out her "true" identity. The women named (and numbered) Marías 14, 17, and 23 depict a particularly striking crisis of identity. And Bruna? All Bruna wants to do is "feel fully human, a person, a woman" ("sentirse plenamente ser humano, persona, mujer," 317). She doesn't want to be a Catovil, a dutiful daughter, a virgin, or any other identity in which her family and the society of the Sleeping City want to imprison her. As María-Elena Angulo observes, "Bruna symbolizes the triumph of 'mestisaje,' the blend of different elements without contradiction."[25] When she decides to rename herself Bruna Illacatu, this is an inversion of her ancestor, Yahuma Illacatu's forced renaming as María, which resulted in the complete erasing of her identity. Try as she might, Bruna cannot escape her double identity as a Catovil and as an Illacatu. She wants to reconcile these two identities, but as this historical struggle still isn't over, the novel remains open-ended. It, too, still isn't over.

The worldwide reemergence of hitherto marginalized ethnicities has brought strong antithetic reactions from those who fear diversity (and dissent) and who favor a single, hegemonic national identity—which is an oppressive fiction in any country, and an impossibility in a society as pluralistic as Ecuador's. To the extent that it is possible to describe it, Ecuador's national "identity" is Spanish *and* Quichua, Incasic *and* Amazonian, Shiri, Cañari, Shuar, Cayapa, Valdivian, Tolitan and Huancavilcan (diverse pre-Colombian cultures), black, white, and *mestizo*, ethnic immigrant (including Chinese, Lebanese, Jewish, etc.), male and female, myth and history—in short, the sum of its many parts.[26] As in so many societies in the majority world, transnational industrialism exists alongside small, subsistence peasant agriculture, and any search for a single "identity" is a negation of the polyglot, plurilinguistic, and authentic national identity.

Macherey notes that dominant narrative is determined by the absence of other narratives.[27] Clearly this is not what is transpiring in the novels of Cárdenas and Yánez Cossío. Rather, what we have here are competing narrative elements, each determined to generate a wholeness that is not possible under such "noisy" conditions.

E. J. Hobsbawm writes that, even for the historian, at times "the mere task of extracting a coherent, ordered and rational account from a mass of doubtful and mutually contradictory facts, is almost overwhelming."[28] It is significant that two of the founding works of the historical novel genre, Scott's *Ivanhoe* and Manzoni's *The Betrothed*, both claim to be based on nonexistent manuscripts encountered by chance. Cárdenas and Yánez Cossío have no such need. As with Hobsbawm's investigations, the "actual" documents are problematic enough. Just as no single person makes history,[29] no single story—documentary or oral—makes history, either. This is in the nature of orality, wherein any speaker can claim the text as her own. (In *Bruna, soroche y los tíos*, rather than contend with each other, María Illacatu refuses to speak so that Bruna can.) The multiple voices in these Ecuadorian novels make for a collective narrative that may be the closest to a true depiction of history in all its multivoiced glory.

Bakhtin writes that the novelistic, nonepic hero should be portrayed as incomplete, "evolving and developing," a person who learns from life, rather than from the prepackaged and unchanging authoritative versions of history.[30] For Bakhtin, the epic valorizes an ideal past in which national ancestors behave like saints: "all the really good things occur only in this past. The epic absolute past is the single source and beginning of everything good for all later times as well."[31] By contrast, in Latin American mock-epic historical novels, the past is usually the source of all that is *wrong* with contemporary society, and clearly these two novels exemplify that stance. Parody of high genres is one way to destroy the homogenizing power of myth over language: "It is precisely laughter which destroys the epic, and in general destroys any hierarchical [distance]."[32] In this sense, *Bruna, soroche y los tíos* is unique. While many contemporary Ecuadorian novels satirize social attitudes toward history and throughout history, *Bruna, soroche y los tíos* is the only one so far that has actually made me laugh out loud. There is very little to laugh at in Ecuador's brutal, violent history, so this is really quite an accomplishment.

As discussed in the previous chapter, humor is frequently an attack on authority: it subverts authoritative logic by introducing upside-down logic or by taking the existing "logic" to its extreme in order to reveal its absurdity; it also often revolves around the breaking of some social taboo, which by extension suggests that other taboos may be flawed or broken. For example, Bandarra, the poet-shoemaker in Scliar's *The Strange Nation of Rafael Mendes*, embarks on an ill-fated attempt to make "the best pair of boots in the world."[33] Like the longest rug in the world, the lifelong project of Bruna's great-uncle Alvaro de Villa-Cató (see *Bruna*, chapter 12), it exemplifies the folly of man's single-minded desire for monumental achievements, for absolute perfection in this world.

Describing the forbidden is usually the domain of political tracts, which choose the path of direct attack, and of humorists, who specialize in making the audience laugh through the bitter tears of truth, while leaving the guilty parties an "out" due to the indirect nature of the attack (although the implied reader is clearly expected to know who the humorist *really* means). This is the modern political extension of a traditional folk humor form, the dirty joke with a two-way punchline, or *double entendre*.

In "Remembrances of Things Future," Mario Szichman breaks another taboo by presenting the extremely serious topics of anti-Jewish pogroms, forced relocation, and ultimately, the Holocaust in a sharp, satiric style that nevertheless has a breezy, comical quality. We are told that in the Ukraine, "the official policy was to drag out the Jews into the main street, chained by the neck, and make them fight the bear while the stationmaster refused to sell them tickets to travel." Once they are refugees, their ships "obtained denials of asylum in Southampton and Reykjavik. . . . Even the Bolivian authorities offered to reject them, despite the fact that their nation lacked any access to the sea."[34]

In *La loca 101*, Alicia Steimberg's character writes a letter describing her dream of walking nude in the street: this is a common enough dream (or nightmare) of self-exposure, but she addresses the letter to the generic authority figure of an unnamed "Rector," thus breaking a second taboo (further exposure), which points toward, and perhaps encourages, the breaking of other taboos.[35]

The veiled criticism of authority through humor is as old as satire itself, but Steimberg's characteristic use of humor shares something with that of Yánez Cossío that suggests a new target: When Steimberg writes, "Now here's where the story really begins" ("Ahora empieza la historia en serio," 15), followed by several pages of the same type of insane, free-associating rambling-with-a-purpose that has preceeded it, she is not only offering a different kind of postmodern fragmentation of linear narrative than many male writers, she seems to be laughing at both linear "male" narrative *and* the highly constructed, "male" intellectual, antinarrative fragmentation that characterizes a work such as Adoum's *Entre Marx y una mujer desnuda*. Instead of offering a text that is so challenging that it "demands that his readers not only participate but suffer the frustration of literary creation,"[36] Steimberg stops short, refusing to describe one character's luxurious apartment, and addresses the female reader as follows:

> La descripción de esos lujos, a mí, personalmente, me pudre. Usted, señora, si estaba interesda en leerla, escríbasela sola. (35)

> [Personally, the description of these luxuries makes me sick. If you were interested in reading it, Madam, write it yourself.]

Steimberg further ridicules the conventions of authorship in a passage that combines the male and female forms of the word, "writer" into a gender-neutral term, "escritor/a." Prominent male writers exhibit a marked preference for the exclusively male form, "escritor":

> Un escritor/a que no se saca una foto con fondo de biblioteca no merece el nombre de tal. (89)

> [A (male or female) writer who doesn't have (his/her) photo taken in front of a bookshelf isn't worthy of the name.]

This suggests a veiled criticism of the narrow-mindedness that unfortunately can be found among many who believe themselves to be radical intellectuals, those who are prepared to remake the world through revolution or at least through textual experimentation: But what is a woman's place in that literary revolution when one of its leading figures, Julio Cortázar, belittles the "passive" reader as "the female reader" ("el lector hembra")?[37]

Steimberg steps into the ultimate taboo when she combines the sacred with surrealistic and scatological humor:

> En sus noches insomnes pensaba sin descanso en niños buenos y niños malos, en hormigas con guantes y perros con anteojos. También pensaba en Dios, me cago en él, perdón, en Él, y enseñaba a los niños a pensar en Él. (47)

> [On sleepless nights he thought tirelessly about good children and bad children, about ants with gloves and dogs with eyeglasses. He also thought about God, I shit on him, excuse me, on Him, and taught the children to think about Him.]

Combining the sacred and the scatological is a patented shock-troop method of shattering existing norms and thereby paving the way for the questioning of other norms, which is precisely what Steimberg does. Disguised as the rambling of an insane fool, Steimberg's *loca* brings up forbidden topics, asking her Argentine audience, "Did you know that night falls in the cemetery too?" (49), and assuring them that the people who have disappeared are not rotting in jail, but rather have become vampires (113). And finally, our "insane" narrator tells us that

> toda historia verdadera o ficticia es truncada por la muerte. Además no hay historias verdaderas. Toda historia es ficticia y trunca por definición. (91)
>
> [all stories whether truthful or fictitious are truncated by death. Besides which there are no true stories. All stories are fictitious and truncated by definition.]

Adoum's resolution of this inevitable truncation is to leave the book in the middle of an unfinished sentence. Cárdenas's answer is to have the main character "live on" in endlessly replicating (and contradictory) legends, and Yánez Cossío's solution is to send her protagonist out into the wide world of possibilities outside of the Sleeping City.

In contrast to the use of humor in *Bruna, soroche y los tíos* is the deadly serious folk-appropriation of the bandit figure in *Polvo y ceniza*. Regarding this, a relevant parallel can be drawn from Clarice Lispector's essay, "Mineirinho" (1964), which chronicles Lispector's reaction to the life and death of a notorious bandit and killer who operated in Rio de Janeiro until he was killed by the police. Lispector begins by asking why she feels so much sorrow at the death of a criminal and suggests that it stems from the contradiction of "not being able to rationalize her feelings" between the "irreducible facts" that he had "murdered far too often."[38] and the sympathy that she feels for him because he was also a fellow human being who had the guts to resist authority when she did not ("I, too, feel desperate," 213). The fact that it took thirty bullets to stop him ("he lived until the thirteenth shot," ibid.) only heightens the tragedy of the already growing myth, which soon becomes martyrdom: "[My] house is standing, and Mineirinho has lived wrath on my behalf" (214). Somehow a man who became a *desperado* "because human speech failed him" (215) was able to exteriorize that "something in us which is capable of disrupting everything—something which understands [the] savage, disarticulated cry" that could only serve him as an utterance (pp. 214, 215). Edgar Allan Poe wrote of the "Imp of the Perverse" within us, that compels us to act irrationally, even self-destructively, if only to escape from the hellish banality of daily routine. Shakespeare articulates this thought when Horatio warns Hamlet about being tempted toward "the dreadful summit of the cliff":

> The very place puts toys of desperation,
> Without more motive, into every brain
> That looks so many fadoms to the sea
> And hears it roar beneath.
> (*Hamlet*, I, iii, 75–78)

For Lispector, Mineirinho has taken that step, and there is something heroic about it, even though "we have to be mad . . . in order to know him." But apparently this is the "madness" of being truly alive, of raging against the machine:

> It is as a madman that I enter this life which often has no door, and it as a madman that I understand what can only be understood at one's peril. It is only as a madman that I feel deep love. . . . Were I not a madman, I should be eight hundred policemen with eight hundred machine-guns, and that would be my claim to honor. (215)

Outside of such "madness," the only positions available are those of the dead rebel, the victorious and bloodstained policemen, or the hand-wringing bystander.

Hobsbawm's studies of social banditry make the crucial point that "bandits belong to remembered history, as distinct from the official history of books."[39] Indeed, the spread of capitalism (banditry on a large scale) changes attitudes toward bandits, who, according to Hobsbawm, are incapable of leading a long-term, organized revolt against the modern capitalist state (not to be confused with long-term, day-to-day peasant resistance to dominant socioeconomic and political forms). This idea is explored in the "Victor Pardo" chapter, where the book-educated poet tells the already-legendary Briones about the Russian Revolution:

> Si me permite, le contaré algo: hace unos años, no muchos, en un lugar que está lejísimos de aquí, la gente pobre ya no quiso ser maltratada y desidió que todos podrían ser iguales y se rebelaron, tumbaron al gobierno, dejaron de creer en su rey porque ese rey nunca había creído que ellos eran iguales a él, y pusieron en su lugar a un gobierno de pobres y

pensaban que la buena suerte podía ser para todos. Y yo me dije ¿por qué no hacer aquí lo mismo, un país sin ricos mandones, sin notables usureros, un país donde nadie necesite volverse bandido para sentirse libre? (125)

[With your permission, I'd like to tell you something: a few years ago, not very many, in a place that's very far away from here, the poor people didn't want to be mistreated anymore and decided that everyone should be equal and they rebelled, they toppled the government, stopped believing in their king because the king had never believed that they were his equals, and replaced him with a government of poor people who thought that good fortune should be for everyone. And I said to myself, why couldn't we do the same thing here?—a country without rich bosses, without usurous gentry, a country where nobody needs to become a bandit to feel free?]

Briones replies

¿Un gobierno donde los pobres tengan razón y manden? . . . yo no sé de gobiernos ni me preocupan: sólo sirvo para robar, matar, asaltar, huir y defenderme. . . . [dijo] que soñaba despierto. (125–26)

[A government where the poor have rights and run things? . . . I don't know anything about governments nor do I care about them: I'm only good for robbing, killing, attacking, escaping and defending myself. . . . You're daydreaming.]

Since one of the more successful goals of modern capitalism has been the elimination of the obvious oppressor-oppressed equation that so permeated the peasant communities that produced Robin Hood, Cartouche, and even Pretty Boy Floyd, bandits are increasingly seen as threats to property and "respectable" people.[40] The carnivalesque celebration of the criminal's challenge to power discussed by Foucault[41] has disappeared from our daily lives but lives on in our myths, especially their current incarnation, the Hollywood film, which typically brims over with overdetermined depictions of exciting-yet-deranged killers.

By far the most "stable" reincarnation of the social bandit is not the mobster (who nevertheless continues to fascinate), but, perhaps paradoxically, the hard-boiled private detective character, who in novel and film has assumed the role of the modern Robin Hood. Who else but the lone detective has a reliable and insatiable desire to see justice done, often in the face of an indifferent or hostile authoritative political structure? Who else sets out to change things single-handedly, to right wrongs—and who else therefore is more worthy to assume the mantle of our modern heroes?

In both of these novels, detective work is being performed. Bruna does it herself, digging up clues to her mysterious past. Regarding Naún Briones, the reader is expected to play detective, to piece together some kind of coherent picture of who this bandit was. The modern replacement of the social bandit hero, Bruna must do her investigating into the reconstruction of the true identity of her own predecessor. But what is she to do with this knowledge? One circle may be closed, but many more remain open.

In the openness of *Polvo y ceniza*, one senses a despair that the cacophonous contention will never cease, and therefore, although the dominant history will always have to co-exist with the subversive, marginal histories, it will still always dominate. History is seen as tragedy (although there is a sense that the struggle between these variant histories is, at least, not over yet). In *Bruna, soroche y los tíos*, however, history is a little closer to farce. Although Bruna's final option is to break open the hellish concentric rings of lies in which her family life is situated, the breaking out is largely accomplished through laughter (and good detective work), and freedom is tasted in its final passages. A glorious, open-ended freedom, full of unrealized possibilities.

Conclusion

Hasta las mayores mentiras pueden tener algo de verdad.

[Even the biggest lies can have some truth in them.]

—Peruvian proverb

It is commonly suggested, especially in the field of Latin American literary criticism, that many fictions are truer than what passes for truth in official histories and other dominant political discourses. When Gabriel García Márquez described the military rulers' slaughtering of thousands of striking banana workers in the late 1920s in *Cien años de soledad* (1967), he was writing in direct opposition to the Colombian government's official version of what occurred (who instigated the violence, the number of casualties, etc.) and aligning himself closely with the version preserved by popular memory. Memory is shown as having the power the change the past in Carlos Fuentes's *The Death of Artemio Cruz* (1962), and Octavio Paz's *Piedra de sol* (1957) places history within a cosmovision in which it, like everything else, is forever moving and changing.

Myths, like all narrative forms, are indeterminate in meaning, and yet, often what makes a myth a myth is precisely its determinacy. The events of history are credible, because they happened, but their meaning is debatable, whereas a myth is authoritative because its meaning is *not* debatable—having a single determinate meaning is thus the definition of a certain kind of myth. For example, that Pearl Harbor was attacked by forces of the Japanese imperial air force on December 7, 1941, is an historical fact. But the common American reading of this event as a "sneak attack," which serves as a paradigm for all Japanese behavior, has, for its believers, the unassailable "truth beyond truth" of myth.

Dorothy Figueira argues that the German myth of an Aryan past in India allowed them to separate themselves from the previously undeniable Hebraic roots of Christianity, replacing the Aryans as the "true" source of their mythic past and permitting the deletion of the Hebrews from that past. To quote:

CONCLUSION

> The Romantic concepts of the degeneration of monotheism into polytheism, and the view of history as an unfolding expression of a people's spirit followed by stagnation and degeneration . . . prepared the ground for the creation of a new mythology: . . . the displacement of the Jews from a central position on the stage of history, theories of the degeneration of peoples and religions, and the idealization of imaginary ancestors and their fictitious descendants [with] disastrous consequences.[1]

Myths of national identity are needed by both traditional authoritarian rulers, to establish and maintain order and loyalty, and by those opposed to authoritarian power who are trying to build unified support among the oppressed classes. In the Andean countries, which have the largest percentage of indigenous populations in South America, this has been a problem for both sides. In this cultural context, official history constantly interacts with oral history, occasionally being displaced by it because of the latter's "mythical dimensions," creating, in effect, "official" oral histories.[2] Goody and Watt write that myths "act as 'charters' of present social institutions rather than as faithful historical records of times past" because of this tendency of oral transmission to mythify.[3] These mythical "charters" can be given total authority. Lord Raglan demonstrated that many purportedly historical facts are "actually traditional in origin."[4]

Thus the dichotomy between written history and oral myth is fairly well deconstructed. But what happens when the two are further conflated in literary transcriptions of oral myth? How does the function of myth itself shift and change? Myths, after all, can supply both cosmic liberation and oppressive stereotypes. Our civilization's distinctions "between truth and falsity, fact and fiction, literature and nonliterature . . . cannot simply be imposed on the narratives of earlier periods,"[5] and this problem is consciously exploited by contemporary Latin American historical novelists. Many of the early efforts at rewriting the myths of Ecuadorian history in the 1930s contain what are today uncomfortably flat, stereotypical depictions of women as obvious symbols of pure, virgin nature constrasted with the corrupt, polluted world of man-made industrial capitalism;[6] in addition, many of the male protagonists, typically undereducated workers and peasants, are portrayed as ignorant, childlike and powerless before both of these forces. One tires rather quickly of these types. In contrast, the works selected for closer examination in this book are interesting precisely because they incorporate a great many elements of literary social realism, but grafted onto a native, mythologizing orality. The result has been called magic realism.

The question then is, Is magic realism "realism" for contemporary Latin America? The answer may be that in the postmodern struggle for self-definition in Latin America, realism is useful for delivering certain kinds of "truth messages," but that any textual performance (like Laurence Olivier's definition of acting), can be a series of lies that adds up to the truth. Such canonical authors as Nathaniel Hawthorne, Robert Louis Stevenson, and Virginia Woolf would have agreed that "romance and the extraordinary give us access to truths that lie beyond the commonplace."[7]

Raymond Williams poses the problem of whether socialist realism errs in presuming that reality is "wholly knowable."[8] In Ecuador, the most influential works of the 1930s and 1940s were fundamentally realist, but, paradoxically, the "realistic" representation of the peasant-class worldview necessarily contained what for a European would be surrealism, myth, magic realism (talking trees, etc.). So is that "realism"? Is the acknowledged fictitiousness of fiction contemporary Ecuador's "realism"? Up to a point, but going too far in the direction of technical experimentation leaves the public behind.

C. Michael Waag writes that realism has "autocthonous roots" in Ecuador, stemming from the Liberal Revolution of 1895.[9] But what kind of "realism" was it? Waag writes that the short story, "La mala hora" (discussed in chapter 2), presents a man-nature symbiosis in a jungle setting that is absent in Rivera's famous and influential work, *La vorágine* (1924), and that the stories collected in *Los que se van* (1930) emphasize "the native way of seeing reality" in contrast with the "white" boss "who has no appreciation for the forest, yet is bent on bringing it under his control and rendering it profitable . . . [who] can utilize the forest only by destroying it and the people who are physically and spiritually part of it"[10] (unfortunately, there is nothing new under the sun here; this is still going on, most visibly in the Amazon, but in every other region of the country as well).

Whereas in *La vorágine* anthropomorphism is framed narratively within the realist convention of jungle-inspired hallucinations, *Los que se van* contains a paradigm shift in this regard. Aguilera Malta's story "El cholo que se castró" ("The *Cholo* Who Castrated Himself") begins by making use of poetic metaphors so traditional in style that Homer would have felt quite at home with them: A character is shaking with emotion (cause), and as a result, "The rocks *seemed* to be walking" (effect; "Las piedras parecían caminar").[11] Later, "an enchanted shrimp *seems* to be laughing" at him ("Un camarón brujo parece reir," 180; emphasis mine). This shift to the present tense, and the "enchanted" quality of the shrimp ("brujo" is literally "male witch"), begin to approach the strangeness of another reality. But it is in the middle of the story that the most radical shift takes place: "The mangrove trees bellowed with laughter" ("Los mangles se reían a carcajadas," 178). They did not "seem to" take on anthropomorphic qualities, as so many natural objects do in these stories, they *do* it. This simple removal of a single word in Spanish, the "seem to" verb, the result of this textualization of the *montuvio*'s mythifying, oral culture, is the beginning of magic realism in Ecuadorian fiction. Aguilera Malta's 1933 novel *Don Goyo*, is "often cited as the earliest manifestation of the magic realist mode,"[12] presumably because it is the first full-length work in which the realist-framing "seem to" has been removed.

It is important to collapse somewhat this apparent binary between "European" realism and "autocthonous" Latin American realism by noting that there is nothing univocal or monolithic about either "pole." We have discussed the breaking up of the European definition, but it is worth quoting Waag at length regarding the striking differences between two works that otherwise exhibit considerable similarities in terms of their settings (jungle) and the countries and periods in which they were written (Colombia in the mid-1920s and Ecuador in the early 1930s):[13]

> *Don Goyo* marks a radical departure from works such as Rivera's *La vorágine* in which a protagonist of European origin . . . "struggles" against a seemingly chaotic environment with which he is culturally unequipped to cope, and ultimately is consumed, defeated, or "devoured" by it. . . . The word "struggle" is inappropriate to a description of the relationship between Don Goyo and his environment. He is very much aware of himself and the community as an integral part of an ever cycling ecological system, although he thinks of the relationship in mythical terms. However, the people of the island lack Don Goyo's profound understanding, and they do not recognize the dangers of removing a primordial element such as the mangrove from the system.[14]

These are the same mangrove trees that speak to Don Goyo and scream when they are cut down (see chapter 2).

One problem is that even "radical" forms can be codified, and to some extent this is happening in Ecuador.[15] That which is called magic realism is sometimes positioned as the only literature that Latin America can, is, or should be producing. Roberto González Echevarría writes, "the constraints of the market deprive the English-languge public of Latin America's best writers, creating a distorted image of the canon."[16] In another context, but related to this issue, George Bernard Shaw expressed his thoughts on the matter in his 1913 preface to the third edition of *The Quintessence of Ibsenism*: He saw canonization, paradoxically, as a form of censorship. By placing the canonized work under glass, one removes it from the world of life and its multiform meanings, and thus from critical debate.

> Now that Ibsen is no longer frantically abused, and is safe in the Pantheon, his message is in worse danger of being forgotten or ignored than when he was in the pillory. . . . the most effective way of shutting our minds against a great man's ideas is to take them for granted and admit that he was great and have done with him.[17]

Is institutionalization necessarily cooptation? Bakhtin has discussed the importance of the "organized anarchy" of the institution of Carnival as a way of defusing potential direct conflict between oppressor and oppressed. Carnival is still very important in Ecuadorian society, especially among the indigenous cultures. The problem is whether this defusing is a healthy "break" from daily oppression, a role-reversing act of resistance, or a false utopian diversion that only serves to keep the oppressive system in place.[18] Frederick Douglass describes how slaves in the pre-war American South were expected to spend the few days of Christmas holiday getting drunk; otherwise they might use the time to plan rebellions or escapes. Not to get drunk was regarded as rejection of the master's "favor," a very dangerous thing indeed.[19] Writing eighty years before Bakhtin (and nearly 140 years before the English translations of Bakhtin), Douglass declares:

> These holidays serve as conductors, or safety-valves, to carry off the rebellious spirit of enslaved humanity. . . . The holidays are part and parcel of the gross fraud, wrong and inhumanity of slavery . . . what our master had deceived us into a belief was freedom.[20]

So, is the temporary concession to the "topsy-turvy" world of Carnival a temporary empowerment or a diverting of potentially dangerous threats to authoritative discourse into a harmless joke? Gerald Graff writes that one of the most important themes of new historicism has been "the idea that societies exert control over their subjects not just by imposing constraints on them but by predetermining the ways they attempt to rebel against those constraints, by co-opting their strategies of dissent."[21] According to Raymond Williams, "authentic breaks" do occur, and therefore the "finite but significant openness of many works of art," requiring persistent and variable signifying responses, is "especially relevant." (Note the similarity to Albert Einstein's declaration, "The universe . . . is finite and yet has no limits"; in other words, the finite nature of the universe does not prevent us from experiencing it as essentially infinite.)[22]

One of those breaks occurs when monolithic linear time is freely and fluidly juxtaposed and intermingled with nonlinear time. Disintegration of linear logic is often a crucial feature of what we are calling magic realism,[23] but its apparent opposite, cyclical, mythic time is often portrayed as nightmarish by Western culture. A brief examination of such "high" works of literature as Samuel Beckett's *Waiting for Godot*, José Triana's *La noche de los asesinos*, and much of the work of Jean Genet, Sam Shepard, and Eugene Ionesco, as well as more popular works of science fiction and *Twilight Zone*-style narratives, will reveal a number of instances of our terror at being made to repeat endlessly the same actions, whether by outside, unseen forces, or by individual "choice." This dichotomy is horrifying indeed, because either extremity leads to a dead end. A balance must be struck: for time is both linear and cyclical. Reality *does* repeat itself (cf. the well-known French proverb "Plus ça change, plus c'est la même chose" ["The more things change, the more they stay the same"] or even Heraclitus [active *cir.* 513 B.C.E.], "There is nothing permanent except change"[24]). Night and day, the phases of the moon, the seasons continually wax and wane, forever leaving and returning, yet time nevertheless moves forward. The cycle of birth and death does not prevent individual subjects from living linear lives that begin with birth and end v ith death. To take an example from science, any wave—such as a sine wave or a light wave—is perpetually oscillating between peak and trough, or on and off, yet the wave also moves forward while simultaneously exhibiting this cyclical quality. (It is merely that our perceptual apparatus does not normally perceive the sixty-cycle-per-second oscillations of electric lights.)

It is nothing new to tell a story "out of order." Homer makes liberal use of extended flashbacks. Nelson Goodman writes that "Cinema and literature alike would be severely handicapped if required always to report incidents in the order of their occurrence."[25] And in the case of myths and other narratives in which the "entire" audience knows the story, there is no need to tell it in a linear way, the same way the observer on the sidelines of a passing parade may look ahead to the baton-twirlers, then back to the marching band, then down the block to get a last look at a departing float without becoming hopelessly confused by the "breakdown of linear logic."

The problem may arise when this remarkable human ability to

maintain a semblance of order in the face of chaotic stimulus is raised to the level of authoritative law. That is, when only one branch of the linear/cyclical fusion is isolated and privileged (this is typically the linear, which tends to reflect our daily lives with more apparent accuracy). "Propp," writes Barthes, "is totally committed to the idea of the irreducibility of the chronological order," when in fact it is the task of narrative "to succeed in giving a structural description of the chronological illusion."[26] In Barthes's argument, narrative "logic" should not be beholden to the prison-house of chronology. Marx was already addressing some of the causes and implications of this issue when he proposed that what had been described as human "nature," rather than being unalterable, with growth occurring by evolutionary means and thought determining being, was in fact alterable (by humans themselves), changing in montage-like jumps, with social being determining thought. But how "able to alter" their reality are oppressed peoples? Emily Hicks writes that one of the major goals of "border writing" (she rejects the term *magic realism*) is "the displacement or 'deterritorialization' of time and space through nonsynchronous memory and 'reterritorialization.' "[27]

One of the functions of such "border" incidents is to parody stable, authoritative discourse (to use Bakhtin's terms), occasionally inverting the terms of that discourse, rendering it unstable. This is typically followed by the absorption of the destabilizing technique by the authoritative discourse, which is then restabilized, rendering it fit to be reparodied in an ongoing cycle.

When it was first introduced in Ecuador in the late 1920s and early 1930s, the social realist style was seen as providing the shocking, terrible truth, in contrast to the disinterested, reactionary modernism it was replacing. Just as Ecuador's modernism was once seen as radical, realism is now seen as an insufficient form to represent the Ecuadorian "reality." But this highly Ecuadorian-flavored brand of social realism was, as we have seen, quite different from what Stalin would have considered to be social realism, because from its very inception it grafted the "social realist" style onto a native mythic oral narrative style and produced something totally new.

It is in the exploration of this conflation of linear, "new," historical time with cyclical, repetitive, mythic time that magic realism comes the closest to fitting the argument that the direct reflection of the real in literature has been replaced by a partial, fragmented, broken mirror that gives the "truer" representation of that reality.[28] Is a direct reflection of the real ever fully possible? Whose reality is to be reflected? Here, too, the goal of magic realism is to reflect multiple realities.

Appendix 1
Translator's Introduction

One of the most difficult problems encountered in translating contemporary Ecuadorian novels is the extreme cultural specificity of so many of the works. It seems fair to generalize that the more established Boom and post-Boom writers were often writing about Latin America for an international audience while in exile in places like Paris and London, and thus kept troublesome cultural specificities to a minimum. Although a handful of Ecuadorian novelists have achieved some measure of international recognition (Icaza, Aguilera Malta, Adoum) or have had at least one or two major works translated into English (Ortiz, Estupiñán Bass, Ubidia), many of them are still writing for a highly culturally specific, Ecuadorian audience. Some writers even aim their work at the implied reader(s) from *a single city*, typically Quito or Guayaquil. This leaves the translator with the problem of how to deal with such specificities.[1] For the sake of simplicity, I will limit my discussion of these issues to the emblematic example of just one of the works included in this appendix, José de la Cuadra's *Los Sangurimas* (1934; discussed at length in chapter 3).

José de la Cuadra was one of the principal Ecuadorian modernists of the 1930s, one of whose primary projects was the replacement of the high lexical social register put in the mouths of illiterates by such nineteenth-century authors as Juan León Mera (e.g., *Cumandá*, 1879) with a naturalism that included reproducing local dialect and describing scenes of violence, ignorance, incest, etc.[2] This poses unique problems for the translator. All of the characters, high and low, speak a similar, nonstandard Spanish. Thus the tone of *Los Sangurimas* is primarily the speech of nonliterate squatters and peasants on Ecuador's tropical coast in the early 1930s. I have chosen a relatively neutral, rarely nonstandard English, because to attempt to recreate the speech of the original in English using some contrived target culture equivalent such as a backwoods Louisiana bayou drawl (and attendant slang) would mark the text with inappropriate cultural associations within U.S. society.

APPENDIX 1. TRANSLATOR'S INTRODUCTION

Generally, with Spanish-to-English translation, the first matter to be engaged is likely to be the Latinate roots of Spanish that often have cognates in English, and which are therefore the first words that might occur to the translator. But these words, which are common in Spanish, sound misplaced in English, where Latinate words belong to a higher register than Anglo-Saxon. Suzanne Jill Levine discusses

> the temptation to choose cognates, Latinate words whose effect in English is often archaic, or even vague, such as *amiable*, whereas the Spanish counterpart *amable* is a common, vivid word. . . . The Spanish language tolerates, even seeks polyvalence, while modern English demands straightforward clarity.[3]

How do we avoid what Bly calls "translatorese"? (There is also Gregory Rabassa's example of the opposite register, how the Spanish *coño* is much more vulgar in English and therefore an inappropriate choice in the context he is discussing.)[4] In the case of *Los Sangurimas* I have translated such words as *interlocutor*, *compadre* and *disimular*, not as "interlocutor," "compatriot" and "dissemble" but as "other speaker" "friend" and "to hide it." Even *documento*, for which "document" seems a perfectly serviceable word, comes from the mouth of a peasant, so I have rendered it as both "pact" (to sound more common) *and* as "document," because Ecuador (like many countries) is so strangled by an inept bureaucracy that it is perfectly appropriate for nonliterates to use what might sound like the high term, *document*, because they would in fact be hearing it all the time.

A *montuvio* is a culture-bound term that I have rendered three different ways. The first time, in an example of meaning-based translation,[5] I chose a detailed explanation, "the *montuvio* people of the coastal lowlands." The next three or four times, I used "*montuvio* people," and subsequently, throughout the translation, I used just *montuvio* (the extract in the appendix begins at this point).

Of course, when a South American uses *invierno* (winter)[6] to refer to the hottest time of the year, it is easy to justify "summer" as a translation, but what of "*Vega en la orilla, no más. Pa dentro, barranco alto todito. Terreno pa invernar*" (18)? What is one to do with the final phrase, which might be rendered into English as "land for getting through the winter"? Leaving aside the regional pronunciation of "pa" for "para," which I generally have attempted to render with displaced, slightly nonstandard English,[7] not all South Americans consider "winter" to be, as it is on Ecuador's coast, the *wettest* as well as the hottest season. I therefore opted for "Low and swampy only down by the river. But inside, high ravines all over. Way 'bove the flood plain."

Finally, there are the extreme cases of local slang and idioms. Native Ecuadorians were able to supply translations of some terms, not in any major Spanish-English dictionary, that are still current in Ecuadorean speech, but there are several terms that require discussion with informed native speakers who are familiar with the 1930s-era slang of Ecuador's coast. De la Cuadra describes a dead person as having "la cara josca" (14), which is an attempt to reproduce the local pronunciation of the initial *t* as the guttural *h* (the word is *tosca*, i.e., stiff with rigor mortis) and "la ley de fuga" ("the law of escape") is invoked against "los comevaca" ("cow-eaters," 15), which turns out to be the shooting of cattle rustlers, and Nicasio Sangurima calls himself a "come bollo-maduro" (25; literally, a "ripe-plantain-ball-eater"). Although the narrative context clearly refers to the destructiveness of greed—overeating may kill you—(a *bollo* is typically made of mashed green plantain and other ingredients rolled into a ball and fried) I was advised, in order to learn the specific regional and temporal meaning of this term, to travel to *a single village* outside Guayaquil, where this expression may still be current. I have yet to make the trip. However, if my experience dealing with this culture is anything to go by, I would probably be supplied with multiple, contradictory meanings. Translators have long been familiar with the problems of such indeterminacy of meaning in source texts.

Appendix 2
The Man Who Was Kicked to Death
PABLO PALACIO

How can we dispose of all those sensational stories of passionate street crimes? Bringing the truth to light is a moral action.
—*El Comercio*, Quito

"Last night, at approximately 12:30 A.M., Police Officer No. 451, who serves this precinct, found a man named Ramírez lying completely flat between Escobedo and García Streets. The unfortunate man's nose was bleeding profusely, and when questioned by the officer he said that he had been the victim of an assault on the part of unknown individuals just because he had asked them for a cigarette. The Officer asked the assault victim to accompany him to the Police Station in order to make a statement that could shed some light on the matter, but Ramírez flatly refused to do so. The Officer, acting according to his duty, then asked one of the drivers at the nearest taxi stand for help, and they drove the injured party to the Police Station, where, in spite of the medical attention of Dr. Ciro Benavidez, he died within a few hours.

"By this morning, the Captain of the 6th Precinct had pursued all the usual formalities, but he was unable to discover anything about the murderers or about Ramírez's identity. The only information known, by chance, was that the deceased had one or two vices.

"We hope to keep our readers up to date, as soon as more is known about this mysterious event."

The *Diario de la Tarde* said no more about the bloody event.

I don't know what I felt then. Except that I laughed my head off. A man kicked to death! As far as I was concerned, that was the funniest, the most hilarious thing that could possibly happen.

I waited until the next day and eagerly leafed through the paper, but there wasn't a line about my man. Nor the next day. I think after ten days nobody even remembered what had happened between Escobedo and García Streets.

But I began to get obsessed. Everywhere I went I was pursued by the hilarious phrase: A man kicked to death! And all the letters danced before my eyes so joyfully that I resolved to reconstruct this street scene or at least penetrate the mystery of why they killed a man in such a ridiculous way.

Caramba, how I would have wanted to do an experimental study, but I've seen in books that such studies only investigate the "How" of things, and between my first idea, which was that of reconstruction, and that of seeking the motives for why certain individuals would attack and kick another, the second seemed to me more original and beneficial for humanity. Well, the "Why" of things is something they say is the domain of philosophy, and in truth I never imagined that my investigation would contain anything philosophical, and besides anything that even *sounds* like that word that annoys me. So, half-fearful and half-discouraged, I lit my pipe.— That is essential, very essential.

The first question that comes up before all the others that muck up these investigations is that of method. All university students, training-college and high school students, and in general all people who want to better themselves have this information at their fingertips. There are two methods: Deduction and induction (see Aristotle and Bacon).

The first, deduction, didn't interest me. I've been told that deduction is a mode of investigation that goes from the best known to the least known. A good method: I confess. But I knew very little about the event and so I had to skip it.

Now, induction is something marvellous. It goes from the least known to the best known. . . . (How does it work? I don't remember. . . . Well, who knows about these things, anyway?) But as I said, this is the method *par excellence*. When you know a little, you have to induce. So induce, kiddo.

Thus resolved, I lit my pipe and with that formidable inductive weapon in my hands, I remained irresolute, not knowing what to do.

All right: And how to apply this marvellous method? I asked myself.

If only I had studied logic! I was going to remain ignorant of the famous events of Escobedo and García Streets all because of the damn idleness of my early years.

Discouraged, I picked up the *Diario de la Tarde* of January 13— the unlucky paper had never left my desk—and taking vigorous puffs on my fired-up, big-assed pipe, I reread the bit of sensational journalism reproduced above. I had to wrinkle my brow like all studious men—a deep line between the eyebrows is the unequivocal sign of attention!

I read and I read until I was struck by something almost dazzling.

The penultimate paragraph, the one that said, "By this morning, the Captain of the 6th . . ." was the one that especially amazed me. The last sentence made my eyes sparkle: "The only information known, by chance, was that the deceased had one or two vices." And I, by means of a secret power that you wouldn't understand, read it like this: HAD ONE OR TWO VICES, in prodigiously large letters.

I believe it was a revelation from the goddess Astarte. From then on the only point that interested me was to verify what class of weakness the dead Ramírez had. Intuitively I discovered that he was . . . no, I won't say it so as not to ruin his memory with women. . . .

And what I had to do was verify through reasoning, and if possible, with proof, what I knew intuitively.

For that, I went down to see the Captain of the 6th, who would be able to give me the revealing data. The police authority hadn't cleared up anything. He even had trouble figuring out what I wanted. After my lengthy explanations he said to me, scratching his forehead:

"Oh! Yes . . . that Ramírez business. . . . You see how we've already given up. . . . It was such a weird turn of events! But, sit down; why don't you sit down, *señor*. . . . As you perhaps know already, they brought him in about one o'clock and he died a few hours later. . . . Poor guy. We took two photos, just in case . . . some relative . . . Are you related to *señor* Ramírez? You have my sympathy . . . my most sincere . . ."

"No, *señor*," I said indignantly, "I didn't even know him. I'm a man who is interested in justice and nothing else."

And I smiled deep down inside. What a well-chosen phrase! Huh? "I'm a man who is interested in justice and nothing else." How it tormented the Captain! In order not to embarass him more, I quickly added: "You said you have two photos. If I might see them . . ."

The dignified civil servant pulled open a drawer of his desk and turned over some papers. Then he opened another and turned over some other papers. In a third, already growing heated, he finally found them.

And he was very proper about it:

"You are interested in this affair. You may have them, sir. . . . That is, as long as you return them," he said, nodding his head up and down as he said these last words, taking pleasure in showing me his yellow teeth. . . .

I thanked him profusely, and kept the photos.

"And tell me, *señor* Captain, you wouldn't be able to remember something special about the deceased, some piece of information that might be revealing?"

"Something special . . . some piece of information . . . No, no. Well, he was a completely ordinary man. More or less my height—" The Captain was a bit on the tall side "—thick, with flabby flesh. But something special . . . no . . . at least as far as I can remember. . . ."

Since the Captain couldn't tell me any more, I left, thanking him again.

I hurried home; I shut myself in my study; I lit my pipe and took out the photos, which along with the newspaper article were precious documents.

I was sure of not being able to find any others, and I resolved to work with what fate had placed within my grasp.

The first thing to do is to study the man, I told myself. And I went to work.

I examined and reexamined the photos, one by one, making a complete study of them. I brought them close to my eyes; I separated them, stretching out my arm; I tried to discover their secrets.

Until, having them in front of me for so long, I managed to memorize every hidden feature.

That protuberance from his face; that large and strange nose—it looked so much like the crystal stopper in the water carafe in my cheap little diner!—those large and limp whiskers, that little pointed beard; that straight, messy hair.

I took a piece of paper, and traced the lines that make up the dead Ramírez's face. Later, when the drawing was finished, I noticed that something was missing; because what I was looking at wasn't him; that some completing and indispensible detail had escaped me. . . . Yes! I picked up the pen and finished his chest, a magnificent chest which if it had been made of plaster would have fit right in in some academy. A chest whose breasts have something womanly about them.

Then . . . then I treated him with savage cruelty. I put a halo on him! A halo that you nail to the cranium, just like they nail them to the effigies of saints in churches.

The dead Ramírez had a magnificent face!

But, why did this happen? I tried . . . I tried to learn why they killed him; yes, why they killed him. . . .

Then I concocted the following logical conclusions:
The deceased Ramírez was named Octavio Ramírez (anyone with a nose like that couldn't have had another name);
Octavio Ramírez was forty-two years old;
Octavio Ramírez had very little money;
Octavio Ramírez was poorly dressed; and, finally, our deceased was a foreigner.
With these precious data, his personality was totally reconstructed.
The only thing that was missing, then, was this business of a motive, which for me gradually began to take on the quality of hard evidence. Intuition revealed everything to me. The only thing I had to do, as a small point of honor, was to eliminate all the other possibilities. The first, his own declaration, this issue of the cigarette, wasn't even worth considering. It's absolutely absurd that someone should be victimized in such a vile way for such a trivial thing. He had lied, he had hidden the truth; I would even say he had murdered the truth, and he had done so because he didn't, he couldn't speak it.
Was the dead Ramírez drunk? No, that couldn't be, because the police would have noticed that immediately and the newspaper story would have confirmed it, without a doubt, or, if it wasn't on record because of the reporter's incompetence, the Police Captain would have revealed it to me without any hesitation.
What other weaknesses could our unhappy victim have had? Because he certainly had one, nobody could convince me otherwise. The proof of that was his stubborn refusal to state the reasons for the assault. Any other reason could have been explained without embarassment. For example, what shame would there be in the following confessions:
"Some guy tricked my daughter; I found him tonight in the street; I went blind with rage, treated him like the scum he is; I grabbed him by the throat, and he, helped by his friends, did this to me" or
"My wife cheated on me with a man who I tried to kill, but he was stronger than me, and started to kick me furiously" or
"I had an affair with a women whose husband took revenge by cowardly attacking me with his friends"?
If he had said something like that no one would have thought it strange.
It also would have been very easy to say:
"We had a fight."
But I'm wasting time, these hypotheses are untenable: In the first

two cases, the family of the unfortunate man would have said something; in the third his confession would have been inevitable, because the first two would have still been honorable deaths; and the fourth we would already know because, wanting vengeance, he would surely have given the names of his assailants.

Nothing, which had caused my brow to wrinkle with so much thinking, was obvious. I had no more room in my head for more reasoning. So, gathering up all my conclusions, I reconstructed, in brief, the tragic events that occurred between Escobedo and García Streets, in the following way:

Octavio Ramírez, an individual of unknown nationality, forty-two years old, of mediocre build, lived in a modest, lower-class hotel until the 12th of January of this year.

It seems that this Ramírez had some income, certainly very little; he did not allow himself excessive expenses, much less extravagant ones, especially with women. Ever since childhood he had a small misdirection of his instincts, which soon degenerated to the point that, by a fatal impulse, they had to end with the tragic results that concern us.

For better clarity, it is on record that the individual had arrived only a few days before in the city that was to be the theater of these events.

The night of January 12th, while he ate in a cheap, filthy diner, he felt a familiar urge that bothered him more and more. At 8:00, when he left the diner, he was agitated by all the torments of this desire. In a strange city, the difficulty of satisfying it, because of his unfamiliarity with the area, urged him on powerfully. He wandered almost desperately, for two hours, through the central streets, anxiously fixing his sparkling eyes on the backs of the men he encountered; he followed them closely, hoping to take advantage of any opportunity, but afraid of being turned down.

By about 11:00 P.M. it became an immense torture. His body trembled and there was a painful emptiness in his eyes.

Deciding that it was pointless walking from street to street, he turned towards the slums, always looking twice at the passers-by, saying hello with a trembling voice, stopping now and then, not knowing what to do, like a beggar.

When he got to Escobedo Street he couldn't take it any more. He wanted to throw himself at the first man who passed by. To whimper, to tearfully tell him about his tortures . . .

He heard, far off, quiet, measured footsteps; his heart beat violently. He stood against the wall of a house and waited. In a few moments the hard body of a worker filled the sidewalk. Ramírez went pale; when the other came close, he reached out and touched his elbow. The worker quickly turned and looked at him. Ramírez tried a sweet smile, a hungry message abandoned in the gutter: The other let out a guffaw and a dirty word; then he kept on walking, slowly, making the heels of his shoes ring out loudly against the stones. After a half-hour another man appeared. Our unfortunate man, shaking all over, risked a flirtatious comment that the passer-by answered with a vigorous shove. Ramírez got scared and left quickly.

Then, after walking two blocks, he found himself in García Street. Ready to collapse, his mouth dry, he looked from one side of the street to the other. A short distance away a fourteen-year-old boy was hurrying along. He followed him.

"Psst! Psst!"

The boy stopped.

"Hey, cutie. What are you doing out this late?"

"I'm going home. What do you want?"

"Nothing, nothing.... But don't go so soon, pretty one...."

And he took the boy's arm.

The boy tried to pull away.

"Let go! I already told you I'm going home."

He wanted to run. But Ramírez gave a lunge and hugged him. Then the frightened street-boy started screaming:

"*Papá! Papá!*"

Almost immediately, a few feet away, a door opened, suddenly throwing some light into the street. A tall man appeared. It was the worker who had passed by before on Escobedo Street.

Seeing Ramírez he threw himself on him. Our poor man stood there staring back at him, with eyes as big and fixed as plates, trembling and silent.

"What do you want, you dirty bastard?"

And he gave him a furious kick in the stomach. Octavio Ramírez collapsed, with a long painful gasp of desire.

Epaminondas, which must be the worker's name, seeing the prick on the ground, considered that one kick was too little punishment, and gave him two more, splendid and marvellous ones, in that large nose that provoked him like a sausage.

How those marvellous kicks must have sounded!

Like the splattering of an orange, vigorously thrown against a wall; like the collapse of an umbrella whose ribs smack and shiver; like a nut cracked between two fingers; or better like the encounter of another firm soul of a shoe against another nose!

Like this:

Whack!
        with a delicious space between.
Whack!
And then: How Epaminondas became greedy for flesh, driven by the instinct of perversity that makes murderers riddle their victims with stab wounds! That same instinct that pushes some innocent fingers, just for fun, to squeeze harder and harder around friends' throats until they turn purple and their eyes blaze!

How the soul of Epaminondas's shoe slammed against Octavio Ramírez's nose!

Whack!
Whack!   dizzyingly,
Whack!
until a thousand points of light like needles pierced the darkness.

Appendix 3
The Sangurimas (Excerpt)
JOSÉ DE LA CUADRA

Legends

The stories they told about ño* Nicasio were savage and wild.[1] In the kitchens of the *montuvio* shacks, after supper, when the evening coffee was being served, frightful stories were told.

The woodsmen in the outlying clearings found much material for their chats in the supposed acts of ño Sangurima, sitting around the fire between meal-time and bedtime, staring up at the sky, on the slashed and burned earth.

The canoe-men who bring the fruit down from the plantations upriver always started to tell legends about the old man whenever they approached the Sangurimas' land.

But they talked about him the most at wakes. . . .

Friendship from Beyond the Grave

The dead man was laid out on a flaky, crumbling mat that was too short for the corpse, whose long limbs spilled onto the bare cane floor. Resting on the mat that had served him as a bed before, the deceased awaited, with an appropriately otherworldly calm, the canoe in which he would embark on the great voyage.

On the porch down below, a few friends were making the coffin, helped along by the master carpenter from the neighboring village.

Bottles of grain liquor were passed around the room, and gulped down straight.

An old woman reacted to a joke one of them made:

"See how good Don Sofronio looks!"

What she said implied a multitude of words.

"Ha! Ha! Ha! How good he looks. . . ."

---
*Ño, ña: contractions of *señor* and *señora*.

Another old woman, after a tremendous puff on her Daule cigar, tasty as bread to her, muttered, alluding to the peaceful corpse:

"Look how he died, now, ño Victorino. . . ."

Another old woman put in:

"The same for the rest of us! . . ."

The conversation generalized.

"Ño Victorino was such a wiseass!"

"That's true, all right."

"And now, with his face so stiff."

"Death brings respect."

"That's true, all right."

The widow tearfully intervened:

"How he liked coconut milk!"

"Really?"

"Yes. A few days before he died, he made Juan cut one down from a palm tree. My poor little dead one wanted to go up himself. . . . Now the palm tree's all full of worms."

The chatting turned again to the seriousness of death.

"Let me tell you! You know what Sangurima did, the old man, one time in Pechichal Chico?"

"No."

"What'd he do?"

"A friend of his died, Ceferino Pintado, remember?"

"Ah! Ceferino? The one they say shacked up with his own mother?"

"Him. . . . He was real close with ño Sangurima. They got drunk together."

"Right. One day in Chilintomo . . ."

"Don't interrupt. Let ña Petita tell her story."

Ña Petita went on:

"The afternoon Ceferino died ño Sangurima came to the wake. There were a lot of us at that wake. Because Pintado, even though he was a real bastard, he had a lot of friends. So ño Sangurima shows up. 'Everybody outside, I want to be alone with my *compadre*.' So we all got up and left. He stayed in the room and shut all the doors. So we hear him start to laugh and talk real slow. But that's nothing. All of a sudden we hear Ceferino talking and laughing too. We didn't understand one bit of it. We all ran downstairs as fast as we could, afraid. We shouted up: 'What's going on, ño Sangurima?' He appeared in the window. At his side was the dead man, with his arm around him. The old man said: 'Don't be scared. Come on up. I'll put my friend back in the box. We were just saying goodbye. But he's already gone back to where God has sent him.

Come on up so he can tell you about it. It's a riot.' We went up. Ño Sangurima opened the doors. We went in, Ceferino was in his canoe. His face looked like he was still laughing. . . . Ño Sangurima said goodbye to him, taking his hand: '*Hasta la vista, compadre.* Take care!' He jumped on his horse and went. . . . I think he was drunk."

"He must have been drunk."

Someone in the circle murmured.

"The one who's drunk is ña Petita. The grain liquor's gotten her tipsy."

"That's right, yeah."

Captain Jaén

Someone else always followed with another story about the old man:

"Let me tell you what he did in Quevedo—and he wasn't drunk. He was stone cold sober."

"And what about it?"

"Ño Sangurima was allied with Captain Jaén, remember? And Venancio Ramos' mountaineers had thrown Jaén in some faraway jail. They wanted to kill him, because Jaén was with the Rurals who shot mountaineers for trying to escape just like they was cattle rustlers."

"Good man, Jaén! No?"

"Aha. . . . So ño Sangurima heard and said a prayer to the Just Judge: 'Now you'll see how Jaén'll go free,' he said. And he took out his revolver and shot into the air. He laughed. 'That bullet has hit that damned Ramos right through the heart. . . .' The next day Captain Jaén arrived from Quevedo. 'How'd you get away, Jaén?' 'Well, you see, I don't even know.' 'And how's that bastard Venancio?' 'Worm food. A bullet came from somewhere in the hills and killed him.' Ño Sangurima asked: 'Where'd the bullet hit him?' 'Right through his chest. I think it got him in the heart.' Ño Sangurima slapped his belly with gusto. 'I'm still a good shot, goddammit,' he said."

Such were the stories that they told about ño Sangurima.

Satanic Pact

The *montuvios* swore that ño Nicasio had signed a pact with the devil.

"Really?"
"Sure."
"That kind of thing only happened a long time ago. Doesn't happen any more."
"Ah, you folks don't know anything. Ño Nicasio is really old."
"Older than the itch?"
"Don't push me! . . . He's older than the big *matapalo* tree out at the Solises' plantation."
"Ah! . . ."
Something brought up the form of this pact:
"My granddad worked on ño Sangurima's plantation, he saw it. It was on the skin of a calf who wasn't born where it's supposed to get born."
"What?"
"Yes, on a calf taken out by cutting open the mom cow's gut. . . . There it was. . . . Written with human blood."
"Ño Nicasio's?"
"No, a menstruating virgin's."
"Ah!"
"And where's this document kept?"
"In a coffin. They say it's in the Salitre cemetery. Buried."
"Why's that, huh?"
"The devil can't go into the cemetery. It's sacred. So he can't collect on it from ño Sangurima. Ño Sangurima laughs at the devil. When he comes for his soul, he says to him: 'Bring the bill so I can pay you.' And the devil bites his tail with rage, because he can't go onto sacred ground to get the pact. But he gets even by letting ño Sangurima live. Ño Sangurima wants to die so he can rest. He's lived longer than any man around here. The devil doesn't let him die. That's how he gets even."
"But they say ño Sangurima is dead inside."
"It must be like that, for sure."

The Price

Some curious person asked about the price of the sale.
"And how much did Old Cloven-hoof give ño Sangurima for his soul?"
"Uy! Land, money, cows, women . . ."
So some old *montuvio* intervened:
"You know how ño Sangurima's plantation—'La Hondura' [The Depths]—is now? Low and swampy only down by the river. But

inside, high ravines all over. Way 'bove the flood plain. Hilly. It wasn't like that before."

"And how was it?"

"My papa said that when he was young the whole place was one big quagmire. That's why they called it 'La Hondura,' and the name stuck."

"Ah!"

"When ño Sangurima put ashore with the Evil One, he bought the quagmire. . . . You know how much? . . . For 20 pesos. . . . To hide it he now says that his mama left it to him. . . . But that's not how it is. . . . And right after that the swamp started to dry up and land sprouted all by itself. . . . Just like flesh grows back over a wound. You've seen that?"

"Bucking hell!"

"It was the devil's magic."

"That—well—that must be it."

"They say when ño Sangurima dies, the land will sink again, and overflow with the water that's under it all, waiting."

"That's how it must be, for sure."

"That's how it must be."

Buried Treasure

There was another legend of riches gotten by extraordinary means.

This one was about a buried treasure that ño Nicasio is supposed to have discovered.

"Of course it was another deal with the devil, like all the others."

"And what happened this time?"

"You'll see. From the moment he signed that evil pact, ño Sangurima could speak with the dead.

"One time he saw a flame burning in a cane grove. So he went up and said to the glow: 'What can I do for you?' The flame turned into a man and said to him: 'I am the renowned Riguberto Zambrano, who lived in these parts ages ago. I have silver hidden, which is for thee. Take it.' Ño Sangurima said all right, and he asked what he had to do. The dead man asked him to request 30 masses to Saint Gregorio and three to the Holy Trinity. Ño Sangurima agreed. 'And what else, *señor* dead person?' he inquired. Now came the big one. The evil vision said that in order to remove the treasure he'd have to sprinkle the earth above it with the blood of a three-month-old boy who hadn't been baptized yet."

"And what'd Ño Sangurima do?"

"He started looking for just such a little one. They say he told people: 'Don't think about it, just sell it to me: I'll pay you well. More than the finest horse.' But nobody wanted to."

"Of course."

"So they say Ño Sangurima caught on and said: 'I'll have to make this baby myself.' He didn't have a wife and kids yet. They say he was very young."

"Aha."

"So he went and found his sweet little Jesús Torres, who was a virgin girl, and he made her produce. She gave birth to a boy just like she was supposed to. And when the kid was three months old, Ño Sangurima took him to the spot where the treasure was buried. Then he stuck a knife into the little one, wet the earth and dug up the dead man's wealth. They say it was a huge one, Spanish silver."

"Ah!"

"And what'd his sweet little Jesús Torres do?"

"When she found out she went crazy, of course. They took her to Guayaquil. She died in the madhouse, years ago."

"How many?"

The narrator remained pensive. He rolled his eyes up to the whites. And finally he stammered,

"According to my reckoning, at least a hundred...."

The most credulous of his listeners supplied the indispensable suffix:

"That's how it must be, all right."

Corrections

When Ño Nicasio Sangurima was asked about his sweet little Jesús Torres his face took on a disgusted look.

"Somebody's told you a lot of stupid stories, *amigo*. I don't know why the *montuvios* jabber so much. I'd really like to damn up their mouths like we damn up creeks to catch us some fish. Just like that. We'd all be better off."

He smiled freely, almost childishly.

"You see, there's some truth in that. But not like they say!"

"So what's the truth, ño Nicasio?"

"I took my sweet little Jesús Torres, who was the daughter of one of my godparents, from right around here, and I made her a baby. That child was plenty sickly. One night he looked just like he was going to die. I grabbed him and ran to take him to my *compadre* José Jurado, who could work cures. On the way, the little angel kicked the bucket; so I went back home to his mama. My sweet one saw the dead kid, latched on to him and wouldn't let go. She held him for two days. We couldn't get it away from her. The little corpse already smelled and we had to pull it away by force. So my sweet little one started to scream: 'Give me my child!' and no one could stop her. She screamed for the longest time. . . . And that's how she went mad. I sent her to Guayaquil, to the 'Lorenzo Ponce' asylum. And that's where she settled her account with God about three years after."

"Ah . . ."

"You see, *amigo*, what tales people invent . . ."

"That's how it is, ño Sangurima."

Funereal Customs

Don Nicasio maintained the respectful memory of his two deceased wives.

He didn't want to bury them in any cemetery.

"Why, ño Nicasio?"

"The poor things! There are so many people in there, especially on Judgment Day, how are they supposed to find their graves? They who were so helpless, how are they going to get by all by themselves? I'll have to help them."

Probably in order to help them in the future, for awhile, he had them buried in a hill in "La Hondura," near the big house.

Later he exhumed the cadavers and put the bones in boxes that were big enough for them.

He kept the two boxes that contained the remains of his wives under his bed, next to the empty coffin that he had made expressly for himself.

On every anniversary of one of their deaths, he took out their remains and cleaned them with alcohol. His third wife helped at this as best she could.

The coffin that was reserved for him was crafted of fine *amarillo* mimosa wood, and was very elegant. He kept it lined with newspaper.

"When I die, I'm not gonna screw up anybody by having them run around. I've got the canoe right under the bed. They pull it out, ship me off and *hasta la vuelta*. That's best."

When he polished the boxes of remains he also polished his casket with careful attention, and he changed the lining of newspaper.

Apparitions

Ño Sangurima swore that his two dead wives appeared at night, climbing out of their boxes, and lay down peacefully, one on one side, the other on the other, together in bed with the man who belonged to both of them.

"I hear their cold bones clack together. And they talk to me. They make conversation with me."

"And aren't you afraid, Don Nicasio?"

"One is afraid of what one doesn't know; but what you know, no. Why should I be afraid of my women! Wouldn't you say I know them as deeply as one can. . . . I remember how they were in life. And I caress them. . . . The sad thing is that where they were plump before, now they're nothing but bones, poor things! . . ."

Appendix 4
Bruna, soroche y los tíos (Bruna and Her Family)
ALICIA YÁNEZ COSSÍO

Chapter 2 (Excerpt)

Bruna was descended from a disloyal race that was still hurt and humiliated by its mixed blood, with all the pain and repression of original sin.

"We don't have a drop of Indian blood."
"Neither do we."
"On the other hand . . . they do."
"All you have to do is look at the color of their faces."
"We all know each other here."

Bruna thought about the great majority of people who lived in the city and who silenced their ancestors if they didn't have an illustrious last name, a last name on top of which they could reconstruct according to their taste a brilliant past, whose foolish wisps were hammered into shape by means of a history forged during afternoon gatherings.

"Which Garcías are you related to?"
"The first ones to come to America."
"Which ones?"
"The founders, of course."
"The family of [President] García Moreno?"
"Yes, exactly, the very same! Our great-grandfather was married to . . ."

The story of her last name was a very common story in those days.... A man [came] from the other side of the ocean, thirsty for adventures and gold—because they were the ones who actually did the colonizing, helped along by some laws that fell into the sea and sank. [The man] married an Indian [princess]. She was the daughter of a chief who owned mountains of gold and emeralds. The white man saw the sky open up.... Men such as he forged and fed the legend of El Dorado for centuries, and spread it around the world re-awakening the greed that had been latent since the days of Ali Baba. The Indian's name was María Illacatu.

"I baptize you, Yahuma, with the name María. In the name of the Father, the Son, and the ..."

And she was named María from the moment they spilled water over her bowed head and washed away the idea of the Sun God, chilling her heart, which had been warmed by the fire of his rays, and told her about some unknown god who seemed to get angry much more often than he should have.

"Idol-worshipper! God will punish you! You're going to go to hell! You're going to be condemned!"
"... ?"

María Illacatu's children were much more their father's children than their mother's. They were aware how much prestige the so-easily-gotten gold brought them and they changed their innocuous name García to Villacatu.

"Here in Spain everyone's García...."
"It's a noble name...."
"Our name is Villacatu. Our mother was of royal blood."

They grew up in their father's land, in a tiny village, and the fact that they were Spanish-American surrounded them with a halo of dignity that accompanied them even in their most private and ordinary acts.

Their children grew up in their mother's land and therefore cursed the day that their fathers changed their name. In the land they were living everything was still waiting to be made, so they adopted the name of Villa-Cató, and in turn, the children of the

Villa-Catós settled the long-debated question of lineage by calling themselves Catovil.

"Villacatu is Indian, pure Quichua...."
"We own six *villas*."
"Villa-Cató doesn't sound bad...!"
"Catovil sounds better!"
"That's it! What a relief to be rid of that Villacatu!"

⁂

Bruna's family preserved like a treasure—without knowing who it was—a painting of the Indian grandmother. She was dressed like a great lady as a result of her unfortunate marriage. The man who did the portrait painted her as she was. But influenced by the conventions of the era, he removed her skin, and thus flayed, he gave her living flesh the skin her husband lent her so she could pose. María Illacatu lost her coppery skin on the canvas with the same stoicism with which she lost her reason for living. Her face, her neck, her arms were all milky white, unreal, as if they had undergone plastic surgery, like the new skin transplants that were now arriving in the city. She was the image of what they wished she had been.

"This is your great-great-grandmother...."
"That's a lie! My great-great-grandmother was an Indian!"
"But can't you see that she's not an Indian?"
"Then it's not her...."

⁂

María Illacatu had succumbed long before they made the portrait. She didn't resist the tragic process of being transplanted and adapting to the world of the whites. Her centuries-old customs, inherited along with the earth by racial privilege, were supposed to have been erased overnight as if they were stigmas.

"We have to put a corset on the Indian so she can pose."
"And you're going to spend so much money getting her picture painted?"
"So that my grandchildren won't say that..."
"Oh, now I understand!"

She learned the whites' language but she refused to speak it, the words born in her throat had a different meaning. When she sensed that she was the target of the city dwellers' looks, she felt such a sensation of contempt that it was as if a thousand shoes were trampling on her face, and in spite of the fact that she knew the meaning of the new words, she never spoke them: it was a small compensation. . . .

"Don't say 'huasi,' say ho-o-use. Don't say 'alpa,' say e-e-earth. Don't say 'rumi,' say sto-o-one. Don't say 'cari,' say ma-a-an. Don't say 'huarmi,' say wo-man. Don't say 'tanda,' say bread. Don't say 'ashcu,' say do-o-og. Don't say 'misi,' say ca-a-at. Don't say, don't say, don't say . . ."

When María Illacatu's children [returned to] the city [. . .] they had the disagreeable surprise of finding that there weren't any more rich Indians for them to marry and later repudiate. What they found were women who knew how to handle a fork and raise their little fingers when drinking tea. How to paint snowy landscapes that they had never seen. How to go to Mass every day with an Indian servant girl carrying the kneeling bench on her back through the cobblestone streets, while older ones showed their devotion by kneeling on large silk pillows that they also sat on to listen to long sermons in which they discussed and condemned the sins of the flesh, called the devil all kinds of names, and begged for clemency for a corrupt world. . . . The women of the city also knew how to handle a fan, behind which they practiced their first, insipient lessons in coquetry. They urinated between five and six times a day in golden chamberpots and spent the rest of the day yawning and dreaming of marrying a noble, rich, and elegant gentleman. They were completely the opposite of what their unknown mother had been.

Once they possessed the riches inherited from their mother's side and the noble title bought by their father's side, the Villacatus remained single for a very short time. The women's fans went into action and perfumed little notes came and went carried next to the breasts of eager, older maids, and under the very eyes of the respective fathers who, long beforehand, had been chattering about how the children should marry. . . .

Nobody ever heard about María Illacatu again, because by mutual agreement they took her and buried her in the box with the dusty memories, from which she would never escape.

It always hurt Bruna to see her Indian ancestor nailed up in the big drawing room, isolated from all contact and tenderness by a wall of silence and mistaken words. Nobody seemed to know anything about her past, and if they kept the painting in an honored place in the house, it was because a superstitious fear kept them from touching or even getting near it. It was said that on moonlit nights, when the rays penetrated through the cracks in the closed windows, sighs and laments could be heard that froze the blood.

There was another truth, the painting was a valuable work of art. The signature that the artist put in the lower right corner had acquired fame with the passing of the years.

When Bruna discovered on her own and through [the maid] Mama Chana's delicious indiscretions the scandal surrounding her distant relatives, she started to venerate her Indian grandmother. She wanted to take the large painting and hang it at the head of her bed to remove her grandmother from memory and give her the warmth that she never had in life. But it was too late now. She was no longer her grandmother. In reality, she never had the slightest relationship with the people who lived in the house. With the passing of time it just became a valuable painting, with an astonishing resemblance to a Bonnat, which represented a great lady from the other side of the ocean and nothing else. . . .

"Who's that?"
"One of our ancestors."
"She's so beautiful!"
"The painting is very valuable, it's been appraised at . . ."
"How distinguished!"
"Of course, she had noble titles!"

Appendix 5
Polvo y Ceniza (Dust and Ashes)
ELIÉCER CÁRDENAS

CHAPTER FOUR: PAJARITO

The old man's horse stopped in the middle of the river, its rump gleaming in the sun, its coat covered with innumerable water droplets, its hoofs testing the clear, rocky bottom of the Catamayo River. The old man bent forward on his mount, letting the reins go, trying not to look back at him. He, keeping a sharp eye out from the riverbank, shouted at him to hurry up, that the Rurals, with their dirty khaki uniforms and their faces streaked with dust from the trail, would soon ride over the hill and gallop across the rocky *pampa*, hurrying towards the river with their swords drawn, their carbines ready. Only a moment before the band of Rurals had raised a cloud of dust on the bald ridge of the farthest hill. The old man, with his huge hat made of fine white straw shading his ruddy, wrinkled face from the sun, showed his profile for a few seconds, displaying, in the tense curve of his body, some unyielding, secret pain. He can't be wounded, he thought, as his horse's hoofs slowly started to splash again in the still water of the river's edge, approaching the silent pain of the old man who had taught him so much. He thought how people say that no bullet can touch Pajarito because he is protected by all the saints of his land. Rose of Lima, black Martin, Jesus of the Miracles; they say that the people from the Peruvian deserts practically can't even touch him when he's running from them. Many say that Pajarito has a pact with he who can't be named and that nobody can harm him. They say that when he was still practically a boy he crossed the border all by himself to rob five hundred head of cattle that some ranch owners in Sullana had bought at the highest price. They say that in '93 he fought alone against a batallion of soldiers and killed them all. They say that he had one hundred women scattered all over the countryside, all of them beautiful and hopelessly in love with him, with his blue eyes and his broken nose. That he burned *haciendas* in Chira, leveled

APPENDIX 5. *POLVO Y CENIZA (DUST AND ASHES)*

farms in Guásimo, that one night, just for fun, he burned an entire neighborhood in Macará, and that in Piura they're offering two hundred gold *soles* for his head. But he denies that all these things are true. They're nothing but lies, old women's tales, he says; that he's just a poor thief who watches out for his own life and who doesn't believe in boundary markers, stockades, fortifications, and flags that divide the world into very large *haciendas* that are called countries. That, for him, the yellow, blue, and red colors of this land and the red and white stripes of his are nothing more than painted rags that trick people into being evil, blind, and bitchy.

Stopping his horse in the middle of the current, reaching out to grab the fallen reins, he looked at his withered profile, time-worn with dark wrinkles. And he saw how, still bent over, he kept his thick, calloused hands around his middle, rolling up his dirty shirt and testing his hairy stomach, cursing, tight-lipped, as if ashamed of showing pain in front of the boy who had learned from him never to complain, ever, to withstand everything that hardened the body with a stubborn smile. It's just a slight pain, here, in the stomach, the old man told him when he tugged on the horse's sweaty reins to guide it to the river's edge. And once on the other side, as the old man, leaning on his horse, let himself be led along, he saw, in the distance, among the bare, sharp, unturned rocks on the hill, the small but unmistakable cloud of dust rising as the Rurals galloped down towards the *pampa*. The old man heard the distant noise and made a shameful and humiliating request not to be abandoned, that he couldn't hold himself up on his horse. He dismounted, lifted Pajarito, put him on his own horse's back, and rode uphill, without saying a word, warmed by the faint waves of heat emanating from the old man's trembling body gripping his. But he didn't figure it was anything serious: a fever, something he picked up long ago, or maybe just some bad air he caught when they passed near a cemetery. Because he couldn't imagine that anything serious would ever happen to this old man who, without even knowing him, had had the patience to wait for an entire night, trusting the barefoot boy who had asked to join the band. As it happened, he didn't show up that night, but five or six months later, when the old man had already forgotten about him, thinking that the boy's desire had only been a sad attempt to defy the hunger and bitterness that showed in his dull eyes in that general store in Cangonamá. But Pajarito did see the boy again, only by then he was more of a man, more filled-out, defiantly riding a fast young sorrel, dressed entirely in white, with large riding boots and silver spurs, quickly crossing the jagged waste-land leading to the shack where Chivo Blanco and his men were hiding out after holding up a mail-coach from the North, only to find, inside the leather bag with the national seal burned into it, nothing but sealed letters, with delicate blue writing on the envelopes, papers that smelled of faraway places, of convents and barracks. Letters that no one in the band wanted to or knew how to read, not even Chivo Blanco, who usually wanted to learn as much as he could about business affairs, love affairs, and the latest deaths from the tiny, cramped writing in the letters. When Pajarito, who was standing out on the porch, saw the intruder riding fearlessly in, he recognized those hard features, arrogant and cheerful at the same time; and he shouted to the triggers, ready to squeeze off some well-aimed shots to bring down the unexpected, unknown figure dressed in white who drew inexorably closer, his horse's hoofbeats kicking up the waste-land's cracked, white earth, as white as his riding clothes. And, without knowing why but sensing somehow that this boy didn't deserve to be shot without being given a chance to explain why he had come, Chivo Blanco's grim-faced highwaymen lowered their sites and let the rider dismount, slowly clean off the trail dust deposited on his clothes, his hat, and listened to him say that he came alone and asked, without explanation, with dauntless determination, to join the group. And Chivo Blanco, blowing a hot breath of air through the musty double-barrel of a shotgun, turned his bald head towards Pajarito, who stood waiting, immobile, to ask him, surprised, who the hell is this brash young boy who came here all alone and wants to be a bandit. A poor boy who wants to be like us, the old man answered. We'll see about that, laughed Chivo Blanco, and he raised his shotgun up to his cheek and let fly a slug of lead at the boy dressed in white who stood waiting for an answer, calmly and patiently, his arms folded across his chest, the tips of the light-blue bandana knotted around his neck billowing in the quiet breeze. The shot, quick and loud, flew near that now uneasy head that moved while he said no, don't shoot at me. Who are you? asked Chivo Blanco, surly and perplexed, not lowering his aim with the old shotgun, crouching on the porch. Pot-bellied and covered with warts. The boy with the white chintz pants, the white linen shirt and white Peruvian hat lit up with a quick smile and said, without raising his voice too much, that his name was Naún, that, due to the injustices of life and fate, he had spent five months in jail and when he got out, he decided to hold up single-handedly a *hacienda* in Catacocha in broad daylight. That he stole a horse, some hemp saddlebags with elegant riding clothes in them, a light-blue silk bandana, a gun and a walnut box full of *pesos*. The *pesos* were spent on cane liquor and cockfights. That he knew of Chivo Blanco's fame, and the only reason he was here was to ask if he could ride with them, through ravines, mountains, and valleys, assaulting and cutting, killing and fleeing. Chivo Blanco twisted his bulging bloodshot eyes towards the old man. You know him, Pajarito? he asked, uneasily, one finger toying with the trigger of his shotgun. The old man answered yes, that one time in Cangonamá this same boy dressed all in white saved my life and that he's not even afraid of bullets fired at him from close range. And the bandit chief, believing him because the old man had the reputation of never lying, ever, lowered the aim of his double-barreled shotgun from the boy's body, and told the boy dressed in white that he could enter the shack. And from that moment on, and for many years after, Naún Briones was part of that famous, fearsome band, Chivo Blanco's criminal gang that robbed and killed so many in the face of the astonished rage, the desperate impotence of the Provincial Deputies, *hacienda* foremen, the heads of garrisons and military detachments. And Pajarito, that old man who was now holding on to him for support, feverish, worn-out, and groaning, was the one who taught Naún how to hide his hard, stony face in market-day crowds, to disguise his voice and the recognizable gestures, to sense the hoofbeats of a handful of guards on some robber's trail; to close the right eye without having the left one blink or cloud over, and to keep his hand steady, and to choose the part of the body that brought death quickest: the nipple near the heart or the broadest part of the forehead. How to shoot and hit the mark every time, because if the first one doesn't hit, then you shouldn't be a bandit. And if you don't learn how to change the sound of your voice at all the right times, such as encounters with strangers, you run the risk of those sounds being remembered and denounced to the first detachment of Rurals, to the nearest Deputy's Office. Because, if one pretends to be a farmer, or a cattleman, a simple, peaceful woodcutter among the crowds circulating at the fairs to buy much-needed equipment, nobody would pay any attention to those heavy footsteps, that hard look, those hands twitching near the pouch where a revolver sleeps, that announce the unmistakable presence of a *bandido*. Because you can't always be on the run, hiding in mountains, unpopulated forests, caves, thickets. That's not living. One needs other people, and that should never be forgotten. He also taught him how robbing the poor, those who have nothing, wasn't worth it, because one got very little robbing a poor person, and, in exchange, earned a lot of hatred. And the rich never lose too much when one puts the bite on them, a robbery, no matter how big, could never finish off their wealth. Because they are not only rich because of what they own but also because of what they represent. We are also poor, Pajarito told him, we who weren't baptized in long, velvet gowns, we who could never learn the alphabet, who live to pay off debts, who work other people's fields, who serve those who need us more than we need them; because all a poor person needs is that little bit that once in a while slips through his fingers while a rich person's needs are like a bottomless pit. And then he knew that he would never stop being poor, even though years later they would say, in newspapers and in the conversations of ostentatious ranch-owners and properous businessmen, in trials and lawsuits brought by corrupt lawyers, that he, Naún Briones, had trunks full of money and jewelry, silk shirts, three-piece suits of English cashmere, patent leather shoes.

With the old bandit's sick warmth still stuck to his ribs like a living arm, he rode over the band's fresh tracks on the dry trail, sensing the guards' distant approach, hot and thirsty, dust covering his wide-brimmed white straw hat, his light-blue bandana tied around his throat and his brown half-boots. When the noonday sun glowed in the middle of a cloudless, windless sky, he caught sight of two small houses leg-lost among some plantains whose leaves were yellowing from drought, and far-off but recognizable, he made out Octavio's profile, one of Chivo Blanco's men, his body half-hidden among the fractures of a big rock that was sending out tiny sparkles of sunlight. Chivo Blanco, moving his heavily and uneasily, went out to meet them, going as far as the parched plantains that surrounded the two miserable huts. He, justifying their delay, explained that the old man had a fever and couldn't keep riding. He let Pajarito down from his horse's back and helped carry him inside the hut that Chivo Blanco and his men were using, temporarily transformed into a fortress and a place of uneasy rest. The old man was shaking, cursing under his breath, as if he were ashamed that they were seeing him like this, panting for breath, bent over, useless, the men who he had taught how to sack, kill, and run. He propped up the old man's head on a saddle placed on the dirt floor, wiped the thickly flowing sweat from his brow. But Chivo Blanco, after staying behind, beyond the withered plantains, to watch the narrow, irregular horizon of the nearby hills for any ominous sign of the pursuing cavalcade of guards, came back to the hut and, squatting down next to the old man, felt his cheeks lightly, suspicious and fearing the worst; he unbuttoned his shirt, loosened his pants, and saw the black blotches on Pajarito's belly, the hard, green lumps spread across his hairy groin. And opening his fearful eyes wide, shouted loudly, so that all could hear, plague, the old man's got the plague. The nine cattle rustlers, alarmed, quickly grabbed their saddle-bags, saddles, horse blankets, and weapons and rushed into the oppressively hot air outside. They've got the plague in Utuana, one of them suddenly remembered, terrorized, and we went through there three days ago. There's been a lot of deaths, recalled another, they were burning houses with the sick still in them, there's no escape from the plague. The old man squirmed, pale, bothered, grabbing at the air as if clawing for his life. Chivo Blanco moved quickly, picking up his shotgun, his saddle and bags, giving direct, frightened orders, saddle up, grab the stuff, and let's get out of here. Nobody can help him, he apologized, not the doctors, not the Holy Pope in person could save him now. And everyone obeyed, saddled up as quickly as they could, hurriedly gathered up their belongings. Except him, he didn't want to leave the old man now, stretched out on the hard dirt floor, his eyes rolled up to the whites, who was starting to remember old prayers, long lost in his memory. Idiot, Chivo Blanco yelled at him, seeing his calm decision to remain behind, you'll catch it from him, you'll die too, nobody, nobody gets cured from the plague, which is the worst punishment God can send a man. But he didn't move from the old man's prayers, his strangled groans, and said that he was staying. Because he didn't want to leave him to die alone, to abandon him now wouldn't be right. Chivo Blanco didn't insist and, ready to dig his steel spurs into his horse's veined belly, told him they would wait for him in Espíndola, with some trustworthy friends that he knew there. But don't even think of going, he told him, if you notice that you're getting feverish or if your body gets covered with black spots, in that case you'd better stay here to die with Pajarito. He answered by nodding yes.

It's not good to remember the past, Pajarito had said one afternoon while taking swallows of the muddy, slightly briny water that El Chira had carried over what everyone else called the national border but which Pajarito, contemptuously and mockingly, called the national fuck-up. Because the things that one has lived through, if good, are better off not being remembered: that way they'll always remain good. If bad, never think about them: sometimes evil comes back in the form of a simple memory. But if you really want to remember, ask your memory not to betray you with frankness and accuracy. Some people say that memories let you to live twice: your own life and the life of their own that memories have. I don't believe that. For me, memories are like buzzards of the soul, circling overhead, black, hungry, waiting to carry off the weakest thing that passes by. One day a friend in Ayabaca told me that one time a famous *señor*, one of those who writes with those pretty words that nobody ever uses, wanted to make a book out of my memories, which would make me live again, even after I had been dead for many years, between the dry pages of a book. That people who haven't even been born yet would talk about me as if they had known me. And I, laughing, answered my friend that the man who wrote about me would be a liar, because if one's own memories are lies, someone else's memories would be even bigger lies. To me, a memory is like the soul of an unburied body: it wanders around, bothering and frightening and fucking people up by haunting them until they find the remains and bury them deep. It's well known that there are people who seek out fame by sticking their noses into other people's memories, they think they're going to cheat death that way, cheat the dust and ashes, which is the oblivion of forgetting all things. But nobody cheats death, who is the only one that never forgets. And, with time, when the men who remembered the actions of men who wanted to be remembered are themselves dust and ashes, people won't know who were the rememberers and who were the remembered. Things happen without needing to be remembered. The sun shines without needing anybody to be polite enough to remember it. Don't ever hope to be remembered by anyone. It's better to be forgotten. That way, the things that happen have to stay what they are: pure lies.

When the afternoon shadows of the plantains lengthened along the dusty, golden ground, he approached the old man and felt his breathing, like a faraway, broken bellows; he looked at the big, dirty blotches spread across his stomach's quivering skin and felt the fear that came thanklessly over him. It was that fear of dying that we all have and, also, the specific horror of leaving life behind so quickly, without reason or hope, falling before the onslaught of a thoroughly mortal, inexplicable disease. Only moments before he had decided to get away from there, to leave the old man alone with his unjust and unending agony. Or to run after stopping his breathing with a single, expert bullet in the back of the neck. But, on the point of leaving, of killing Pajarito as a dark form of thanks, he was held back by those watery, light-blue eyes that watched the sunset without bitterness. An old man's eyes, gravely ill, meek and empty, fixed on what would remain after they had gone: the big sun polishing the colors of the earth and sky, the faded plantain leaves, the hut's dusty, ruined eaves; the horses, patiently waiting, displaying their rumps, their ears, their tails swishing carelessly in the still atmosphere of sundown. And, somewhere inside those resigned eyes, the rush of years leaving those tired memories of hardships behind without nostalgia: through the eyes through which the years had entered. And he couldn't go now, nor kill him, it was too painful. He sat through the harsh, rough sounds that came after, satisfied the parched lips that begged for water: one last swallow that almost didn't make it down his throat. And he allowed the final, warm cowardice of the old man's hand grabbing his shoulder for support, not wanting to die, anguished and hard, feeling, moments later, that Pajarito, that old bandit who didn't like memories or borders, was going off into death's eternal letting go, into that never again, into the growing rigidness after the one, lonely second in which we all meet our end.

Chapter Five: His Face

They say that very few people ever saw his face more than twice. That the majority of his victims never saw him again or that they suddenly forgot what his features looked like out of pure fear that they would see him again someday. That when they killed him, Major Deifilio ordered his face to be covered with a piece of cloth, and so, without a face for anyone to remember him by, he was taken to Loja where, without cutting into his belly or sawing open his skull, because there was no need to do it, he was buried somewhere—nobody can tell you precisely where. But I saw him face to face many times, his real face, round, a little pale in spite of his living outdoors, on mountain roads and open-air hideouts. His round face, a bit aloof from always having to keep it covered from friends and enemies, from the light of day and the oil lamps of night. His face had thick, unforgettable lines that looked like they had been carved in wood or stone; shining eyes hidden between thick, bushy eyebrows: eyes that moved gloomily and threateningly, or happily and openly; almost always hardened in a fixed stare that looked right through you, guessing the intentions of those they were contemplating. They weren't dark, they had that light brown color of cane syrup, a little more golden because of their brilliance, not big but deep, a bit slanted, with quick, heavy lids. His wide, straight nose. His lips, almost always tightened with fatigue or anger, never with contempt, although they might suddenly open up in a roar of laughter that shook his whole body, a roar of laughter that was his badge, his trademark during robberies, flight, sudden appearances. Not a happy or mocking laugh: just plain full of life, or manly challenge. His teeth were very white; even, strong teeth that gleamed with each roar of laughter like a collection of flint washed in the river. I only saw him a few times without his thick, bristly beard, reddish-brown like his uncombed hair. He always said he never had time to shave. Only when he went down into the towns to have some fun, wanting to amuse himself without making any trouble, did he shave off that beard which was the mark of all of the bandits in the region: short and dirty. Then, in the villages, without the beard, with his cheeks smooth and round, and without the roars of laughter, nobody recognized him. He was actually rather small: his legs were short and thick, each step heavy and sure; his waist was thick and his hands small and hairy, his fingers crowded with rings: rings were his only extravagance, he was crazy about them, he put two on each finger, he polished them on his clothes so they were always shiny, flashy. Thick rings with carved relief or set with stones or plain, thin rings of cheap gold that he stole because he liked them. That's how he looked: unmistakable, different from any other surly, violent, and abusive bandit. I don't know why Major Deifilio ordered his face covered when they brought his cadaver into the city of Loja. Maybe he was afraid that if people got a look at him they would never forget him and would turn him into some kind of hero or saint, and would pray to him, or invoke him, remembering his round, robust face, his bright white teeth, his week-old beard, dirty with dry sweat, with thistle, and with bits of thread. But after he was dead and buried the people always managed to invent faces similar to the one he had: friendly faces. And legendary. They carved his face in wood, modeled it in clay, painted it on walls, traced it with pencils. They made it survive in spite of the fact that Major Deifilio covered his face, trying to abolish him. In vain.

Notes

INTRODUCTION: Narrative Theory, Ideology, and Literary Production

1. Humberto Robles, among others, rejects the term *Magic Realism*, preferring to use *Mythic Realism* to describe the culture of Ecuador's coastal hinterland where *Los Sangurimas* takes place, a world in which the quotidian and the extraordinary co-exist, an amalgam of the real and the marvellous, a reality full of fascinating exploits (Humberto E. Robles, *Testimonio y tendendcia mítica en la obra de José de la Cuadra*, [Quito: Casa de la Cultura, 1976], 189, 249, 106–9). Regarding "Marvellous Realism" (meaning "extraordinary realism"), Alejo Carpentier repeated for more than 25 years his view that the "marvellous" was obtained in Europe by tricks and formulas while Americans had daily contact with it, that it was fabricated and prefabricated in Europe but a spontaneous translation of the American ambience (Alejo Carpentier, Introduction to *El reino de ese mundo*, *Obras completas:* Vol. 2 [Mexico: Siglo XXI, 1983], 14, 16; and Carpentier, *Tientos y diferencias y otros ensayos* [Barcelona: Plaza & Janes, 1987], 115, 117–18; essays originally published in 1949 and 1975, respectively). These are excessively totalizing statements that must be historicized: e.g., Carpentier includes the legends of the Knights of the Round Table as examples of artificially constructed European fantasy (Introduction to *El reino*, 13), but surely even the most conventionally textualized versions of these legends contain some transmission of marvellous oral tales "natural" to some of the culture's inhabitants.

2. For example, the reader is expected to know that "the foreign general," "the intermittent leader," and "the bloodstained rat" refer to the historical figures of Ecuadorian presidents Juan José Flores, José María Velasco Ibarra and Gabriel García Moreno (see Pablo Martínez, "Strategies of (Re)presentation in the New Ecuadorian Novel: Between Marx and a Naked Woman and the Aesthetics of Violence," *New Novel Review/Nueva Novela/Nouveau Roman* 3, no. 1 [October.1995]: 84). Writers living in insecurity may use such indirection out of necessity. But the usage of this technique may also reproduce a literary "insiderism" that occasionally works against some of the "new" Ecuadorian novel's internationalist goals.

3. Erich Auerbach, *Mimesis* (Princeton: Princeton University Press, 1968), 20.

4. Perhaps a better term would be *suppressive*: The narrational creation of order would appear to be linked to other physiological perceptual apparatuses that help us make sense of the world. As Seymour Chatman notes, "a narrative . . . can never be totally 'complete,'" however, "The audience's capacity to supply plausible details is virtually limitless," which "explains the technique by which the reader 'fills in' gaps in the text" (Seymour Chatman, *Story and Discourse: Narrative Structure in Fiction and Film* [Ithaca: Cornell University Press, 1978], 29, 49). Physiological psychology explains that our visual perception owes a great deal of its success as a system to the suppression and integration of potentially chaotic

stimuli. The rods and cones in our retinas, those receptors of light and color, are point sources, much like the tiny dots which make up a photograph. There are gaps between them which the visual system suppresses, just as it normally supresses what would otherwise be the highly interruptive process of blinking and the blind spot in our eyes created by the bundle of receptor neurons passing through the funnel-like fovea to the brain. In other words, it is normal and "correct" procedure for our perceptual apparatus to suppress and ignore discontinuities in stimuli in favor of a "seamless" depiction of sensory events. Hence some forms of psychosis (or the effects of psychomimetic drugs), which seem to remove that "normal" channels of suppression and inhibition of multiform stimuli, can leave the subject "hearing" the walls breathe, "feeling" colors and "seeing" music.

In other words, too many gaps produce an incoherent narrative, but not enough gaps can mimic psychosis. Effective narrative would therefore seem to be that which has just the "right" number of gaps.

Thus the brain's apparently inherent urge to narrate would be seen as a healthy preventor of psychosis. Yet Eagleton, using Freud and Habermas, discusses narrative as a form of neurosis (Terry Eagleton, *Ideology: An Introduction* [London: Verso, 1991], 132–36). If neurosis is the price of preventing psychosis, so be it. Perhaps this "neurosis" refers to taking the urge to order through narration to the extreme. Or does it refer to all fictional narration, which could be described as spinning a web out of nothing—surely a neurotic act.

5. Jorge Enrique Adoum, Prologue to *Narradores ecuatorianos del 30* (Caracas: Biblioteca Ayacucho, 1982), ix.

6. In terms of reaching the readers, Kurt Vonnegut writes, "If I broke all the rules of punctuation, had words mean whatever I wanted them to mean, and strung them together higgledy-piggledy, I would simply not be understood. . . . Readers want our pages to look very much like pages they have seen before" (Kurt Vonnegut, "How to Write with Style," in *How to Use the Power of the Printed Word* [New York: Anchor, 1985], 37). This would seem to complicate Barbara Herrnstein Smith's confident statement that "the narrator always has the option of subverting the conventions and thwarting the operations of any or all . . . cognitive tendencies." See W.J.T. Mitchell, ed., *On Narrative* (Chicago: University of Chicago Press, 1981), 227.

7. Karl Marx and Frederick Engels, *Marx and Engels on Literature and Art*, Lee Baxandall and Stefan Morawski, eds. (New York: International General, 1974), 114.

8. Stuart Hall, "Notes on Deconstructing 'The Popular,' " in *People's History and Socialist Theory*, ed. Raphael Samuel (London: Routledge & Kegan Paul, 1981), 239.

9. Michael J. Toolan, *Narrative: A Critical Linguistic Introduction* (London: Routledge, 1991), 173.

10. Ibid., 174.

11. Georg Lukács writes: "the great mission of true literature is to awaken men to consciousness of themselves. In order to fulfill this mission it must have popular appeal. But such popularity does not mean the blunting of problems or the transformation of literature into propaganda. The popularity of truly great literature should rest on the fact that it expresses genuine problems on the highest possible level and digs down to the deepest roots of human suffering, feeling, thought, and action" (Georg Lukács, *Studies in European Realism* [New York: Grosset & Dunlap, 1964], 85, 218).

This "popular-*but*-high-level" paradigm is of the utmost relevance. While the terms *popular* and *high* are often used by traditional critics as if they were synonymous with *simple* and *complex*, respectively, Bakhtinian theory allows critics to posit quite the opposite: multivoiced complexity in the popular and monolingual sterility in the "high."

In *Literature and Revolution* (1924), Leon Trotsky addresses these issues, and his conclusions are useful in this context. He praises the Russian Futurist experiments with form, noting that "a purely logical approach destroys the question of artistic form. One must judge . . . not with one's reason . . . but with one's whole mind, which includes the irrational." See Leon Trotsky, *Literature and Revolution* (New York: Russell & Russell, 1957), 143. He also notes, "If one cannot get along without a mirror, even in shaving oneself, how can one reconstruct oneself or one's life, without seeing oneself in the 'mirror' of literature? Of course no one speaks about an exact mirror. No one even thinks of asking the new literature to have a mirror-like impassivity" (ibid., 137). Note the similarity to the post-structuralist examination of the "mirror" itself, rather than the world that the mirror was traditionally seen as impassively reflecting. But Trotsky still cautions against the Futurist call to make a complete break with the past: literature must include elements of an "irrational, inexact mirror" to be effective, however, *for now* the way to reach the masses is through realism. Perhaps in some utopian future we can move beyond convention, but for now, "A work of art must show gradual growth of an image . . . and must not throw the reader about from one end to another" (ibid., 152). Do not write "above their heads. . . . the masses are culturally and aesthetically unprepared, and will rise only slowly" (ibid., 159).

12. Angel Rama, *Transculturación narrativa en América Latina*, 3rd ed. (Mexico City: Siglo XXI, 1987), 75–76, 125.

13. M. M. Bakhtin, *The Dialogic Imagination*, ed. Michael Holquist, trans. Caryl Emerson and Michael Holquist (Austin: University of Texas Press, 1981), 11, 15, 23, 35.

14. Rama writes that some Latin American societies may contain more than nine linguistic subcultures:

"1) indias tribales; 2) indias modernas; 3) campesinas; 4) y 5) plantación de ingenio y plantación de fábrica; 6) citadinas; 7), 8) y 9) clase alta metropolitana, clase media metropolitana y proletariado urbana" (Rama, *Transculturación*, 62). [1) tribal indians; 2) modern indians; 3) rural peasants; 4) and 5) (laborers at) small and industrial plantations; 6) small towns; 7), 8) and 9) metropolitan upper class, metropolitan middle class and urban proletarians.] In addition, the "tribal" groupings must be understood as containing further subgroups. However, indigenous populations have been able to suppress enough of their differences to form a powerful union, CONAIE (Confederación de Nacionalidades Indígenas del Ecuador/ The Ecuadorian Confederation of Indigenous Peoples), and have also learned how to speak the "master's" language to such an extent that their unity can effectively mount a strike that interrupts most interprovincial travel (although this is not quite as hard as it sounds in a country with few paved roads) *and* conduct a press conference about it as well. They probably do so privately, and may soon employ their numerous distinct languages publicly as part of a carnivalesque attack on the univocality of a singular official discourse (see Louise O. Vasvari, "Pitas Pajas: Popular Phonosymbolism," *Revista de Estudios Hispánicos* 26 [1992]: 144). They are beginning to force that most resistant of powers, the reactionary oligarchy and their protectors defending their wealth and privilege, to begin to learn just a little bit of *their* language. As Fred Weinstein has written, "The interpretation of people's actions must be rendered in two languages, the language of the people themselves (because that is one of the really crucial sources for their subjective sense of things and still the most important source for understanding what they have done) and the language of the observer. . . . Choosing only one of the two languages distorts the experience of one of the two groups of people involved, a situation that must lead to ideologically contaminated conclusions" (Fred Weinstein, *History and Theory after the Fall: An Essay on Interpretation* [Chicago: University of Chicago Press, 1990], 80). Unfortunately for previous generations of oppressed Ecuadorians, the "observers" have been quite content to live with their "ideologically contaminated conclusions."

15. The work of Walter Ong has been instrumental in highlighting the differences between oral and written narratives, and the intriguing possibilities that may arise when authors mix elements of the two. On the one hand, oral compositions such as the Homeric epics are understood to be the "creations of a whole people" (Walter Ong, *Orality and Literacy: The Technologizing of the Word* [London: Routledge, 1989], 19), and thus considerably more democratic than the finished texts produced by individual artists or government committees. Moreover, the episodic structure of such epic works produces less "oppressive" closure, much in keeping with the desires of many recent anti-novelists: "If we take the climactic linear plot as the paradigm of plot, the epic has no plot" (ibid., 144). On the other hand, orality may also be instrumental in freezing thought processes in preexisting, circumscribed channels. The burden placed on the memory by the performance of oral epics leaves little room for freedom of thought. By taking up this burden, "the text frees the mind of conservative tasks, that is, of its memory work, and thus enables the mind to turn itself to new speculation" (Havelock quoted in Ong, *Orality*, 41). Viewed in this way, it is the oral mind that "totalizes" rather than the narratives themselves (ibid., 175). This issue is of particular interest in relation to the project of a mid-1970s experimentalist novel such as Jorge Enrique Adoum's, *Entre Marx y una mujer desnuda* (discussed in chapter 5), which goes to great length to resist closure, and to remain open-ended. Ong concludes that language cannot be structured to be a perfectly consistent, and therefore closed, system: "There are no closed systems and never have been. The illusion that logic is a closed system has been encouraged by writing and even more by print" (ibid., 169). Or, as Gabriel García Márquez said, traditional realist texts are all "books which finish on the last page" ("son libros que acaban en la última página"; Gabriel García Márquez, *El olor de la guayaba: Conversacions con Plinio Apuleyo Mendoza* [Barcelona: Bruguera, 1982], 82).

16. Norman E. Whitten, Jr., ed., *Cultural Transformations and Ethnicity in Modern Ecuador* (Urbana: University of Illinois Press, 1981), 16.

17. Eagleton, *Ideology*, 114.

18. See also Gramsci, "Every conception has its thinkers and experts to put forward, and authority does not belong to one side." Antonio Gramsci, *Selections from the Prison Notebooks* (New York: International Publishers, 1971), 338.

19. Eagleton, *Ideology*, 123.

20. Alberto Flores Galindo, *Buscando un Inca: Identidad y utopia en los Andes* (Lima: Instituto de Apoyo Agrario, 1987), 279–280.

21. As a footnote, I have spent three years in Cuenca, and can verify that the local Spanish is peppered with Quichua *and* English (though an English that native speakers of English might not recognize at first, e.g., "Estar full," meaning *not being able to take it anymore*, and "Hacer jafana jafana," *to split something fifty-fifty*," where "jafana" is a phonetic rendition of the English *half and half*), a further indication of the heterogeneity of Ecuadorian urban society due to literal and figurative border crossings.

22. British Petroleum has been pumping oil from the Santa Elena peninsula on the Pacific coast of Ecuador since the 1920s, but after the 1967 war in the Middle East, aggressive exploitation of the Amazonian oil fields began (see Jaime Galarza, *El festín del petroleo*, 3rd ed. [Cuenca: Ediciones Solitierra, 1974]), with results that should be familiar to anyone who reads the papers: the rivers are poisoned, the natives are relocated, the land is slashed and burned so that the oil can be shipped to the United States to be refined, then shipped back and resold to the producing nation at an outrageous markup. Many Ecuadorians have expressed to me that the Amazonian oil should never have been discovered, for the vicious exploitation of it has only served to impoverish them further.

23. In the realm of mass art, virtually all film and television is imported. Ecuador has some independent film production, but no film industry. The Ecuadorian-made television shows consist of relatively inexpensive variety shows, quiz shows, and the occasional *telenovela* or made-for-TV movie, but almost all the narrative television shows—comedies and dramas—are imports as well, mostly from the United States, Mexico, Venezuela, and Brazil. I have come to appreciate the low production values of the cheaper *telenovelas*—single-source lighting and sound, etc.—which make them look very "fake": the audience is well aware of the "fakeness" of the *telenovelas*, and therefore many of them consider it absurd to spend millions of dollars, as they do in Hollywood, trying to make these popular fictions seem that much more "real." A refreshing attitude, in its way.

24. M. M. Bakhtin, *Speech Genres and other Late Essays*, eds. Caryl Emerson and Michael Holquist, trans. Vern W. McGee (Austin: University of Texas Press, 1986), 79–80. It is interesting to note that even "radical" avant-garde styles can assume their own mantle of authority, which opens them for parody as well.

25. Jan Kott, *The Eating of the Gods* (Evanston, Ill.: Northwestern University Press, 1987), 105.

Chapter 1

1. See Alejo Carpentier, Introduction to *El reino de este mundo*, *Obras completas*, vol. 2 (Mexico: Siglo XXI, 1983).

2. Klaus Müller-Bergh, "Corrientes vanguardistas y surrealismo en la obra de Alejo Carpentier," *Asedios a Carpentier: Once ensayos críticos sobre el novelist cubano*, ed. Klaus Müller-Bergh (Santiago: Universitaria, 1972), 16–17.

3. André Breton, Introduction to *Mad Love*, trans. Mary Ann Caws (Lincoln: University of Nebraska Press, 1987), xii–xiv.

4. Emma Marras, "Robert Bly's Reading of South American Poets: A Challenge to North American Poetic Practice," *Translation Review* 14 (1984): 36.

5. Gonzalo Celorio, *El surrealismo y lo real-maravilloso americano* (Mexico City: SepSetentas, 1976), 71. Note: All unreferenced translations throughout this book are mine.

6. Ibid., 104, 112.

7. Carlos Martín, *Hispanoamerica: Mito y surrealismo* (Bogota: Procultura, 1986), 253.

8. Jorge Carrera Andrade, *Reflections on Spanish-American Poetry*, trans. Don C. Bliss and Gabriela de C. Bliss (Albany: SUNY Press, 1973), 45.

9. Yes, such a term is justified. Humberto Robles finds himself in a similar situation discussing "traditional vanguardists." See Humberto Robles, "La noción de vanguardia en el Ecuador: Recepción y trayectoria (1918–1934)," *Revista*

Iberoamericana 54 (1988): 667. One part of the dialectic of literary production is that yesterday's avant-garde technique is today's convention and tomorrow's cliché.

10. Alejo Carpentier, *Obras completas*, vol. 9, *Crónicas 2: Arte, literatura, política* (Mexico: Siglo XXI, 1986), 122, 128–29.

11. See Anna Balakian, "Latin-American Poets and the Surrealist Heritage," in *Surrealismo/Surrealismos: Latinoamerica y España*, eds. Peter G. Earle and Germán Gullón (Philadelphia: University of Pennsylvania Press, 1977), p. 13.

12. Isabel Allende, interview with the author (15 May 1991). This anecdote may be apocryphal, but the alternate reality it represents is nevertheless possible.

13. Balakian, 11; see also Stefan Baciu, *Antología de la poesía surrealista latinoamericana* (Valparaíso: Ediciones Universitarias, 1981), 139 ff.

14. Gerald J. Langowski, *El surrealismo en la ficción hispano-americana* (Madrid: Gredos, 1982), 27. Robles challenges this equation.

15. Emir Rodriguez Monegal, "Surrealism, Magical Realism, Magical Fiction: A Study in Confusion," in *Surrealismo/Surrealismos: Latinoamerica y España*, eds. Peter G. Earle and Germán Gullón (Philadelphia: University of Pennsylvania Press, 1977), 27–28.

16. Carrera Andrade, *Reflections*, 47.

17. Carpentier, *Crónicas 2*, 298–301 (translation mine).

18. The authors also seem to be unaware that the Brazilian modernists had been combining surrealism with nativism for several years.

19. Pedro Lastra, "Aproximaciones a ¡*Écue-Yamba-Ó!*" *Asedios a Carpentier: Once ensayos críticos sobre el novelist cubano*, ed. Klaus Müller-Bergh (Santiago: Universitaria, 1972), 40.

20. Langowski, 89–90.

21. Ibid., 93.

22. Octavio Paz, "Sobre el surrealismo hispanoamericano: El fin de las habladurías." Introduction to *Surrealismo Latinoamericano: Preguntas y respuestas*, ed. Stefan Baciu (Valparaíso: Ediciones Universitarias, 1979), 12.

23. Baciu, *Antología de la poesía surrealista latinoamericana*, 148.

24. Langowski, 191–92.

25. Arthur Rimbaud, *Oeuvres*, (Paris: Garnier, 1960), 251 (emphasis mine).

26. J. Enrique Ojeda, "Jorge Carrera Andrade y la vanguardia," *Revista Iberoamericana* 54 (1988): 678–79.

27. Ibid., 683.

28. Carlos Martín, *Hispanoamerica: mito y surrealismo*, (Bogota: Procultura, 1986), 259; and Paz, "Sobre el surrealismo hispanoamericano," 14.

29. The characteristics inherent in a strict definition of "socialist realism"—a logical, real forward movement of history, "an aesthetic of transparency and clarity, a monologic dream of cultural and ideological homogeneity, and a very specific figuration, the positive hero" (Régine Robin, *Socialist Realism: An Impossible Aesthetic*, trans. Catherine Porter [Stanford: Stanford University Press, 1992], 299)—are largely absent from the works examined herein, hence the distinction between socialist realism and social realism (although Gabriel García Márquez's *One Hundred Years of Solitude* has been stretched to fit some critics' definitions of socialist realism; see ibid. and Thomas Lahusen, Introduction [special issue], *South Atlantic Quarterly* 94, no. 3 [1995]: 669). José de la Cuadra even ascribes the socialist realist qualities of nationalism and patriotic virtues to Fascist literature, as opposed to "revolutionary literature," which reveals the injustices and contradictions within a society (José de la Cuadra, *Obras completas* [Quito: Casa de

la Cultura, 1958], 965–66), although elsewhere he declares that a literature that depicts "reality and nothing but reality" ("la realidad y nada más que la realidad"; ibid., 807) is sufficient to accomplish this goal, a statement that is not far from the "educational mission" of socialist realism to depict truly "what is" (Lahusen, 667).

30. Irlemar Chiampi, *El realismo maravilloso: Forma e ideología en la novela hispanoamericana* (Caracas: Monte Avila, 1983), 166.

31. That Lautréamont spent the first thirteen years of his life in Montevideo offers the possibility of further complications to the discussion of two-way influence between Latin American and European literary traditions.

32. Robles, "La noción de vanguardia en el Ecuador," 651–54.

33. Such literary cosmopolitanism was in fact quite established. For example, Rubén Darío spent many years in Madrid and Paris, publishing five books there between 1901 and 1914.

34. For example, in the journal *Llamarada*. See María del Carmen Fernández, *El realismo abierto de Pablo Palacio en la encrucijada de los 30* (Quito: Libri Mundi, 1991), 64–68.

35. Robles, "La noción de vanguardia en el Ecuador," 664–65.

36. Fernández, 34, 57.

37. Ibid., 76.

38. Ojeda, 688.

39. Massimo Bontempelli, *L'avventura novecentista* (Firenze: Vallecchi, 1974), 187, 321. Note that these two statements were made in 1929 and 1935, respectively.

40. Ojeda, 690.

41. Carrera Andrade, *Reflections*, 49.

42. Alfredo Pareja Diezcanseco, "El reino de la libertad en Pablo Palacio," *Casa de las Américas* 22 (1981): 3–4.

43. Ibid., 19.

44. Ibid.

45. Agustín Cueva, *La literatura Ecuatoriana* (Buenos Aires: Centro Editor de América Latina, 1968), 54. There also seems to be concrete evidence that Palacio read Pirandello. See Antonio Sacoto, *Quatorze novelas claves de la literatura ecuatoriana* (Cuenca: Universidad de Cuenca, 1990), 135.

46. Sacoto, 144.

47. Agustín Cueva, "Literatura y sociedad en el Ecuador, 1920–1960," *Revista Iberoamericana* 54 (1988): 632.

48. Humberto E. Robles, *Testimonio y tendendcia mítica en la obra de José de la Cuadra* (Quito: Casa de la Cultura, 1976), 30.

49. Humberto E. Robles, "Pablo Palacio: El anhelo insatisfecho," *Cultura* [Quito] 7, no. 20 (1984): 67.

50. Fernández, 53.

51. Ibid, 59.

52. Pablo Palacio, *Obras completas* (Quito: El Conejo, 1986), 37. All subsequent references are from this edition.

53. Providing an accurate translation of this term proved to be very challenging, since in Spanish *vicioso* can mean either that one has fairly serious "vices" (such as criminal activity) or relatively innocuous ones, such as smoking cigarettes. The ambiguity is in all likelihood deliberate. At first I tried the obvious, "had his vices," but that was too strong, since in English usage the word tends toward the former meaning, so I watered it down to "had his weaknesses," but that was, well,

too weak, so I finally settled on the relative in-between state of "one or two vices," which contains the strong word *vices*, but appears to dilute it somewhat. The story contains several other instances of the deliberate use of terms that are ambiguous in Spanish, as when a police officer describes the victim as "un hombre vulgar," which, again, can either mean the obvious cognate, "vulgar," or quite innocently, "ordinary, common."

Chapter 2

1. For those who may require some background in Ecuadorian history, one figure dominates modern politics: José María Velasco Ibarra. Elected five times to the presidency (1934, 1944, 1952, 1960, 1968) and overthrown four times for attempting to establish a dictatorship, this self-proclaimed "liberal" manipulated election-year rhetoric so effectively that his most famous quote is "Dadme un balcón, y el pueblo será mío" ("Give me a balcony, and the people will be mine"). See C. Michael Waag, "Sátira política a través de la historia mitificada: *El secuestro del general*, de Demetrio Aguilera Malta," *Revista Iberoamericana* 54 (1988): 771.

A popular joke places him in the Andean city of Riobamba, speaking from a just such a balcony to an ecstatic crowd, making the absurd campaign promise of constructing a seaport to transform the city into an international center of trade. The crowd roars its approval, but an aide asks how the candidate intends to build a port eight thousand feet up in the mountains: "On this sea of idiots!" he answers.

Though such self-deprecating political humor is probably a worldwide phenomenon, Ecuadorians have exceptionally valid historical reasons for not taking their politicians' words at face value and for openly acknowledging the yawning gap between their country's rhetoric and its reality. Yet many Ecuadorians face aspects of their history more honestly than Americans do. Most openly acknowledge that their first elected leader, Juan José Flores, was not a particularly good president. The primary difference is that the United States generally emerged victorious from such events as the invasion of Mexico and the near total annihilation of Native Americans and thus was able to suppress or shape their discussion as part of the glorious myths of Manifest Destiny, Spheres of Influence, and continual, progressive expansion. Ecuador keeps *losing* wars. Instead of expanding, Ecuador keeps losing territory to Colombia and Peru; today it is reduced to almost one-quarter the size it was in 1740 (See Lilo Linke, *Ecuador: Country of Contrasts*, 3rd ed. [London: Oxford University Press, 1960], 178; one Ecuadorian history text puts the southern boundary in 1830 at the Madre de Diós River, which flows between Peru and northern Bolivia on today's maps). Ecuador has had eight civil wars, one as recently as 1932. In 120 years as an independent nation (1830–1950), Ecuador had sixty-two different governments (twenty-three of them between 1925 and 1948 alone), and a dozen constitutions that were suspended almost before the ink was dry (the current Ecuadorian constitution dates from 1978). In 1961, when the military forced Velasco Ibarra out for the third time, the head of the Supreme Court took over illegally; he was president for approximately twenty-four hours. Since 1964, the military have ousted five governments and backed President Velasco Ibarra's seizing of extra-constitutional powers in 1970. See J. Samuel Fitch, "The Military Coup d'État as Political Process: A General Framework and the Ecuadorean Case," in *Armies and Politics in Latin America*, eds. Abraham F. Lowenthal and J. Samuel Fitch (New York: Holmes & Meier, 1986), 152.

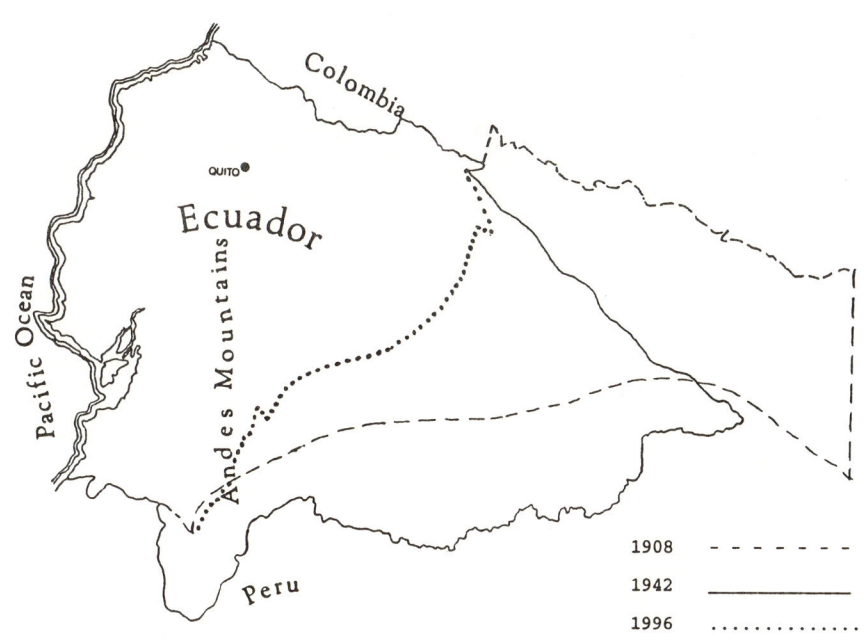

Map of Ecuador. Showing the approximate locations of the eastern border. Ecuador's western border, the Pacific coastline, has remained largely the same.

Ecuador's historical performance of simultaneous worship and disregard of idealized constitutional language bears closer examination. The first constitution (1830) declared that the president had to be an Ecuadorian citizen. So Venezuelan General Juan José Flores had a clause added that conferred citizenship on all who had fought for independence, got elected president by the Constitutional Convention (*not* by popular vote) and promptly established a military dictatorship (see Edwin E. Erickson et al., *Area Handbook for Ecuador* [Washington D.C.: Government Printing Office, August 1966], 44). Flores anticipated his own overthrow by installing the second president, Vicente Rocafuerte, but the real power stayed with Flores. The second constitution (1835) prohibited immediate reelection so that Rocafuerte could not run, and Flores became president again in 1839. Limited to four years by the second constitution, he had a third constitution drawn up that doubled the presidential term to eight years. By 1895 disregarding the constitution (the tenth) was a well-established tradition. When Velasco Ibarra was reelected in 1946, he suspended the 1945 Constitution and had another one written that was more to his liking (ibid., 57).

2. See Alfredo Pareja Diezcanseco, "Los narradores de la generación del treinta: El grupo de Guayaquil," *Revista Iberoamericana* 54 (1988): 92–93; Agustín Cueva, "El método materialista histórico aplicado al la periodización de la historia de la literatura Ecuatoriana: Algunas consideraciones teóricas," *Casa de las Americas* 22 (1981): 34; and Agustín Cueva, "Literatura y sociedad en el Ecuador; 1920–1960," *Revista Iberoamericana* 54 (1988): 630.

3. Agustín Cueva, *The Process of Political Domination in Ecuador*, trans. Danielle Salti (New Brunswick, N.J.: Transaction Books, 1982), 4.

168

NOTES

4. Linda Alexander Rodriguez, *The Search for Public Policy: Regional Politics and Government Finances in Ecuador, 1830–1940*, (Berkeley: University of California Press, 1985), 54.

5. See David Corkhill and David Cubitt, *Ecuador: Fragile Democracy* (London: Latin American Bureau, 1988), 11; Rodriguez *The Search for Public Policy*, 88, 104; and Corkhill and Cubitt, 13, 17.

6. Rodriguez, *The Search for Public Policy*, 99, 113.

7. E.J. Hobsbawm, *The Age of Revolution, 1789–1848* (New York: Mentor, 1962), 45.

8. Anthony Burgess, *English Literature: A Survey for Students* (London: Longman, 1974), 11.

9. Clementine Christos Rabassa, *Demetrio Aguilera-Malta and Social Justice: The Tertiary Phase of Epic Tradition in Latin American Literature* (Rutherford, N.J.: Fairleigh Dickinson University Press, 1980), 20.

10. Rodriguez, *The Search for Public Policy*, 16.

11. These figures come from Corkhill and Cubitt, *Ecuador: Fragile Democracy*, 95, 92.

12. Georg Lukács, *The Historical Novel*, trans. Hannah and Stanley Mitchell (Lincoln: University of Nebraska Press, 1983), 21.

13. Rodriguez, *The Search for Public Policy*, 28.

14. It is increasingly common in Ecuador to speak of "indigenous populations." However, *Indian (indio)* is the term used in most of the literature and is still commonly used in the language of current politics. Since many of the textual citations refer to "Indians," I have opted to keep that term relatively constant throughout the commentary.

15. Cueva, "El método materialista histórico," p. 41; and Cueva, "Literatura y sociedad en el Ecuador, 1920–1960," 638, 640–41.

16. All subsequent citations in Spanish are to the following editions: Demetrio Aguilera Malta, *Don Goyo* (Buenos Aires: Editorial Platina, 1958); Enrique Gil Gilbert, *Nuestro pan*, 2 vols. (Guayaquil: Clasicos Ariel, 1975); Jorge Icaza, *Huasipungo* (Quito: Libresa, 1990). All citations in English are to the following editions: Demetrio Aguilera Malta, *Don Goyo*, trans. John and Carolyn Brushwood (Clifton, N.J.: The Humana Press, 1980); Enrique Gil Gilbert, *Our Daily Bread*, trans. Dudley Poore (New York: Farrar & Rinehart, 1943); Jorge Icaza, *The Villagers*, trans. Bernard M. Dulsey (Carbondale: Southern Illinois University Press, 1964). All words or brief quotations cited in English only are from the English editions. Since these three novels are available in English, translations are not included in the Appendix. I am therefore supplying plot summaries:

Demetrio Aguilera Malta's Don Goyo *(1933)*

Aguilera Malta's first novel, published the same year as Alejo Carpentier's *Ecue-Yamba-O*, shares many similar elements—a belief in magic, particularly animism, the idea that "inanimate" objects contain souls and spirits that think, speak, and move.

The plot begins with an inland Indian, Cusumbo, fleeing to the islands after he has hacked his girlfriend and the white boss to pieces after finding the two of them in bed together. It is never explained that she was probably coerced, and once again we have male characters who are all instantaneous explosive emotion, like children, with no concept as to the consequences of their actions. Indeed, for the rest of the tale, Cusumbo never thinks back to this event, never shows remorse for it.

His new surroundings are on an island whose people make their living cutting *mangle* wood (mangrove) and shipping it to Guayaquil to sell it and buy rice, bananas, etc. Don Goyo is first seen sitting high in a tree watching the world go by. It is said that he is over one hundred years old and is the progenitor of half of the inhabitants of the island (a motif that is also in *Nuestro Pan*—as is the motif of the murderer fleeing to the jungle where the police will never find him, although in Gil's novel the man *is* plagued by guilt).

One day the spirits of the *mangle* trees speak to Don Goyo and tell him that as the humans' lives are intertwined with those of the trees, if they continue to cut *mangle*, they will all end up working for the evil white men, denude the island of vegetation, and then be left homeless and without a means to live. The inhabitants all revere and respect Don Goyo, so they try their hand at fishing, but they are not good at it and cannot catch anything worth traveling to Guayaquil to sell. The people tell Don Goyo that they must return to cutting *mangle*. He basically tells them to go ahead and do whatever they want, but he will not be responsible. Then he disappears.

He is found a few days later, dead, sitting in the oldest *mangle* tree on the island, which has fallen into the water. The villagers put Don Goyo in a coffin and take him in a canoe to bury him on the mainland. Then two villagers watching from the island see Don Goyo alive, swimming with a stream of sharks who "appeared to follow him submissively" (192), before they lose sight of him in the waves. The funereal canoers come back to tell everyone that while they were rowing, they heard a splash and when they looked back both Don Goyo and the coffin were gone.

Jorge Icaza's Huasipungo *(1934)*

Icaza's novel begins with Don Alfonso Pereira, an upper-class Quiteño, being confronted by his rich and powerful uncle and creditor over some overdue bills, and a deal is made regarding opening some of their lands to foreign investment. This requires that a road be built through some of the roughest, most inhospitable land in the high sierra. Icaza follows the corrupt collusion of the rich landowner, his sherrif, and the vicious local priest—who tells the Indians that they will not get into heaven unless they purchase one of the more expensive burial plots closer to the church!—in comparison with the daily struggle of a poor Indian *huasipungero*, Andrés Chiliquinga. When Andrés is forcibly separated from his wife, Chunchi, to go work clearing for the road, and Cunshi is removed to the *hacienda* to nurse the landowner's grandchild without letting Andrés know, Andrés returns to find his hut empty, and in his rage and despair, scrambles back to work late, then cuts a huge gash in his foot.

The landowner pursuades the engineer to save time and money by going through a swamp, which has to be drained, even though they both know this will cost 10 or 20 Indian lives. However, the landowner makes a cost-effectiveness estimate (each Indian, he figures, only cost him about 5 sucres), and decides that it is more than worth it. Another problem is that the engineer has said that the *huasipungos* near the river must be cleared away. The landowner decides that the easiest thing to do would just be not to take the steps that are taken every year to prevent the river from overflowing. Soon enough, torrential downpours turn the river into a muddy-red monster that washes all the *huasipungos* away. Many lives are lost, but the road is finished, and Pereira is toasted in the press as a national hero.

However, Pereira has become so contemptuous of the Indians that he denies them the *socorros* (bushels of corn or barley) all *huasipungeros* have always gotten as a "barbaric custom" (151), and when an ox is found dead and decaying, he orders it buried rather than distributed to the Indians, because "once they taste it they get to like it and then we're really screwed. Every day they'd make me slaughter an animal" (159). The animal is buried, but that night the Indians dig it up and eat it. Andrés wakes up and vomits, but he forces Cunshi not to "give back the food of Taita Dios." ("God the Father" in Quichua and Spanish; 169) Cunshi gets sick and dies. Andrés must steal a cow and sell it in order to afford to bury his beloved Cunshi in the priest's luxury gravesite. He is caught and whipped. And so the day the *gringo* investors come to lay out their plans for forestry exploitation and oil prospecting, the Indians revolt. The army is called out and all of the Indians—men, women, children—are slaughtered, even as the last one of them cries out "Ñucanchic huasipungo!"—The *huasipungos* are ours!

Enrique Gil Gilbert's Nuestro Pan *(1942)*

Gil Gilbert's work does not lend itself easily to a simple plot outline. In a sense it resembles a Chekhov play in which there is very little "action"—only one world ends and another begins. The first section describes the arrival of settlers by canoe in a patch of untouched tropical jungle on Ecuador's coast and their clearing a rice field by hand with machetes. The work is hard, but once the men get their cane houses built, the women arrive and life seems pretty good. Conditions are so primitive that it isn't until a gasoline can is mentioned (57) that the reader knows for sure what century it is.

In the second section we jump back about twenty years to 1912, when the landlord of the rice field was a young guerrilla Captain Sandoval under General Alfaro, the Liberal revolutionary. The Captain is an expert and heroic leader who ruthlessly ends lives in order to save many others. Thinking only of his men, he leads them to safety, only to learn that the government troops have killed Alfaro, permanently ending the revolution. With no where else to go, he stays on, marries a landowner's daughter, and soon becomes head of the ranch.

In the third section, we return to the 1930s, and Sandoval's son is now a law student at the University of Guayaquil, determined to modernize the awful conditions of the rice plantation with tractors and other machinery. Since it is time for the harvest, we also follow the trail of several dirt-poor mountain Indians leaving for the coast in search of high-paying harvest work. But these Indians sicken and die in the terribly oppressive tropical climate. Working a rice paddy without rubber boots gives one huge open running sores on the legs that soon fill with maggots.

The novel's complexity arises not only from its continual time-jumping structure, but also from the content. We do not have the poor-but-noble peasants and the forever-evil landowners of Icaza and others. The workers are presented unromantically, as people who work hard, can identify forty different species of animal by their smell in the jungle wind, but who also are irresponsible—the men often act like big children, never thinking anything through, always reacting with their fists first, or worse, their machetes. They get drunk, start fights, and abandon the women they have gotten pregnant. Yet other peasants are the poor-but-noble type with a sense of honor. And the landowners are far from one-dimensional. Captain Sandoval is clearly a "liberal" among Ecuador's elite. Fighting for Alfaro was only part of it. The old rich of the sierra look down on the coastal rich the same way the landed nobility of Europe looked down on the emerging mercantile bourgeoisie, and the older rich of the coast are no better—being of "pure" European blood, they look down on Sandoval with his "mixed" blood.

So while the Sandoval family members are no heroes to the peasants, they are clearly drawn as the best hope in terms of the elite from which Ecuador's leaders are always drawn. The son's desire to modernize the agriculture is portrayed as a good thing, because it will produce more crops and save workers' lives. In a way, they novel is part "one day in the life of a rice paddy peasant" and part chronicle of the rise of one coastal landowning family. At the end the river rises and begins washing away the rice harvest, but the son, confident that the future of Ecuador lies with him, does not despair.

17. This is still happening today: In 1984 the Ecuadorian government gave 100 percent tax relief to foreign oil companies as part of a drive to double known oil reserves (Corkhill and Cubitt, *Ecuador: Fragile Democracy*, 78), oil which lies under land that the Shuar Indians have lived on since before the appearance of agriculture in the ancient Near East. But do the Shuars "own" it? Where are their documents? The government has papers showing that the Shuars never "own" any land once it has been found to be valuable.

18. See for example chapter 3, "Jorge Icaza," in Agustín Cueva, *Lecturas y rupturas* (Quito: Planeta, 1986); and Arturo Torres-Rioseco, *The Epic of Latin American Literature* (Berkeley: University of California Press, 1959), 189.

19. E.g., "envejecido," "mecaniza[do]," "agota[do]," "monótono," "gastado." See Irlemar Chiampi, *El realismo maravilloso: Forma e ideología en la novela hispanoamericana* (Caracas: Monte Avila, 1983), 21–22.

20. Alberto Flores Galindo, *Buscando un Inca: Identidad y utopia en los Andes* (Lima: Instituto de Apoyo Agrario, 1987), 294–95.

21. José María Arguedas, *Yawar Fiesta*, trans. Frances Horning Barraclough (Austin: University of Texas Press, 1985), 6.

22. Alberto Flores Galindo, *Europa y el país de los Incas: La utopía Andina* (Lima: Instituto de Apoyo Agrario, 1986), 44.

23. Raymond Williams, *Marxism and Literature* (Oxford: Oxford University Press, 1977), 167–78; 39.

24. See ibid., 13.

25. As Terry Eagleton writes, "To place one's credence in the slogan as rhetorically valid is to perform a fictional act, whereas to take it literally is to fall victim to a myth." Terry Eagleton, *Ideology: An Introduction* (London: Verso, 1991), 191.

26. John Steinbeck, *The Grapes of Wrath* (New York: Bantam, 1972), 40. All subsequent references are to this edition.

27. M. M. Bakhtin, *The Dialogic Imagination*, ed. Michael Holquist, trans. Caryl Emerson and Michael Holquist (Austin: University of Texas Press, 1981), 223.

28. Ibid., 271.

29. Ibid., 361.

30. Ibid., 401.

31. Nicola Chiaromonte, *The Paradox of History: Stendhal, Tolstoy, Pasternak, and others* (Philadelphia: University of Pennsylvania Press, 1985), 111.

32. Sherry B. Ortner, "Is Female to Male as Nature Is to Culture?" in *Woman, Culture, and Society*, eds. Michelle Zimbalist Rosaldo and Louise Lamphere (Stanford: Stanford University Press, 1974), 68.

33. Classic historical novels tend toward the reverse—centering the human subject as representative of nature, rather than marginalizing humanity's place in nature, as Ecuadorian literature (and history) tend to do. In Walter Scott's *Ivanhoe*,

Urfried embodies Saxon England: "I was free, was happy, was honoured, loved and was beloved. I am now a slave, miserable and degraded, the sport of my masters' passions while I had yet beauty, the object of their contempt, scorn and hatred, since it has passed away" (Sir Walter Scott, *Ivanhoe* [New York: Signet Classics, 1962], 258), while in Manzoni's *The Betrothed*, the Unnamed is so powerful that even nature reflects him. Having had his soul inflamed with religious awakening by Lucia: "He stood at the window again for a while.... Then he gazed up up at the sun, which at that moment was just vanishing behind the mountain; and then at the clouds just above it. Black a moment before, they had suddenly turned to flame" (Alessandro Manzoni, *The Betrothed*, trans. Bruce Penman [London: Penguin, 1972], 380). Later, "The Unnamed's thoughts could be seen passing across his face, like clouds on a stormy day sweeping across the face of the sun" (ibid., 429).

34. Another interesting parallel between *The Grapes of Wrath* and other Latin American texts occurs when Grampa Joad refuses to leave their home, declaring, "This country ain't no good, but it's my country" (121); he is paraphrasing José Marti's famous quote, "Our wine is bitter, but it's ours" ("Nuestro vino es agrio, pero es nuestro").

35. Ortner, "Is Female to Male as Nature Is to Culture?" 75.

36. Liberation theologist Leonardo Boff has pointed out in speeches that the Spanish *conquistadores* and their descendants have long claimed that they brought "civilization" to the Americas—yet Tenochtitlan was larger with more advanced sanitation than any European city at that time.

37. Pareja Diezcanseco, "Los narradores de la generación del treinta," pp. 696–99; and Cueva, "Literatura y sociedad en el Ecuador: 1920–1960," 642–43.

38. Cueva, "El método materialista histórico," 39.

39. Ibid., 34.

40. Cueva, "Literatura y sociedad en el Ecuador: 1920–1960," 643.

41. Waag, "Sátira política a través de la historia mitificada," 777.

42. Ibid., 778.

43. Note the similarity to the red harvest of human arms at the end of *Huasipungo*.

44. See Jorge Enrique Adoum, "El realismo de la otra realidad," in *America Latina en su literatura*, ed. César Fernández Moreno (Mexico City: Siglo XXI, 1972); also in *Sin ambages* (Quito: Planeta, 1989).

45. See Adina Cruz, "Similitud y contraste en las novelas *Huasipungo* y *The Pearl*," *Kañina* 4, no. 2 (1980): 109–15.

46. Pareja Diezcanseco, "Los narradores de la generación del treinta," 699.

47. For example, "It is often surprising for people outside Latin America to learn that the literary figures who constitute the ill-defined 'boom' in Latin American fiction in the last two or three decades took many of their cues from the United States, from Ernest Hemingway, John Dos Passos and especially William Faulkner" (Nicholas Shrady, "Why He Jilted Sartre," a review of Mario Vargas Llosa's *A Writer's Reality*, *New York Times Book Review* [10 March 1991]: 13). Also, in his review of Carlos Fuentes's *The Campaign*, Roberto González Echevarría refers to a perceived evolution of Fuentes's style over the years: "He has been Joycean in *Christopher Unborn*, Jamesian in *Aura*, Faulknerian in *The Death of Artemio Cruz*, baroque in *Terra Nostra*, realistic in *The Good Conscience*, mythical in *Where the Air is Clear* and camp in *Cumpleaños*." (*New York Times Book Review* [6 October 1991]: 24)

48. Cunshi, an Indian woman, is at the absolute lowest rung of the social scale.

Paradoxically, this also means that everything rests on top of her. The gap left by her death precipitates the apocalyptic disasters that collapses the entire local society. In *The Grapes of Wrath*, Ma Joad is described similarly: "She seemed to know that if she swayed the family shook, and if she ever really deeply wavered or despaired the family would fall, the family will to function would be gone" (80). This is exactly the role she plays throughout the novel.

49. See Bakhtin, *The Dialogic Imagination*, 163–64.

50. Leopoldo Benítez Vinueza, "La mala hora," in *Cuento de la generacion de los 30*, vol. 1 (Guayaquil: Clasicos Ariel, 1975), 44. All references are to this edition.

Chapter 3

1. José de la Cuadra, *Los Sangurimas* (Quito: Editorial El Conejo, 1986), 2. All subsequent references are to this edition.

2. José Arcadio Buendía's murder of his best friend Prudencio Aguilar and Nicasio Sangurima's mother's murder of her uncle. For further discussion of these issues, see Galo F. González, "José de la Cuadra: Nicasio Sangurima, un patriarcha olvidado," *Revista Iberoamericana* 54 (1988): 739–51.

3. José Arcadio with Prudencio Aguilar (Gabriel García Márquez, *One Hundred Years of Solitude*, trans. Gregory Rabassa [New York: Avon, 1978], 30; all subsequent references are to this edition), Nicasio Sangurima with Ceferino Pintado (de la Cuadra, 14). As Rebeca carries a bag of her parents' bones with her to Macondo (García Márquez, 79) and shuttles them around endlessly from place to place, so Nicasio Sangurima keeps the skeletons of his first two wives under his bed, sleeps between them at night, and converses with them (de la Cuadra, 22–23).

4. "The Mexican Revolution" (García Márquez, 278), "the party of García Moreno" and "the wars with Colombia" (de la Cuadra, 10) are about as close as one gets, but these are not reducible to an exact date within either narrative. Robles has pointed out the significance of the implied chronology of *Los Sangurimas*, namely, the hundred-year-history of the Republic of Ecuador from its independence in the 1830s to the 1930s when the novel was written ("más o menos los cien años de existencia de la República del Ecuador"). See Humberto E. Robles, *Testimonio y tendendcia mítica en la obra de José de la Cuadra* (Quito: Casa de la Cultura, 1976), 204–6.

5. For further discussion of these interrelations, see Jacques Gilard, "De *Los Sangurimas* a *Cien años de soledad*," *Universidad de Medellín* 21 (1976): 183–96; González, "José de la Cuadra"; and Humberto E. Robles, "De San Borondón a Samborondón: Sobre la poética de José de la Cuadra," *Nuevo Texto Crítico* 4, no. 8 (1991): 173–83.

6. "Sangurima . . . isn't a *gringo* name. *Gringo*s have names like Juay, names like Jones; but Sangurima, no" ("Sangurima . . . no es nombre gringo. Los gringos se mientan Juay, se mientan Jones; pero Sangurima, no," 10)

7. It is also possible to read fascinating foreshadowings in one of the first descriptions of Don Nicasio: "There were no grey hairs in his thicket of fine curly threads. Which, by their absence, denoted the remote presence of the African race." ("Las canas estaban ausentes de esa mata de hilos ensortijados. Por ahí, en esa ausencia, denotaba su presencia remota la raza de Africa," 9). Not only is the "purity" of Nicasio's blood that is so essential to his self-indentification dis-

counted, but it is precisely the "absence" of grey hairs that denotes the "presence" of this self-negation.

8. For example, "Look now toward heaven, and count the stars, if thou be able to number them: and He said to him, So shall thy seed be" (Gen. 15:5), or, "And thy seed shall be as the dust of the earth" (Gen. 28:14).

9. José de la Cuadra, *Obras completas* (Quito: Casa de la Cultura, 1958), 873; and Robles, *Testimonio y tendendcia mítica*, 205.

10. Antonio Sacoto, *Quatorze novelas claves de la literatura ecuatoriana* (Cuenca: Universidad de Cuenca, 1990), 184.

11. Ibid., 185.

12. Agustin Cueva, "Literatura y sociedad en el Ecuador, 1920–1960," *Revista Iberoamericana* 54 (1988): 638, 640–41.

13. Interestingly, he changes the wording of his original statement, underscoring the unreliability of oral communication: "—You see, I told you: 'Take care of those girls.' Why didn't you let them marry? It would've been better" ("—Ya ves, yo te dije: 'Cuida a las muchachas esas.' ¿Y por qué no las dejastes casar? Más mejor hubiera sido," 72). Note also the introduction of a conditional verb form (*pretérito pluscuamperfecto*); this is the first trickle in what will soon become a torrential flood of conditional verbs.

14. "They had nailed a pointed shaft of dark wood through her sex . . . in the form of a cross" ("Le habían clavado en el sexo una rama puntona de palo-prieto . . . formando una cruz," 73).

15. Benedict Anderson, *Imagined Communities: Reflections on the Origin and Spread of Nationalism* (New York: Verso, 1991), 74.

16. Luisa Valenzuela makes use of a similar absence in *The Lizard's Tail*. The expected "river of blood" never appears because the expected crowds never show, the massacred and the disappeared are inexplicably absent. See Luisa Valenzuela, *The Lizard's Tail*, trans. Gregory Rabassa (London: Serpent's Tail, 1991), 273.

17. See Mario Vargas Llosa, *García Márquez: Historia de un deicidio* (Barcelona: Barral Editores, 1971), 16–20.

18. Cueva, "Literatura y sociedad en el Ecuador, 1920–1960," 638–39.

19. Humberto E. Robles, "Genesis y vigencia de 'Los Sangurimas,' " *Revista Iberoamericana* 45 (1979): 87.

20. Regina Janes, *One Hundred Years of Solitude: Modes of Reading* (Boston: G. K. Hall, 1991), 10.

Chapter 4

1. Mircea Eliade, "Time and Eternity in Indian Thought," in *Man and Time: Papers from the Eranos Yearbooks*, vol. 3, ed. Joseph Campbell, trans. Ralph Manheim (New York: Bollingen Series XXX, Pantheon, 1957), 173. Eliade also suggests the possibility of using *pranayama*, the Indian "rhythmization of breathing," under the heading, "Techniques of Escape from Time." See ibid., 195; and Mircea Eliade, *Two Tales of the Occult*, trans. William Ames Coates (New York: Herder and Herder), 177ff.

2. In other words, either there is no "physical" gap between them (for they overlap the same space) and this nonexistent gap is therefore utterly unbridgeable, or there *is* a gap, equally unbridgeable, but the gap is unperceived.

3. Gerardo Luzuriaga, *Del realismo al expresionismo: El teatro de Demetrio Aguilera-Malta* (Madrid: Plaza Mayor, 1971), p. 93.

4. *Zambo* commonly means "curly haired" in Ecuadorian speech, but it also refers to that other *mestizaje*, the mixture of African and Indian that is generally given less national attention than the dominant *mestizaje* of Indian and European. This would certainly suggest the further marginalization of Zambo Aguayo's character.

5. Ecuador does not have true "tigers," which are Asian. The word *tigre* is used colloquially to refer to any of the large felines—leopards, panthers, pumas, jaguars, etc.—which are native to Ecuador. Since the exact species is not specified in the text, I have translated *tigre* as "tiger."

6. Juan Guerrero Zamora, *Historia del teatro contemporáneo*, vol. 4 (Barcelona: Juan Flors, 1967), 560–61.

7. Luzuriaga, *Del realismo al expresionismo*, 93.

8. Henri-Charles Puech, "Gnosis and Time," in *Man and Time: Papers from the Eranos Yearbooks,* vol. 3, ed. Joseph Campbell, trans. Ralph Manheim (New York: Bollingen Series XXX, Pantheon, 1957), 50–51.

9. Mircea Eliade, *The Myth of the Eternal Return: Or, Cosmos and History*, trans. Willard R. Trask (Bollingen Series, XLVI. Princeton: Princeton University Press, 1991), 9–11.

10. Demetrio Aguilera Malta, "El tigre," in *Teatro completo* (Mexico City: Finisterre, 1970), 181. All subsequent references are to this edition.

11. Eugene O'Neill, "The Emperor Jones," in *Nine Plays* (New York: Modern Library, 1959), 9. All subsequent references are to this edition.

12. Interestingly, Eliade's fiction is full of doubt in the power of words to bridge the gap between realities, to arrive at truth, intentionality, or to describe the experience of transcendence: "His words didn't reassure us," "I asked her whether her husband had ever been in India. 'That's hard to say,' she whispered hesitantly," "Dr. Zerlendi had become convinced . . . that many of Honigberger's statements, which had been accepted without question by his contemporary biographers, were based on false data or on documents which were purposely falsified later on," "Everything I found out later I stumbled on by accident." See Eliade, *Two Tales of the Occult*, 20, 70, 81, 82.

13. Eliade, "Time and Eternity in Indian Thought," 199–200.

14. Ibid.

15. Puech, "Gnosis and Time," 76–77.

16. Eliade, *The Myth of the Eternal Return*, 162.

17. Eliade, "Time and Eternity in Indian Thought," 175, 193).

18. More specificaly, how do we react to a confident statement such as Jean-Claude Antoine's about the cycles of Nature, "When we apply irregular pulsations to a swing, in the end we maintain its motion without profoundly altering its inherent rhythm" ("Lorsque nous donnons des impulsions irrégulières à une balançoire, nous en entretenons finalement le mouvement sans en perturber très profondément le rhythme propre," Jean-Claude Antoine, "L'Éternel Retour de l'Histoire Deviendra-t-il Objet de Science?" *Critique* 4, no. 27 [1948]: 738), when we now realize that modern industrial short-sightedness *can* irreparably destroy the natural balance? In other words, when do all these searches for breaks and transcendence negate themselves? The answer may be: When one looks at them in their profane (that is, historical) context.

19. Dorothy Figueira has pointed out that the Theosophists' visions of racial purity and dominance "supported belief in a cyclical historical process" precisely because their interpretation of that process put them in a superior position (Dorothy Figueira, "Aryan Ancestors, Pariahs and the Lunatic Fringe," *The Compara-

tive Civilizations Review 25 [1991]: 7). According to Figueira, Theosophy fed into race theory of the late nineteenth and early twentieth centuries, which eventually was handed down, through a series of recursions, to Adolph Hitler and the Nazi party. So an examination of Eliade's "Techniques of Escape from Time" (Eliade, "Time and Eternity in Indian Thought," 195) might tell us more about Eliade's personal problems with his own unsavory history than it would tell us about some universally valid application of *pranayama*.

20. Eliade, "Time and Eternity in Indian Thought," 191.
21. Eliade, *Two Tales of the Occult*, 114.
22. Van der Leeuw comes closer to the timely space of *El tigre* when he writes that, "Spatial time . . . is an experience of time that we have organized spatially, a homogeneous . . . sequence of segments. In reality there are no segments. . . . Real time is a river" (G. van der Leeuw, "Primordial Time and Final Time," in *Man and Time: Papers from the Eranos Yearbooks*, vol. 3, ed. Joseph Campbell, trans. Ralph Manheim [Bollingen Series XXX, New York: Pantheon, 1957], 325–26). But the example he cites—"The images that a motion-picture projector casts on the screen in swift succession may not simply appear one after the other, they must fuse into one image" (ibid.)—contains an illusory continuity: cinematic projection consists of a series of still pictures that flash on screen faster than our perception is able to separate and so a false fusion of motion is created precisely where none exists.
23. What has changed from pagan times to ours? Why is the endless repetition that was so comforting (apparently) to the ancients so terrifying for moderns, if Kafka, Ionesco, and episodes of *The Twilight Zone* are to be believed? For Eliade, this terror of the cycle without end is the terror of History without goal, without God. The main difference between what we have come to know as Eastern and Western approaches to the endless cycles is that in the West they are endless because they are identical. In the "East," however, Buddhism sees "many cycles of dissolution of the universe, many cycles of its evolution" (Freny Mistry, *Nietzsche and Buddhism: Prolegomenon to a Comparative Study* [New York: Walter de Gruyter, 1981], 148–49). Thus the cycles repeat in a wheel-of-fortune-like *samsara*, but they are different every time, and the effort is gradually to work one's way out. Interestingly, Jewish mysticism includes related, contrasting concepts such as the idea that "before making this world God made many others and destroyed them because he did not like them" (Gershom G. Scholem, *Major Trends in Jewish Mysticism* [New York: Schocken, 1961], 32). The cycles may be endless, but they are *not* identical (the previous cycles may have been necessary, but they were corrupt; ibid., 355).
24. Eliade, *The Myth of the Eternal Return*, 156–57.
25. Nietzsche, 1052; translation in Mistry, *Nietzsche and Buddhism*, 157.
26. Paul Ricoeur, *Time and Narrative*, vol. 1, trans. Kathleen McLaughlin and David Pellauer (Chicago: University of Chicago Press, 1984), 44.
27. Ibid., 76.
28. See for example René Girard, "The Demons of Gerasa," in *The Daemonic Imagination: Biblical Text and Secular Story*, eds. Robert Detweiler and William G. Doty (Atlanta: Scholars Press, 1990).

CHAPTER 5

1. Jorge Enrique Adoum, "El realismo de la otra realidad" ("The Realism of the Other Reality" [1972]), in *Sin ambages* (Quito: Planeta, 1989), 108.

2. Eduardo Giordano, "Entrevista a Jorge Enrique Adoum," *Plural* 187 (1987): 10.

3. Jorge Enrique Adoum, correspondence with the author, 22 May 1997.

4. Charles Issawi, "The Historical Background of Lebanese Emigration, 1800–1914," in *The Lebanese in the World: A Century of Emigration*, eds. Albert Hourani and Nadim Shehadi (London: I. B. Tauris & Co., 1992), 31, 27.

5. Kohei Hashimoto, "Lebanese Population Movement, 1920–1939: Towards a Study," in *The Lebanese in the World*, eds. Albert Hourani and Nadim Shehadi (London: I. B. Tauris & Co., 1992), 92, 95.

6. These terms are from Norman E. Whitten, Jr., ed., *Cultural Transformations and Ethnicity in Modern Ecuador* (Urbana: University of Illinois Press, 1981), 49.

7. Ronald Stutzman, "*El Mestizaje*: An All-Inclusive Ideology of Exclusion," in *Cultural Transformations and Ethnicity in Modern Ecuador*, ed. Norman E. Whitten, Jr. (Urbana: University of Illinois Press, 1981), 59.

8. Wendy B. Faris, "Scheherazade's Children: Magical Realism and Postmodern Fiction," in *Magical Realism: Theory, History, Community*, eds. Lois Parkinson Zamora and Wendy B. Faris (Durham: Duke University Press, 1995), 172.

9. Jorge Enrique Adoum, *El tiempo y las palabras* (Quito: Libresa, 1992), 189–90.

10. Stutzman, "*El Mestizaje*," 47, 82.

11. Whitten, *Cultural Transformations and Ethnicity in Modern Ecuador*, 15.

12. A parallel moment that seems to sum up Adoum's structural paradigm occurs in *The Strange Nation of Rafael Mendes* by Moacyr Scliar, the Brazilian-Jewish writer, when the main character pauses to stare at the maid's body, "a nice piece of tail," he observes, before he locks the door to his study, picks up the second volume of a hand-written notebook, and attempts to rebuild his history. See Moacyr Scliar, *The Strange Nation of Rafael Mendes*, trans. Eloah F. Giacomelli (New York: Harmony, 1988), 204. All subsequent references are to this edition.

13. Carlos Calderón Chico, *Literatura, autores y algo más* . . . (Guayaquil: Offset Graba, 1984), 27.

14. A similar collage motif, including newspaper articles and reproductions of official documents such as birth certificates, is employed in *The Fragmented Life of Don Jacobo Lerner*, by the Peruvian-Jewish author, Isaac Goldemberg. In addition, the image of being "at sea" is used repeatedly as a metaphor for the "betweenness" of their condition by Goldemberg and other Latin American Jewish writers such as Scliar, Elisa Lerner, and Mario Szichman. See for example, Isaac Goldemberg, *The Fragmented Life of Don Jacobo Lerner*, trans. Robert S. Picciotto (New York: Persea, 1976), 99; Moacyr Scliar, *The Volunteers*, trans. Eloah F. Giacomelli (New York: Ballantine, 1988), 1, 16, 17; Scliar, *Mendes*, 23, 75, 133; Elisa Lerner, "Papa's Friends," in *Tropical Synagogues*, ed. Ilan Stavans (New York: Holmes & Meier, 1994), 142; and Mario Szichman, "Remembrances of Things Future," in *Tropical Synagogues*, ed. Ilan Stavans (New York: Holmes & Meier, 1994), 108.

15. Jorge Enrique Adoum, *Entre Marx y una mujer desnuda* (Quito/Bogota: El Conejo/Oveja Negra, 1987), 2. All subsequent references are to this edition.

16. Alicia Steimberg, *La loca 101* (Buenos Aires: Ediciones de la Flor, 1995), 28–29. All subsequent references are to this edition.

17. Stutzman, "*El Mestizaje*," 45.

18. Gerardo Mario Goloboff, "The Passion According to San Martín," in *Tropical Synagogues*, ed. Ilan Stavans (New York: Holmes & Meier, 1994), 84–85.

19. Amaryll Chanady, "The Territorialization of the Imagery in Latin America:

Self-Affirmation and Resistance to Metropolitan Paradigms," in *Magical Realism: Theory, History, Community*, eds. Lois Parkinson Zamora and Wendy B. Faris (Durham: Duke University Press, 1995), 133.

20. Isaac Goldemberg, *Play by Play*, trans. Hardie St. Martin (New York: Persea, 1985), 65.

21. Lois Parkinson Zamora, "Magical Romance/Magical Realism: Ghosts in U.S. and Latin American Fiction," in *Magical Realism: Theory, History, Community*, eds. Lois Parkinson Zamora and Wendy B. Faris (Durham: Duke University Press, 1995), 544.

22. "El gran poeta chileno Mahfud Massís," *Nivel* 113 (31 May 1972): 1. This article is an assembly of several short comments about Mahfud Massís by numerous writers. This quote is attributed to Dionisio Aymara.

23. See Giordano, "Entrevista a Jorge Enrique Adoum."

24. Jorge Enrique Adoum, correspondence with the author, 22 May 1997.

25. Giordano, "Entrevista a Jorge Enrique Adoum," 11. Scliar's *The Volunteers* contains two scenes in which the folly of trying to maintain one's original culture intact in a new environment is embodied in the character of a gaucho who rides a horse down the middle of a crowded city street (and ends up killing the horse), and who later uses a lasso to snare a woman escaping by boat from the harbor, thus messing up the central character's well-laid plans to travel to Jerusalem (10–11, 136).

26. Werner Sollors, *Beyond Ethnicity: Consent and Descent in American Culture* (New York: Oxford University Press, 1986), 151.

27. "El Hombre de Punín" refers to a skull unearthed by archaeologists in 1923 near the village of Punín, high in the Andes, near the snow-covered volcanic peak of Chimborazo. Although of "uncertain age, it is believed to be approximately ten to twelve thousand years old (Jorge Enrique Adoum, correspondence with the author, 6 October 1997).

28. Giordano, "Entrevista a Jorge Enrique Adoum," 11.

29. Bakhtin writes: "The essential principle of grotesque realism is degradation, that is, the lowering of all that is high, spiritual, ideal, abstract; it is a transfer to the material level, to the sphere of the earth and body. . . . [Degradation] relates to acts of defecation and copulation, conception, pregnancy, and birth. Degradation digs a bodily grave for a new birth; it has not only a destructive, negative aspect, but also a regenerating one. To degrade an object does not imply merely hurtling it into the void of nonexistence, into absolute destruction, but to hurl it down to the reproductive lower stratum, the zone in which conception and a new birth takes place." See M. M. Bakhtin, *Rabelais and His World*, trans. Hélène Iswolsky (Bloomington: Indiana University Press, 1984), 19, 21.

30. Adoum, *Sin ambages*, 111.

31. Mahfud Massís, *Leyendas del cristo negro*, 5th ed. (Santiago: Orfeo, 1969), 8. All subsequent references are to this edition.

32. A similar image also occurs in Mário de Andrade's *Macunaíma* (Brazil, 1928).

33. "El gran poeta chileno Mahfud Massís," 2. This quote is attributed to Benedicto Chuaqui.

34. Pablo Martínez, "Strategies of (Re)presentation in the New Ecuadorian Novel: Between Marx and a Naked Woman and the Aesthetics of Violence," *New Novel Review/Nueva Novela/Nouveau Roman* 3, no. 1 (1995): 87.

35. Adoum, *Sin ambages*, 106–7.

36. Ibid., 76

37. Dolores Aguilera, "Jorge Enrique Adoum," *Quimera* 5 (1981): 9.
38. See Laura Hidalgo, "*Entre Marx y una mujer desnuda*, de Jorge Enrique Adoum," *Revista Iberamericana* 144–45 (1988): 886–87.
39. Lois Parkinson Zamora and Wendy B. Faris, Introduction to *Magical Realism: Theory, History, Community*, eds. Lois Parkinson Zamora and Wendy B. Faris (Durham: Duke University Press, 1995), 3–4.
40. In this regard, Adoum criticizes Jorge Luis Borges's literary conception of "a completely finished world, in which nothing remains to be done, that is, perfect and immutable: Isn't that the best definition of conservative ideology—and politics?" ("un mundo completamente acabado, en el que ya no hay nada que hacer, o sea, perfecto e inmutable: ¿no es ésta la mejor definición de una ideología—y de una política—conservadora?") See Giordano, "Entrevista a Jorge Enrique Adoum," 16.
41. See Alicia Steimberg, "Cecilia's Last Will and Testament," in *Tropical Synagogues*, ed. Ilan Stavans (New York: Holmes & Meier, 1994).
42. Adoum, *Sin ambages*, 114.
43. Frederick Douglass's *Narrative of the Life of Frederick Douglass, an American Slave* (1845) sold 30,000 copies in five years, compared with Harriet Beecher Stowe's *Uncle Tom's Cabin*, which sold 1.5 million copies in eight years. See Harriet Beecher Stowe, *Uncle Tom's Cabin* (New York: Signet Classic, 1981), 480.
44. Calderón Chico, *Literatura, autores y algo más* . . . , p. 23.
45. Etienne Decroux, interview with the author, 12 March 1982.
46. Clarice Lispector, *The Hour of the Star*, trans. Giovanni Pontiero (New York: Carcanet, 1987), 8. All subsequent references are to this edition.
47. Clarice Lispector, *The Foreign Legion*, trans. Giovanni Pontiero (Manchester: Carcanet, 1986), 75. All subsequent references are to this edition.
48. See Fred Weinstein, *History and Theory after the Fall: An Essay on Interpretation* (Chicago: University of Chicago Press, 1990), 97–102.
49. Adoum, *Sin ambages*, 147.

CHAPTER 6

1. Josefina Ludmer, "Quién educa," *Filologia* 20, no. 1 (1985): 103.
2. Josefina Ludmer, "La lengua como arma: Fundamentos del género gauchesco," in *Homenaje a Ana María Barrenechea*, eds. Lía Schwartz Lerner and Isaías Lerner (Madrid: Castalia, 1984), 476.
3. See Dick Gerdes, "An Embattled Society: Orality versus Writing in Alicia Yánez Cossío's *La cofradia del mullo del vestido de la virgen pipona*," *Latin American Literary Review* 18, no. 36 (1990): 50.
4. Orality can even self-consciously reproduce doubt about its own validity as a form. For example, the term *cuentista*, which can be used to mean either "storyteller" or "liar," depending on the speaker's intent.
5. Alicia Yánez Cossío, *Bruna, soroche y los tíos* (Quito: Libresa, 1991), back cover. All subsequent references are to this edition.
6. María-Elena Angulo, "Entrevista: Alicia Yánez Cossío," *Hispamerica* 58 (1991): 53–54.
7. M. M. Bakhtin, *Speech Genres and Other Late Essays*, eds. Caryl Emerson and Michael Holquist, trans. Vern W. McGee (Austin: University of Texas Press, 1986), 79–80.

8. Raymond Williams, *Marxism and Literature* (Oxford: Oxford University Press, 1977), 127.

9. Like Isabel Allende's *House of the Spirits* (Chile), Gabriel García Márquez's *One Hundred Years of Solitude* (Colombia) and Moacyr Scliar's *The Strange Nation of Rafael Mendes* (Brazil), and other novels of related scope, *Bruna, soroche y los tíos* tells the "story of Ecuador" from one family's perspective. In this genre of novel, history "is a ghost to be confronted, exorcised, used, overcome." See Lois Parkinson Zamora, "Magical Romance/Magical Realism: Ghosts in U.S. and Latin American Fiction," in *Magical Realism: Theory, History, Community*, eds. Lois Parkinson Zamora and Wendy B. Faris (Durham: Duke University Press, 1995), 503.

10. Mercedes M. Robles, "To the Rescue of a Concealed History: Eliécer Cárdenas' *Polvo y ceniza*," in *The Historical Novel in Latin America: A Symposium*, ed. Daniel Balderston (Gaithersburg, Md: Ediciones Hispamerica, 1986), 15.

11. Nina Scott, "Alicia Yánez Cossío: Una perpectiva feminina sobre el pasado del Ecuador," *Discurso Literario* 4, no. 2 (1987): 625.

12. Mercedes M. Robles, "To the Rescue of a Concealed History," 151, 152, 154.

13. Raymond Williams, *Marxism and Literature*, 200.

14. One could argue that the historical treatment of the preachings of Jesus Christ are another example of this effect, albeit with far wider consequences.

15. Agustín Cueva, *Lecturas y rupturas* (Quito: Planeta, 1986), 69–71, 107.

16. Francisco Ferrándiz Alborz, *El novelista hispano-americano Jorge Icaza* (Quito: Editora Quito, 1961), 35.

17. Agustín Cueva, *Lecturas y rupturas*, p. 182.

18. Icaza's comments probably refer to his 1958 novel, *El Chulla Romero y Flores*, a precursor to the novels discussed in this chapter in terms of its treatment of identity, ethnicity, polyphony/dialogism, space and hybrids in conflict.

19. Eliécer Cárdenas, interview with the author (19 February 1994).

20. M. M. Bakhtin, *The Dialogic Imagination*, ed. Michael Holquist, trans. Caryl Emerson and Michael Holquist (Austin: University of Texas Press, 1981), 35. This was noted in the Introduction.

21. Eliécer Cárdenas, *Polvo y ceniza* (Quito: Libresa, 1993), 68–69. All subsequent references are to this edition.

22. Carlos Calderón Chico, *Literatura, autores y algo más . . .* (Guayaquil: Offset Graba, 1984), 84.

23. Ibid., 81.

24. This issue merits further investigation. Ethnicities made invisible due to name changes, whether voluntary or coerced by the pressure to conform to the idea of a unified national identity, are also dramatized in such works as Mario Szichman's novel, *At 8:25 Evita Became Immortal*, which describes how the Pechoff family attempts to assimilate within Argentine society by changing their name to Gutiérrez-Anselmi, and Moacyr Scliar has a passage explaining how the thoroughly Hebrew name Moses ben Maimon became "Maimonides, Maimendes, Memendes," and finally, the thoroughly Spanish "Mendes" (Moacyr Scliar, *The Strange Nation of Rafael Mendes*, trans. Eloah F. Giacomelli [New York: Harmony, 1988], 112; there is even a three-act "farce," *El teatro soy yo* [1933], written by the Argentine-Jewish playwright, Israel Zeitlin, *under the pseudonym* of César Tiempo, in which a black character complains that Jews get to fit into Argentine society by changing their names ["truecan sus apellidos"]. See David William Foster, *Cultural Diversity in Latin American Literature* [Albuquerque: University

of New Mexico Press, 1994], 116). Similarly, Lebanese and Syrian immigrants to South America erased their ethnicity, at least on paper, by changing names such as Mohammad and Sulaiman to Manuel and Solomon. Strip away the veneer of conformity, and many societies are a great deal more "diverse" than they realize.

25. María-Elena Angulo, "Ideologeme of 'Mestizaje' and Search for Cultural Identity in *Bruna, soroche y los tíos* by Alicia Yánez Cossío," in *Translating Latin America: Culture as Text: Translation Perspectives VI 1991*, eds. William Luis and Julio Rodríguez-Luis (Binghamton: Center for Research in Translation, SUNY Binghamton, 1991), 206.

26. The supposedly unified national literatures of Western Europe emerged when the oral languages became textualized, with the appearance of stitched-together collections of fables, fairy tales, myths, proverbs and tall tales. In the contemporary Ecuadorian novels of Eliécer Cárdenas, Alicia Yánez Cossío, and others, "old" forms such as the historical novel can be seen as new. (Raymond Williams sees this phenomenon occurring in societies that are undergoing major social transformations [Williams, *Marxism and Literature*, 189].) Local discourse still resists the totalizing interpretation of the Latin American "narrative." Roberto González Echeverría believes that conscious self-reflexivity can be a way of disassembling the mediation through which Latin America is narrated. See Roberto González Echeverría, *Myth and Archive: A Theory of Latin American Narrative* (Cambridge: Cambridge University Press, 1990), 28.

27. See for example Pierre Macherey, *A Theory of Literary Production*, trans. Geoffrey Wall (London: Routledge & Kegan Paul, 1978), 256.

28. E. J. Hobsbawm, *Social Bandits and Primitive Rebels* (Glencoe, Ill.: Free Press, 1959), 9.

29. Boris Pasternak, quoted in Nicola Chiaromonte, *The Paradox of History: Stendhal, Tolstoy, Pasternak, and Others* (Philadelphia: University of Pennsylvania Press, 1985), 121.

30. Bakhtin, *The Dialogic Imagination*, 10.

31. Ibid., 15.

32. Ibid., 60, 23 (as noted in the Introduction).

33. Scliar, *The Strange Nation of Rafael Mendes*, 113.

34. Mario Szichman, "Remembrances of Things Future," in *Tropical Synagogues*, ed. Ilan Stavans (New York: Holmes & Meier, 1994), 103, 102, 108.

35. See Alicia Steimberg, *La loca 101* (Buenos Aires: Ediciones de la Flor, 1995), 74. All subsequent references are to this edition.

36. C. Michael Waag, "Frustration and Rage in Jorge Enrique Adoum's *Entre Marx y una mujer desnuda*," *Perspectives on Contemporary Literature* 10 (1984): 96.

37. Antonio Sacoto, *Quatorze novelas claves de la literatura ecuatoriana* (Cuenca: University de Cuenca, 1990), 348. In a non-humorous example, *Love and Shadows*, the author, Isabel Allende, rather than challenging her audience at the level of textual experimentation and complexity, offers them a love story that serves as a vehicle for challenging the politics-as-usual ideology of the readers of romances by exposing, in straightforward prose, the political horrors of the Pinochet government.

38. Clarice Lispector, *The Foreign Legion*, trans. Giovanni Pontiero (New York: Carcanet, 1986), 212. All subsequent references are to this edition.

39. E. J. Hobsbawm, *Bandits* (London: Weidenfeld & Nicholson, 1969), 115. "The point about social bandits is that they are peasant outlaws whom the lord and state regard as criminals, but who remain within peasant society, and are consid-

ered by their people as heroes, as champions, avengers, fighters for justice, perhaps even leaders of liberation, and in any case as men to be admired, helped and supported" (ibid., 13). Also, "We need not suppose that they spent all their time fighting, let alone trying to overthrow, the oppressors. The very existence of bands of free men, or of those small patches of rock or reed beyond the reach of any administration, was sufficient achievement" (ibid., 70).

40. Hobsbawm, *Bandits*, 82.

41. See Michel Foucault, *Discipline and Punish: The Birth of the Prison*, trans. Alan Sheridan (New York: Vintage, 1979), 60–68.

Conclusion

1. Dorothy Figueira, "Myth, Ideology and the Authority of an Absent Text," *Yearbook of Comparative and General Literature* 39 (1990–91): 59–60.

2. Alberto Flores Galindo, *Europa y el país de los Incas: La utopía Andina* (Lima: Instituto de Apoyo Agrario, 1986), 20; see also Mark Thurner, "Peasant Politics and Andean Haciendas in the Transition to Capitalism: An Ethnographic History," *Latin American Research Review* 28, no. 3 (1993): 45.

3. J. Goody and I. Watt, "The Consequences of Literacy," in *Language and Social Context*, ed. Pier Paolo Giglioli (New York: Viking Penguin, 1972), 318.

4. Wallace Martin, *Recent Theories of Narrative* (Ithaca: Cornell University Press, 1986), 89.

5. Ibid., 46.

6. Important exceptions are said to include de la Cuadra's "La tigra" (1932) and Pareja Diezcanseco's *Baldomera* (1938), but Ecuadorian feminist critics maintain that "in spite of the authors' intensions, these are not characters that truly break" with tradition ("No son auténticos personajes de ruptura, a pesar de las intenciones de sus autores"). See Cecilia Ansaldo Briones, "Una mirada 'otra' a ciertos personajes femeninos de la narrativa ecuatoriana," *Memorias del quinto encuentro de literatura ecuatoriana*, ed. Alfonso Carrasco Vintimilla (Cuenca: Cuenca University Press, 1995), 248.

7. Martin, *Recent Theories of Narrative*, 63.

8. Raymond Williams, *Marxism and Literature* (Oxford: Oxford University Press, 1977), 102.

9. C. Michael Waag, "The Ecuadorian Novel of the 1970s in the Context of its Historical and Literary Past," doctoral dissertation (University of Illinois at Urbana-Champaign, 1983), 16. Humberto E. Robles discusses a number of important examples, e.g., Roberto Andrade's *Pacho Villamar* (1900), Luis Alberto Martínez's *A la costa* (1904), José Antonio Campos's *Rayos catódicos y fuegos fatuos* (1906–7) and José Rafael Bustamante's *Para matar el gusano* (1912). See Humberto E. Robles, *Testimonio y tendencia mítica en la obra de José de la Cuadra* (Quito: Casa de la Cultura, 1976), chapter 2, especially 30–35.

10. Waag, "The Ecuadorian Novel of the 1970s," 62.

11. Demetrio Aguilera Malta, Joaquín Gallegos Lara and Enrique Gil Gilbert, *Los que se van* (Quito: El Conejo, 1985), 174. All subsequent references are to this edition.

12. Waag, "The Ecuadorian Novel of the 1970s," 273.

13. To be precise, *La vorágine* is set in the Amazon, while *Don Goyo* is set in the jungle along the Pacific coast.

14. Waag, "The Ecuadorian Novel of the 1970s," 73.

15. In spite of a literary history largely characterized by politically engaged writers, today's literary critics still seem to place poetry in a privileged position "above" all else, and poetic prose in the exalted position of second place. The kind of appropriation from genres traditionally labeled "popular," or even "small" (Michael J. Toolan, *Narrative: A Critical Linguistic Introduction* [London: Routledge, 1991], 43) such as newspaper stories, scandal sheets and tabloid journalism, television shows, and ads that has been practiced by many now-canonical Latin American authors still encounters violent resistance from the gatekeepers of Ecuadorian national literary identity and criticism. There is movement toward opening up this area, but it is still very much in its infancy. The largest space within Ecuadorian literature where popular or "smaller" forms can be said to be operating with any vitality and acceptance is precisely in the representation of oral anecdotes, of native cosmological vision, of that oral popular expression that can be poeticized most "acceptably" in its reportage because the appropriated source has been framed as "poetic" to begin with. At the Fifth National "Encuentro Literario" conference at the University of Cuenca, Ecuador, a public debate took place between a younger critic introducing the idea that Ecuadorian tabloid journalism has a recognizable "poetics," and the outraged opposition from more conservative critics. This is clearly new territory to be explored.

16. Roberto González Echevarría, "The Criticism of Latin American Literature Today: Adorno, Molloy, Magnarelli," *Profession* (1987): 10.

17. Bernard Shaw, *The Quintessence of Ibsenism* (New York: Hill & Wang, 1957), 12.

18. See for example Flores Galindo, *Europa y el país de los Incas*, 26.

19. "It was deemed a disgrace not to get drunk at Christmas." See Frederick Douglass, *Narrative of the Life of Frederick Douglass, an American Slave* (Cambridge: Harvard University Press, 1960), 106.

20. Ibid., 107–8. It is therefore possible to suggest that recent increases in the number of Indians who reject the binge-drinking that has traditionally accompanied the celebration of Carnival and other national and religious holidays has potentially empowering significance for those populations (see Thurner, "Peasant Politics and Andean Haciendas in the Transition to Capitalism").

21. Gerald Graff, "Co-optation," in *The New Historicism*, ed. H. Aram Veeser (New York: Routledge, 1989), 168–69.

22. Williams, *Marxism and Literature*, 114; Albert Einstein, *Relativity* (New York: Crown, 1961), 109.

23. One example from *One Hundred Years of Solitude*: At one point we are told that José Arcadio Buendía was left in charge of Macondo, and that *ten months* later the government attacked and liquidated the resistance "in a half hour" (Gabriel García Márquez, *One Hundred Years of Solitude*, trans. Gregory Rabassa [New York: Avon, 1978], 104–5). But soon after the reader is informed, "About the time that Arcadio was named civil and military leader" he had a daughter (113) as a result of his sexual relations with Santa Sofía de la Piedad, which we had just been told came *after* his being named leader. Then we are told that Arcadio ruled for "11 months" and that he has a "six-month-old daughter," which "logically" must mean that at least *15 months* have passed (114). And the next time we read about the resistance being quelled "in less than half an hour," he has an eight-month-old daughter (117–18), which (again) "logically" must mean that at least *17 months* have passed. Thus we have at least four possible trajectories generated by the same point-event in time, through which completely different (and "logically" incompatible) events have occurred. This is mythic time, that lives in variants and accepts "contradictory" tales as belonging to the same story.

24. John Bartlett, *Familiar Quotations*, 13th ed. (Boston: Little, Brown, 1955), 12.

25. Nelson Goodman, "Twisted Tales; or, Story, Study and Symphony," *Critical Inquiry* 7, no. 1 (1980): 104.

26. Roland Barthes, *Image, Music, Text*, trans. Stephen Heath (New York: Hill and Wang, 1977), 98–99.

27. D. Emily Hicks, *Border Writing: The Multidimensional Text* (Minneapolis: University of Minnesota Press, 1991), xxxi.

28. This has been put forth by such diverse critics as Leon Trotsky, Pierre Macherey, and Richard Rorty.

Appendix: Translator's Introduction

1. I do not like wholesale substitutions, for example, turning Eugenio Espejo into Tom Paine in *Bruna, soroche y los tíos*, but sometimes there is no choice. While some culturally specific references can be clarified with a few extra words in the sentence (the authors generally agree with this—they want to be understood!), some, I'm afraid, must be explained with detailed footnotes, a practice I am against in theory because it "breaks the flow," but which in fact I must use when necessary. With the author's consent, I have even invented proverbs in that do not exist in English to replace the Spanish rhymed couplet proverbs *Polvo y ceniza* rather than stick in the "closest" existing recognizable English proverb.

2. Agustín Cueva, "El método materialista histórico aplicado a la periodización de la historia de la literatura Ecuatoriana: Algunas consideraciones teóricas," *Casa de las Americas* 22 (1981): 41; see also Agustín Cueva, "Literatura y sociedad en el Ecuador; 1920–1960," *Revista Iberoamericana* 54 (1988): 638, 640–41.

3. Suzanne Jill Levine, *The Subversive Scribe: Translating Latin American Fiction* (St. Paul: Greywolf Press, 1991), 2–3.

4. Robert Bly, "The Eight Stages of Translation," in *Translation: Literary, Linguistic & Philosophical Perspectives*, ed. W. Frawley (Newark: University of Delaware Press, 1984), 77; Gregory Rabassa, "Words Cannot Express . . . The Translation of Cultures," in *Translating Latin America: Culture as Text*, eds. William Luis and Julio Rodriguez-Luis (Binghamton: SUNY Binghamton Center for Research in Translation, 1991), 43.

5. See Mildred L. Larson, *Meaning-Based Translation: A Guide to Cross-Language Equivalence*, (Lanham, Md: University Press of America, 1984), 181.

6. José de la Cuadra, *Los Sangurimas* (Quito: Editorial El Conejo, 1986), 30. All subsequent references are to this edition.

7. See Levine's example: Original: "La dejé habla así na ma que pa dale coldel y cuando se cansó de metel su descalga yo le dije no que va vieja, tu etás muy euivocada." Translation: "I let her go on and on and on just so she could get to an end and when she got tired of shooting off her big mouth and kinda breathless, I told her but dahling you got it all wrong." Levine, *The Subversive Scribe*, 70.

Bibliography

Adoum, Jorge Enrique. "El realismo de la otra realidad." *America Latina en su literatura*. Edited by César Fernández Moreno. Mexico City: Siglo XXI, 1972.

———. Prologue to *Narradores ecuatorianos del 30*. Caracas: Biblioteca Ayacucho, 1982.

———. *Entre Marx y una mujer desnuda*. Quito/Bogota: El Conejo/Oveja Negra, 1987.

———. *Sin ambages*. Quito: Planeta, 1989.

———. *El tiempo y las palabras*. Quito: Libresa, 1992.

———. Correspondence with the author. 22 May 1997.

———. Correspondence with the author. 6 October 1997.

Aguilera, Dolores. "Jorge Enrique Adoum." *Quimera* 5 (1981): 9–15.

Aguilera Malta, Demetrio. *Don Goyo*. Buenos Aires: Editorial Platina, 1958.

———. "El tigre." *Teatro completo*. Mexico City: Finisterre, 1970.

———. *Don Goyo*. Translated by John and Carolyn Brushwood. Clifton, N.J.: Humana Press, 1980.

Aguilera Malta, Demetrio, Joaquín Gallegos Lara, and Enrique Gil Gilbert. *Los que se van*. Quito: El Conejo, 1985.

Allende, Isabel. *Love and Shadows*. Translated by Margaret Sayers Peden. New York: Bantam, 1988.

Anderson, Benedict. *Imagined Communities: Reflections on the Origin and Spread of Nationalism*. New York: Verso, 1991.

Angulo, María-Elena. "Entrevista: Alicia Yánez Cossío." *Hispamerica* 58 (1991): 45–54.

———. "Ideologeme of 'Mestizaje' and Search for Cultural Identity in *Bruna, soroche y los tíos* by Alicia Yánez Cossío." In *Translating Latin America: Culture as Text: Translation Perspectives VI 1991*, edited by William Luis and Julio Rodríguez-Luis. Binghamton: Center for Research in Translation, SUNY Binghamton, 1991.

Ansaldo Briones, Cecilia. "Una mirada 'otra' a ciertos personajes femeninos de la narrativa ecuatoriana." *Memorias del quinto encuentro de literatura ecuatoriana*. Edited by Alfonso Carrasco Vintimilla. Cuenca: Universidad de Cuenca, 1995.

Antoine, Jean-Claude. "L'Éternel Retour de l'Histoire Deviendra-t-il Objet de Science?" *Critique* 4, no. 27 (1948): 723–38.

Arguedas, José María. *Yawar Fiesta*. Translated by Frances Horning Barraclough. Austin: University of Texas Press, 1985.

Auerbach, Erich. *Mimesis*. Princeton: Princeton University Press, 1968.

Baciu, Stefan. *Antología de la poesía surrealista latinoamericana*. Valparaíso: Ediciones Universitarias, 1981.

Baciu, Stefan, ed. *Surrealismo Latinoamericano: Preguntas y respuestas*. Valparaíso: Ediciones Universitarias, 1979.

Bakhtin, M. M. *The Dialogic Imagination*. Edited by Michael Holquist. Translated by Caryl Emerson and Michael Holquist. Austin: University of Texas Press, 1981.

———. *Rabelais and His World*. Translated by Hélène Iswolsky. Bloomington: Indiana University Press, 1984.

———. *Speech Genres and Other Late Essays*. Edited by Caryl Emerson and Michael Holquist. Translated by Vern W. McGee. Austin: University of Texas Press, 1986.

Balakian, Anna. "Latin-American Poets and the Surrealist Heritage." In *Surrealismo/Surrealismos: Latinoamerica y España*, edited by Peter G. Earle and Germán Gullón. Philadelphia: University of Pennsylvania Press, 1977.

Barthes, Roland. *Image, Music, Text*. Translated by Stephen Heath. New York: Hill and Wang, 1977.

Bartlett, John. *Familiar Quotations*. 13th ed. Boston: Little, Brown, 1955.

Beecher Stowe, Harriet. *Uncle Tom's Cabin*. New York: Signet Classic, 1981.

Benítez Vinueza, Leopoldo. "La mala hora." *Cuento de la generacion de los 30*. Vol. 1. Guayaquil: Clasicos Ariel, 1975.

Bly, Robert. "The Eight Stages of Translation." In *Translation: Literary, Linguistic & Philosophical Perspectives*, edited by W. Frawley. Newark: University of Delaware Press, 1984.

Bontempelli, Massimo. *L'avventura novecentista*. Firenze: Vallecchi, 1974.

Breton, André. *Mad Love*. Translated by Mary Ann Caws. Lincoln: University of Nebraska Press, 1987.

Burgess, Anthony. *English Literature: A Survey for Students*. London: Longman, 1974.

Calderón Chico, Carlos. *Literatura, autores y algo más . . .* Guayaquil: Offset Graba, 1984.

Cárdenas, Eliécer. *Polvo y ceniza*. Quito: Libresa, 1993.

Carpentier, Alejo. Introduction to *El reino de ese mundo*. *Obras completas*. Vol. 2. Mexico: Siglo XXI, 1983.

———. *Obras completas*. Vol. 9. Mexico: Siglo XXI, 1986.

———. *Tientos y diferencias y otros ensayos*. Barcelona: Plaza & Janes, 1987.

Carrera Andrade, Jorge. *Reflections on Spanish-American Poetry*. Translated by Don C. Bliss and Gabriela de C. Bliss. Albany: SUNY Press, 1973.

Celorio, Gonzalo. *El surrealismo y lo real-maravilloso americano*. Mexico City: SepSetentas, 1976.

Chanady, Amaryll. "The Territorialization of the Imagery in Latin America: Self-Affirmation and Resistance to Metropolitan Paradigms." In *Magical Realism: Theory, History, Community*, edited by Lois Parkinson Zamora and Wendy B. Faris. Durham: Duke University Press, 1995.

Chatman, Seymour. *Story and Discourse: Narrative Structure in Fiction and Film*. Ithaca: Cornell University Press, 1978.

Chiampi, Irlemar. *El realismo maravilloso: Forma e ideología en la novela hispanoamericana*. Caracas: Monte Avila, 1983.

Chiaromonte, Nicola. *The Paradox of History: Stendhal, Tolstoy, Pasternak, and others*. Philadelphia: University of Pennsylvania Press, 1985.

Corkhill, David, and David Cubitt. *Ecuador: Fragile Democracy*. London: Latin American Bureau, 1988.

Cruz, Adina. "Similitud y contraste en las novelas *Huasipungo* y *The Pearl*." *Kañina* 4, no. 2 (1980): 109–15.

Cueva, Agustín. *La literatura Ecuatoriana*. Buenos Aires: Centro Editor de América Latina, 1968.

———. "El método materialista histórico aplicado a la periodización de la historia de la literatura Ecuatoriana: Algunas consideraciones teóricas." *Casa de las Americas* 22 (1981): 31–47.

———. *The Process of Political Domination in Ecuador*. Translated by Danielle Salti. New Brunswick, N.J.: Transaction Books, 1982.

———. *Lecturas y rupturas*. Quito: Planeta, 1986.

———. "Literatura y sociedad en el Ecuador: 1920–1960." *Revista Iberoamericana* 54 (1988): 629–47.

De la Cuadra, José. *Obras completas*. Quito: Casa de la Cultura, 1958.

———. *Los Sangurimas*. Quito: Editorial El Conejo, 1986.

Douglass, Frederick. *Narrative of the Life of Frederick Douglass, an American Slave*. Cambridge: Harvard University Press, 1960.

Eagleton, Terry. *Ideology: An Introduction*. London: Verso, 1991.

Einstein, Albert. *Relativity*. New York: Crown, 1961.

"El gran poeta chileno Mahfud Massís." *Nivel* 113 (31 May 1972): 1–2.

Eliade, Mircea. "Time and Eternity in Indian Thought." In *Man and Time: Papers from the Eranos Yearbooks*, edited by Joseph Campbell. Translated by Ralph Manheim. Bollingen Series XXX, vol. 3. New York: Pantheon, 1957.

———. *Two Tales of the Occult*. Translated by William Ames Coates. New York: Herder and Herder, 1970.

———. *The Myth of the Eternal Return: Or, Cosmos and History*. Translated by Willard R. Trask. Bollingen Series, XLVI. Princeton: Princeton University Press, 1991.

Erickson, Edwin E., et al. *Area Handbook for Ecuador*. Washington, D.C.: Government Printing Office, August 1966.

Faris, Wendy B. "Scheherazade's Children: Magical Realism and Postmodern Fiction." In *Magical Realism: Theory, History, Community*, edited by Lois Parkinson Zamora and Wendy B. Faris. Durham: Duke University Press, 1995.

Fernández, María del Carmen. *El realismo abierto de Pablo Palacio en la encrucijada de los 30*. Quito: Libri Mundi, 1991.

Ferrándiz Alborz, Francisco. *El novelista hispano-americano Jorge Icaza*. Quito: Editora Quito, 1961.

Figueira, Dorothy. "Myth, Ideology and the Authority of an Absent Text." *Yearbook of Comparative and General Literature* 39 (1990–91): 54–61.

———. "Aryan Ancestors, Pariahs and the Lunatic Fringe." *The Comparative Civilizations Review* 25 (1991): 1–27.

Fitch, J. Samuel. "The Military Coup d'État as Political Process: A General

Framework and the Ecuadorean Case." In *Armies and Politics in Latin America*, edited by Abraham F. Lowenthal and J. Samuel Fitch. New York: Holmes & Meier, 1986.

Flores Galindo, Alberto. *Europa y el país de los Incas: La utopía Andina.* Lima: Instituto de Apoyo Agrario, 1986.

———. *Buscando un Inca: Identidad y utopia en los Andes.* Lima: Instituto de Apoyo Agrario, 1987.

Foucault, Michel. *Discipline and Punish: The Birth of the Prison.* Translated by Alan Sheridan. New York: Vintage, 1979.

Galarza, Jaime. *El festín del petroleo.* 3rd ed. Cuenca: Ediciones Solitierra, 1974.

García Márquez, Gabriel. *One Hundred Years of Solitude.* Translated by Gregory Rabassa. New York: Avon, 1978.

———. *El olor de la guayaba: Conversacions con Plinio Apuleyo Mendoza.* Barcelona: Bruguera, 1982.

Gerdes, Dick. "An Embattled Society: Orality versus Writing in Alicia Yánez Cossío's *La cofradia del mullo del vestido de la virgen pipona.*" *Latin American Literary Review* 18, no. 36 (1990): 50–58.

Gil Gilbert, Enrique. *Nuestro pan.* 2 vols. Guayaquil: Clasicos Ariel, 1975.

———. *Our Daily Bread.* Translated by Dudley Poore. New York: Farrar & Rinehart, 1943.

Gilard, Jacques. "De *Los Sangurimas* a *Cien años de soledad.*" *Universidad de Medellín* 21 (1976): 183–96.

Giordano, Eduardo. "Entrevista a Jorge Enrique Adoum." *Plural* 187 (1987): 8–17.

Girard, René. "The Demons of Gerasa." In *The Daemonic Imagination: Biblical Text and Secular Story*, edited by Robert Detweiler and William G. Doty. Atlanta: Scholars Press, 1990.

Goldemberg, Isaac. *The Fragmented Life of Don Jacobo Lerner.* Translated by Robert S. Picciotto. New York: Persea, 1976.

———. *Play by Play.* Translated by Hardie St. Martin. New York: Persea, 1985.

Goloboff, Gerardo Mario. "The Passion According to San Martín." In *Tropical Synagogues.* Edited by Ilan Stavans. New York: Holmes & Meier, 1994.

González, Galo F. "José de la Cuadra: Nicasio Sangurima, un patriarcha olvidado." *Revista Iberoamericana* 54 (1988): 739–51.

González Echevarría, Roberto. "The Criticism of Latin American Literature Today: Adorno, Molloy, Magnarelli." *Profession* (1987): 10–13.

———. *Myth and Archive: A Theory of Latin American Narrative.* Cambridge: Cambridge University Press, 1990.

———. Review of Carlos Fuentes's *The Campaign.* *New York Times Book Review*, 6 October 1991, 3+.

Goodman, Nelson. "Twisted Tales; or, Story, Study and Symphony." *Critical Inquiry* 7, no. 1 (1980): 103–19.

Goody, J., and I. Watt. "The Consequences of Literacy." In *Language and Social Context*, edited by Pier Paolo Giglioli. New York: Viking Penguin, 1972.

Graff, Gerald. "Co-optation." In *The New Historicism*, edited by H. Aram Veeser. New York: Routledge, 1989.

Gramsci, Antonio. *Selections from the Prison Notebooks*. New York: International Publishers, 1971.
Guerrero Zamora, Juan. *Historia del teatro contemporáneo*. Vol. 4. Barcelona: Juan Flors, 1967.
Hall, Stuart. "Notes on Deconstructing 'The Popular.' " In *People's History and Socialist Theory*. Edited by Raphael Samuel. London: Routledge & Kegan Paul, 1981.
Hashimoto, Kohei. "Lebanese Population Movement, 1920–1939: Towards a Study." In *The Lebanese in the World: A Century of Emigration*, edited by Albert Hourani and Nadim Shehadi. London: I.B. Tauris & Co., 1992.
Hicks, D. Emily. *Border Writing: The Multidimensional Text*. Minneapolis: University of Minnesota Press, 1991.
Hidalgo, Laura. "*Entre Marx y una mujer desnuda, de Jorge Enrique Adoum.*" *Revista Iberamericana* 144–45 (1988): 875–92.
Hobsbawm, E. J. *Social Bandits and Primitive Rebels*. Glencoe, Ill.: Free Press, 1959.
———. *The Age of Revolution: 1789–1848*. New York: Mentor, 1962.
———. *Bandits*. London: Weidenfeld & Nicholson, 1969.
Hourani, Albert, and Nadim Shehadi, eds. *The Lebanese in the World: A Century of Emigration*. London: I. B. Tauris, 1992.
Icaza, Jorge. *Huasipungo*. Quito: Libresa, 1990.
———. *The Villagers*. Translated by Bernard M. Dulsey. Carbondale: Southern Illinois University Press, 1964.
Indice de la narrativa ecuatoriana. Edited by Gladys Jaramillo Buendía, Raúl Péres Torres, and Simón Zabala Guzmán. Quito: Editora Nacional, 1992.
Issawi, Charles. "The Historical Background of Lebanese Emigration, 1800–1914." In *The Lebanese in the World: A Century of Emigration*. Edited by Albert Hourani and Nadim Shehadi. London: I. B. Tauris, 1992.
Janes, Regina. *One Hundred Years of Solitude: Modes of Reading*. Boston: G. K. Hall, 1991.
The Jerusalem Bible. Jerusalem: Koren, 1984.
Kott, Jan. *The Eating of the Gods*. Evanston: Northwestern University Press, 1987.
Lahusen, Thomas. Introduction to special issue of *South Atlantic Quarterly* 94, no. 3 (1995): 657–85.
Langowski, Gerald J. *El surrealismo en la ficción hispano-americana*. Madrid: Gredos, 1982.
Larson, Mildred L. *Meaning-Based Translation: A Guide to Cross-Language Equivalence*. Lanham, Md.: University Press of America, 1984.
Lastra, Pedro. "Aproximaciones a ¡*Écue-Yamba-Ó!*" In *Asedios a Carpentier: Once ensayos críticos sobre el novelisto cubano*, edited by Klaus Müller-Bergh. Santiago: Universitaria, 1972.
Lerner, Elisa. "Papa's Friends." In *Tropical Synagogues*, edited by Ilan Stavans. New York: Holmes & Meier, 1994.
Levine, Suzanne Jill. *The Subversive Scribe: Translating Latin American Fiction*. St. Paul: Greywolf Press, 1991.
Linke, Lilo. *Ecuador: Country of Contrasts*. 3rd ed. London: Oxford University Press, 1960.

Lispector, Clarice. *The Foreign Legion*. Translated by Giovanni Pontiero. Manchester: Carcanet, 1986.

———. *The Hour of the Star*. Translated by Giovanni Pontiero. New York: Carcanet, 1987.

Ludmer, Josefina. "La lengua como arma: Fundamentos del género gauchesco." In *Homenaje a Ana María Barrenechea*, edited by Lía Schwartz Lerner & Isaías Lerner. Madrid: Castalia, 1984.

———. "Quién educa." *Filologia* 20, no. 1 (1985): 103–16.

Lukács, Georg. *Studies in European Realism*. New York: Grosset & Dunlap, 1964.

———. *The Historical Novel*. Translated by Hannah and Stanley Mitchell. Lincoln: University of Nebraska Press, 1983.

Luzuriaga, Gerardo. *Del realismo al expresionismo: El teatro de Demetrio Aguilera-Malta*. Madrid: Plaza Mayor, 1971.

Macherey, Pierre. *A Theory of Literary Production*. Translated by Geoffrey Wall. London: Routledge & Kegan Paul, 1978.

Manzoni, Alessandro. *The Betrothed*. Translated by Bruce Penman. London: Penguin, 1972.

Marras, Emma. "Robert Bly's Reading of South American Poets: A Challenge to North American Poetic Practice." *Translation Review* 14 (1984): 33–39.

Martín, Carlos. *Hispanoamerica: mito y surrealismo*. Bogota: Procultura, 1986.

Martin, Wallace. *Recent Theories of Narrative*. Ithaca: Cornell University Press, 1986.

Martínez, Pablo. "Strategies of (Re)presentation in the New Ecuadorian Novel: Between Marx and a Naked Woman and the Aesthetics of Violence." *New Novel Review/Nueva Novela/Nouveau Roman* 3, no. 1 (1995): 83–106.

Marx, Karl, and Frederick Engels. *Marx and Engels on Literature and Art*. Edited by Lee Baxandall and Stefan Morawski. New York: International General, 1974.

Massís, Mahfud. *Leyendas del cristo negro*. 5th ed. Santiago: Orfeo, 1969.

Mistry, Freny. *Nietzsche and Buddhism: Prolegomenon to a Comparative Study*. New York: Walter de Gruyter, 1981.

Mitchell, W. J. T., ed. *On Narrative*. Chicago: University of Chicago Press, 1981.

Müller-Bergh, Klaus. "Corrientes vanguardistas y surrealismo en la obra de Alejo Carpentier." In *Asedios a Carpentier: Once ensayos críticos sobre el novelisto cubano*, edited by Klaus Müller-Bergh. Santiago: Universitaria, 1972.

Nietzsche, Friedrich. *Der Wille zur Macht*. Leipzig: Alfred Kröner, 1928.

O'Neill, Eugene. "The Emperor Jones." *Nine Plays*. New York: Modern Library, 1959.

Ojeda, J. Enrique. "Jorge Carrera Andrade y la vanguardia." *Revista Iberoamericana* 54 (1988): 675–90.

Ong, Walter. *Orality and Literacy: The Technologizing of the Word*. London: Routledge, 1989.

Ortner, Sherry B. "Is Female to Male as Nature Is to Culture?" In *Woman, Culture, and Society*, edited by Michelle Zimbalist Rosaldo and Louise Lamphere. Stanford: Stanford University Press, 1974.

Palacio, Pablo. *Obras completas*. Quito: El Conejo, 1986.

Pareja Diezcanseco, Alfredo. "El reino de la libertad en Pablo Palacio." *Casa de las Américas* 22 (1981): 3–20.

———. "Los narradores de la generación del treinta: El grupo de Guayaquil." *Revista Iberoamericana* 54 (1988): 691–707.

Parkinson Zamora, Lois, and Wendy B. Faris, eds. *Magical Realism: Theory, History, Community*. Durham: Duke University Press, 1995.

Paz, Octavio. "Sobre el surrealismo hispanoamericano: El fin de las habladurias." Introduction to *Surrealismo Latinoamericano: Preguntas y respuestas*, edited by Stefan Baciu. Valparaíso: Ediciones Universitarias, 1979.

Puech, Henri-Charles. "Gnosis and Time." In *Man and Time: Papers from the Eranos Yearbooks*, edited by Joseph Campbell. Translated by Ralph Manheim. New York: Bollingen Series XXX, vol. 3, Pantheon, 1957.

Rabassa, Clementine Christos. *Demetrio Aguilera-Malta and Social Justice: The Tertiary Phase of Epic Tradition in Latin American Literature*. Rutherford: Fairleigh Dickinson University Press, 1980.

Rabassa, Gregory. "Words Cannot Express . . . The Translation of Cultures." In *Translating Latin America: Culture as Text*. Edited by William Luis and Julio Rodriguez-Luis. Binghamton: SUNY Binghamton Center for Research in Translation, 1991.

Rama, Angel. *Transculturación narrativa en América Latina*. 3rd ed. Mexico City: Siglo XXI, 1987.

Ricoeur, Paul. *Time and Narrative*. Vol. 1. Translated by Kathleen McLaughlin and David Pellauer. Chicago: University of Chicago Press, 1984.

Rimbaud, Arthur. *Oeuvres*. Paris: Garnier, 1960.

Robin, Régine. *Socialist Realism: An Impossible Aesthetic*. Translated by Catherine Porter. Stanford: Stanford University Press, 1992.

Robles, Humberto E. *Testimonio y tendencia mítica en la obra de José de la Cuadra*. Quito: Casa de la Cultura, 1976.

———. "Genesis y vigencia de 'Los Sangurimas.' " *Revista Iberoamericana* 45 (1979): 85–91.

———. "Pablo Palacio: El anhelo insatisfecho." *Cultura* [Quito] 7, no. 20 (1984): 3–20.

———. "La noción de vanguardia en el Ecuador: Recepción y trayectoria (1918–1934)." *Revista Iberoamericana* 54 (1988): 649–74.

———. "De San Borondón a Samborondón: Sobre la poética de José de la Cuadra." *Nuevo Texto Crítico* 4, no. 8 (1991): 173–83.

Robles, Mercedes M. "To the Rescue of a Concealed History: Eliécer Cárdenas' *Polvo y ceniza*." In *The Historical Novel in Latin America: A Symposium*, edited by Daniel Balderston. Gaithersburg, Md.: Ediciones Hispamerica, 1986.

Rodriguez, Linda Alexander. *The Search for Public Policy: Regional Politics and Government Finances in Ecuador, 1830–1940*. Berkeley: University of California Press, 1985.

Rodriguez Monegal, Emir. "Surrealism, Magical Realism, Magical Fiction: A Study in Confusion." In *Surrealismo/Surrealismos: Latinoamerica y España*, edited by Peter G. Earle and Germán Gullón. Philadelphia: University of Pennsylvania Press, 1977.

Sacoto, Antonio. *Quatorze novelas claves de la literatura ecuatoriana*. Cuenca: Universidad de Cuenca, 1990.

Scholem, Gershom G. *Major Trends in Jewish Mysticism*. New York: Schocken, 1961.

Scliar, Moacyr. *The Strange Nation of Rafael Mendes*. Translated by Eloah F. Giacomelli. New York: Harmony, 1988.

———. *The Volunteers*. Translated by Eloah F. Giacomelli. New York: Ballantine, 1988.

Scott, Nina. "Alicia Yánez Cossío: Una perpectiva feminina sobre el pasado del Ecuador." *Discurso Literario* 4, no. 2 (1987): 623–30.

Scott, Sir Walter. *Ivanhoe*. New York: Signet Classics, 1962.

Shaw, Bernard. *The Quintessence of Ibsenism*. New York: Hill & Wang, 1957.

——— *Plays Unpleasant*. London: Penguin, 1992.

Shrady, Nicholas. "Why He Jilted Sartre." Review of Mario Vargas Llosa's *A Writer's Reality*. *New York Times Book Review*, 10 March 1991, 13.

Sollors, Werner. *Beyond Ethnicity: Consent and Descent in American Culture*. New York: Oxford University Press, 1986.

Stavans, Ilan, ed. *Tropical Synagogues*. New York: Holmes & Meier, 1994.

Steimberg, Alicia. *La loca 101*. Buenos Aires: Ediciones de la Flor, 1995.

Steinbeck, John. *The Grapes of Wrath*. New York: Bantam, 1972.

Stutzman, Ronald. "*El Mestizaje*: An All-Inclusive Ideology of Exclusion." In *Cultural Transformations and Ethnicity in Modern Ecuador*, edited by Norman E. Whitten, Jr. Urbana: University of Illinois Press, 1981.

Szichman, Mario. "Remembrances of Things Future." In *Tropical Synagogues*, edited by Ilan Stavans. New York: Holmes & Meier, 1994.

Thurner, Mark. "Peasant Politics and Andean Haciendas in the Transition to Capitalism: An Ethnographic History." *Latin American Research Review* 28, no. 3 (1993): 41–82.

Toolan, Michael J. *Narrative: A Critical Linguistic Introduction*. London: Routledge, 1991.

Torres-Rioseco, Arturo. *The Epic of Latin American Literature*. Berkeley: University of California Press, 1959.

Trotsky, Leon. *Literature and Revolution*. New York: Russell & Russell, 1957.

Valenzuela, Luisa. *The Lizard's Tail*. Translated by Gregory Rabassa. London: Serpent's Tail, 1991

van der Leeuw, G. "Primordial Time and Final Time." In *Man and Time: Papers from the Eranos Yearbooks*, edited by Joseph Campbell. Translated by Ralph Manheim. Bollingen Series XXX, vol. 3. New York: Pantheon, 1957.

Vargas Llosa, Mario. *García Márquez: Historia de un deicidio*. Barcelona: Barral Editores, 1971.

Vasvari, Louise O. "Pitas Pajas: Popular Phonosymbolism." *Revista de Estudios Hispánicos* 26 (1992): 135–62.

Vonnegut, Kurt. "How to Write with Style." *How to Use the Power of the Printed Word*. New York: Anchor, 1985.

Waag, C. Michael. "The Ecuadorian Novel of the 1970s in the Context of Its Historical and Literary Past." Doctoral dissertation, University of Illinois at Urbana-Champaign, 1983.

———. "Frustration and Rage in Jorge Enrique Adoum's *Entre Marx y una mujer desnuda*." *Perspectives on Contemporary Literature* 10 (1984): 95–101.

———. "Sátira política a través de la historia mitificada: *El secuestro del general*, de Demetrio Aguilera Malta." *Revista Iberoamericana* 54 (1988): 771–78.

Weinstein, Fred. *History and Theory after the Fall: An Essay on Interpretation.* Chicago: University of Chicago Press, 1990.

Whitten, Norman E., Jr., ed. *Cultural Transformations and Ethnicity in Modern Ecuador.* Urbana: University of Illinois Press, 1981.

Williams, Raymond. *Marxism and Literature.* Oxford: Oxford University Press, 1977.

Yánez Cossío, Alicia. *Bruna, soroche y los tíos.* Quito: Libresa, 1991.

Index

A la costa (Martínez), 30, 182 n. 9
Adoum, Jorge Enrique, 13, 30, 113, 115, 126, 162 n. 15; on art and politics, 100–101, 102; critique of Borges, 179 n. 40; and ethnicity, 7; and Neruda, 93; self-imposed exile, 87; *Los cuadernos de la tierra*, 87; *Entre Marx y una mujer desnuda*, 7, 9, 85, 90–101, 113, 162 n. 15; "Mestizaje," 87–89
agriculture: banana crop failure, 67; export markets, 39; feudalistic system of, 12, 39, 40
Aguilera, María Dolores, 99
Aguilera Malta, Demetrio, 8, 26, 126; early magical realism of, 41; narrative technique of, 54–55, 68–69; "*El cholo que se castró*," 121–22; *Don Goyo*, 8, 13, 41, 49–55, 69, 75, 122, 168–69 n. 16; *La isla virgen*, 53, 75; *Los que se van*, 13, 41, 75, 121; *El secuestro del general*, 13, 54; *El tigre*, 8, 13, 74–84
Alfaristas, 42
Alfaro, Eloy, 39, 106
Allende, Isabel, 22; *Love and Shadows*, 181 n. 37
Anderson, Benedict, 72
Angulo, María-Elena, 111
anthropomorphism, 44, 48; in *Don Goyo*, 53; in *Huasipungo*, 51; in *Nuestro pan*, 55
anti-realism: in the work of Palacio, 30–31, 38
Antoine, Jean-Claude, 175 n. 18
Apollinaire, Guillaume, 25, 26, 27
Arguedas, José María, 12; *Yawar fiesta*, 45, 46
Aristotle, 33; poetics of, 83
Arsenal, 63
Asturias, Miguel Angel, 21
Auerbach, Erich, 9

Baciu, Stefan, 22, 24
Bakhtin, Mikhail, 7, 11, 13; on carnival, 123; dialogism, 14; epic conventions, 107, 112; grotesque realism, 178 n. 29; realist emblematic, 46, unitary language, 47
Bakhtinian, 11, 45; dialogics, 58, 105; innocents, 61, 62; satiric language, 106
Balakian, Anna, 22
banditry, social, 115–18; modern Robin Hood and, 117
Barbusse, Henri, 26
Barthes, Roland, 125
Bataille, Georges, 22
Battle of Pichincha (24 May 1822), 111
Beckett, Samuel: *Waiting for Godot*, 124
Benítez Vinueza, Leopoldo, 63; "*La mala hora*," 63–64, 121
Betrothed, The (Manzoni), 112, 172 n. 33
blanqueamiento. See ethnicity, "whitening"
Bly, Robert, 20, 127
Boff, Leonardo, 172 n. 36
Bontempelli, Massimo, 19, 28
Boom literature, 65, 172 n. 47; and post-Boom, 126
Borges, Jorge Luis, 22, 179 n. 40
Borgesian, 32
Breton, André, 19, 21, 25; *Mad Love*, 19; *Manifesto of Surrealism*, 21
British Petroleum, 163 n. 22
Bruna, soroche y los tíos (Yánez Cossío [*Bruna and Her Family*]), 9, 11, 103–18; detective work in, 118; elastic time in, 110; humor in, 112; *mestizaje* in, 111; oppositional narratives in, 105; orality in, 105
Bucaram, Abdala, 87
Burgess, Anthony, 40

195

INDEX

Caldwell, Erskine, 41
Campaign, The (Fuentes), 172n. 47
canonization: and market forces, 122; as suppression, 106, 123
capital, 56, 57, 58, 95
capitalism: banditry and, 116–17; consumer, 10; masculine industrial, 120; peripherally-modern, 12; "savage," 73; uniformity under, 15
capitalist, 13, 78, 116
cara del Inca, La, 52
Cárdenas, Eliécer, 9, 11, 13; epic conventions of, 107; *Polvo y ceniza*, 103–18
Caricatura, 26
Carpentier, Alejo, 14, 53, 159n. 1; on surrealism, 19–25, *Ecue-Yamba-O*, 168n. 16; *El reino de este mundo*, 19–20, 25, 159n. 1
Carrera Andrade, Jorge, 21–22, 24, 25; on surrealism, 28–29
Celorio, Gonzalo, 25
Chants de Maldoror, Les (Lautréamont), 26
Chiampi, Irlemar: on *Huasipungo*, 45; on marvellous realism, 26
Chimborazo (volcano), 48–49
"*cholo que se castró, El*" (Aguilera Malta), 121–22
cholos, 41, 42; in *Don Goyo*, 49, 55
Christianity: capitalist, 13; and the cultivation of chaos, 84; and ethnicity, 86; as "foreign" doctrine, 92; Hebraic roots of, 119; and mythology, 77–78; and older forces, 78; popular representations of Jesus, 96–98; tradition of comic testimonials, 100
Chronicle of a Death Foretold (García Márquez), 53
civil war: of 1895–96, 38; of 1912, 42; of 1932, 39
Como agua para chocolate, 15
Communist Party, 25, 26
Conquest, 41, 105
conquistadores, 87, 105, 172n. 36
Cortázar, Julio: and the "female" reader, 114
cuadernos de la tierra, Los (Adoum), 87
Cuba, 22
Cuenca, 27, 40

Cueva, Agustín, 30, 106; on *Don Goyo*, 51; on magical realism in Ecuador, 53; on the *mestizo*, 106–07; on modernism, 73; on social realism, 56
Cumandá (Mera), 126

Dadaism, 26, 27
Darío, Rubén, 165n. 33
de la Cuadra, José, 8, 11, 26, 97, 126, 128; on revolutionary literature, 164–65n. 29; translation issues in, 126–28; *Los Sangurimas*, 65–73, 126–28
Death of Artemio Cruz, The (Fuentes), 119
Decroux, Etienne, 101
Desnos, Robert, 22
detectives: in literature, 35, 118; readers as, 118
dialogism. *See* Bakhtin
dialogue, decontextualization of, 110
Don Goyo (Aguilera Malta), 8, 41, 49–55; compared to *Los Sangurimas*, 69; heteroglossia in, 13; plot summary of, 168–69n. 16; as proto-magical realist text, 51, 75, 122
Dos Passos, John, 57, 172n. 47
Douglass, Frederick, 123

Eagleton, Terry, 14
economy: agriculture-based, 39; control of cultural production, 14; depression, 73; free market, 14; natural disasters and, 39, 67; single-product, 15–16
economic analysis: Marxist, 29–30
Ecuador: map, *167*; seal of, 49, *50*
Ecue-Yamba-O (Carpentier), 168n. 16
Einstein, Albert, 124
Eisenstein, Sergei M., 10; and montage technique, 110
Eliade, Mircea, 74; and chaos, 78; and time, 76, 81–82; *The Secret of Dr. Honigberger*, 82
Emperor Jones, The (O'Neill), 8, 75–77, 79–82, 84; compared to *El tigre*, 76; performative power in, 79
Engels, Frederick, 10, 100
Entre Marx y una mujer desnuda (Adoum), 7, 9, 85, 90–101, 113; audience for, 98–99; criticism of Chil-

ean dictatorship in, 92; humor in, 95–96, 98; multiple perspectives in, 90; neologisms in, 99; open-endedness in, 162n. 15; parentage and identity in, 94–95
Escudero, Gonzalo, 27, 31
Estupiñán Bass, Nelson, 126
ethnicity: and assimilation, 92; and "betweenness," 85–86; and generational conflict, 93–94; and language, 99; and name-changing, 109–10, 180–81n. 24; and nationality, 87, 89, 91, 111; and universality, 92; and "whitening," 89
expressionism: in Germany, 22; in *El tigre*, 74–75

Faris, Wendy B., 99
Faulkner, William, 57, 172n. 47
feminism: challenging official history, 104–5; gender-neutral terms, 114; reconstruction of identity, 110–11; reconstruction of the past, 109; satirizing "male" narrative forms, 113–14; stereotypical depictions of women, 120, 182n. 6; suppression of women's voices, 104
Fernández, María del Carmen, 27, 31
feudalism, 16, 53, 73; oil wealth and, 16; patriarchy and, 72. See also agriculture
Figueira, Dorothy, 119, 175–76n. 19
Flores Galindo, Alberto, 15; on violence, 45
Floyd, Pretty Boy, 62, 117
Foucauldian, 14
Foucault, Michel, 117
Fragmented Life of Don Jacobo Lerner, The (Goldemberg), 92; collage in, 177n. 14
France, Anatole, 26
Franco, General Francisco, 95
Fuentes, Carlos: *The Campaign*, 172n. 47; *The Death of Artemio Cruz*, 119

Galarza, Jaime: *El festín del petroleo*, 163
Gallegos Lara, Joaquín, 26, 29, 41; *Los que se van*, 13, 41, 75, 121
García Márquez, Gabriel, 8, 119, 162n. 15; *Chronicle of a Death Foretold*, 53; *One Hundred Years of Solitude*, 8, 53, 65–73, 95–96, 119, 164n. 29, 183n. 23
general strike (15 Nov. 1922), 39, 73, 111
Genet, Jean, 124
Gil Gilbert, Enrique, 8, 41; *Los que se van*, 13, 41, 75, 121; *Nuestro pan*, 8, 13, 41, 48–49, 55, 170–71n. 16
Girard, René, 84
Goldemberg, Isaac, 92; *The Fragmented Life of Don Jacobo Lerner*, 92, 177n. 14; *Play by Play*, 92
Goloboff, Gerardo Mario, 92; "The Passion According to San Martín," 92
González Echevarría, Roberto, 122, 172n. 47
Goodman, Nelson, 124
Goody, J., and I. Watt, 120
Gospel According to Luke, The, 63
Graff, Gerald, 123
Grapes of Wrath, The (Steinbeck), 8, 46, 57–64; anthropomorphism in, 48; compared to *Huasipungo*, 57–58; and José Martí, 172n. 34; mythic realism in, 57; orality in, 59–61
grupo de Guayaquil, El, 29, 57
Guayaquil, 40, 126; as business center, 49; as source of legal authority, 72
Guayas (river): in *Nuestro pan*, 48–49; in *El tigre*, 78
Guerrero Zamora, Juan, 75

Hall, Stuart, 11
Hamlet, 116
hegemony: in discourse, 11; in education, 91–92; in *Entre Marx y una mujer desnuda*, 90; in narrative, 10; and national identity, 111; in oral and written texts, 104–5, 110; racial, in *The Grapes of Wrath*, 58
Hélice, 27
Hemingway, Ernest, 57, 172n. 47
Heraclitus, 124
Hicks, D. Emily, 125
historical novels, 112, 171–72n. 33, 181n. 26. See also *Bruna, soroche y los tíos*; *Polvo y ceniza*
history: Ecuadorian (general back-

ground), 166–67 n. 1; and myth, 119; and popular memory, 119–20
Hobsbawm, E. J., 112; on banditry, 116, 181–82 n. 39
Holmes, Sherlock, 32
Holmesian, 36
"*hombre muerto a puntapiés, Un.*" See "The Man Who Was Kicked to Death"
Homer, 107, 121, 124; *The Iliad*, 107
Hour of the Star, The (Lispector), 101
Huasipungo (Icaza), 8, 41, 43–46; anthropomorphism in, 51; compared to *The Grapes of Wrath*, 57–58; heteroglossia in, 13, 43; as international best-seller, 57–58; plot summary of, 169–70 n. 16; social realism in, 56
huasipungo, 41, 43–44, 46–47, 59, 169–70 n. 16
Huidobro, Vicente, 21
humor, 91; criticism of authority through, 112–13; in *One Hundred Years of Solitude*, 95–96; sacred and scatological, 114–15; in testaments, 100

Icaza, Jorge, 8, 13, 45, 126; and the "*mestizo* soul," 107; representation of indigenous culture in, 46; *Huasipungo*, 8, 13, 41, 43–46, 51, 56–58, 169–70 n. 16
identity: through ancestry, 94–95, 109–10; crisis of, 67, 70, 106–7; national, 111, 120; in *Los Sangurimas*, 66, 69. See also ethnicity
ideology: hybridization of, 14; and narrative, 7; through realism, 9
Iliad, The, 107
Illuminations (Rimbaud), 25
Indice de la narrativa ecuatoriana, 92–93
indigenism, 58
indigenists, 12, 45; and "new language," 73; and social realism, 53
indigenous culture: and Christianity, 14, 45–46; and immigrant ethnicity, 86; and loyalty to national authority, 120
indigenous populations: of Bolivia, 12; and hybridization, 14; of Peru, 12. See also native Ecuadorians

Inti, 14
Ionesco, Eugene, 124, 176 n. 23
isla virgen, La (Aguilera Malta): anthropomorphism in, 53; as source of *El tigre*, 75
Ivanhoe (Scott), 112, 171–72 n. 33

Jacob, Max, 26
Jews: Brazilian authors, 101; ethnicity of, 92, 111; humor as weapon of, 113; immigration of, 87; and mysticism, 176 n. 23; mythology of, 77–78; Talmudic textual analysis of, 101; transformation and survival of, 100
Joyce, James, *Ulysses*, 53

Kafka, Franz, 176 n. 23
Kott, Jan, 16

Langowski, Gerald J., 24
language: and anti-realist neologisms, 99; and ethnicity, 99; and humor, 91; "new," of indigenists, 73; and power, 46. See also orality; writing
Lautréamont, Count of (Isidore Ducasse), 21, 26, 31; *Les Chants de Maldoror*, 26
law, written and oral, 103
Lebanese: Ecuadorian ethnicity of, 111; immigration of, 86-87. See also ethnicity
Lenin, Vladimir, 102
Letras, 25
Levi-Straussian, 77
Levine, Suzanne Jill, 127
Leyendas del cristo negro (Massís [*Legends of the Black Christ*]), 96–98
Liberal Revolution, 39, 105, 106, 121
Lispector, Clarice, 101: on banditry (in "Mineirinho"), 115-16; "The Fifth Story," 101; *The Hour of the Star*, 101
literacy, economics of, 15, 98–99. See also writing
Lizard's Tail, The (Valenzuela), 174 n. 16
loca 101, La (Steimberg), 91, 98; criticism of authority through humor in, 113–15; sacred and scatological

INDEX

humor in, 114–15; satirizing "male" narrative forms, 113–14
Los que se van (Aguilera Malta, Gallegos Lara, Gil Gilbert [*Those Who Leave*]), 41, 75; heteroglossia in, 13; magical realism in, 121
Love and Shadows (Allende), 181 n. 37
Ludmer, Josefina, 103–4
Lukács, Georg, 41, 160 n. 11
Luzuriaga, Gerardo, 75, 76

Macherey, Pierre, 111
Mad Love (Breton), 19
Madrid, 22, 165 n. 33
Magic Mountain, The (Mann), 53
magical realism, 7, 120–25; against colonialism, 92; definition of, 19–20; early uses of, 75; elements of, 26, 120; first appearance in Ecuadorian literature, 122; first use referring to literature, 28; multiple realities in, 125; as "natural" phenomenon, 19–25, 53, 122, 159 n. 1; neologisms in, 99; as non-chronological history, 51; non-linear time in, 48, 124; and popular forms, 99
Mahuad, Jamil, 87
"*mala hora, La*" (Benítez Vinueza), 63–64, 121
"Man Who Was Kicked to Death, The" (Palacio), 31–38, 109
Mañana, 27
Manifesto of Surrealism (Breton), 21
Mann, Thomas, *The Magic Mountain*, 53
Manzoni, Alessandro, *The Betrothed*, 112, 172 n. 33
Martí, José, 172 n. 34
Martín, Carlos, 25
Martínez, Luis A., *A la costa*, 30, 182 n. 9
marvellous realism, 14, 19, 159 n. 1
Marx, Karl, 125. *See also* economic analysis
mass production: of art, 163 n. 23; and uniformity, 15
Massís, Mahfud, 93, 96–98; *Leyendas del cristo negro*, 96–98
Mayo, Hugo, 27
Menchu, Rigoberta, 12
Menem, Carlos Saúl, 87

Mera, Juan León, 96, 126; *Cumandá*, 126
"*Mestizaje*" (Adoum), 87–89
mestizaje, 13, 16, 175 n. 4; in *Bruna, soroche y los tíos*, 111; as "burden," 89; as literary theme, 8; the myth of, 87, as rape, 87–89
mestizo, 45, 51, 53, 54; in *Don Goyo*, 55; identities of, 106–7, 111
metric system, 15
Moby Dick (Melville), 80
modernism, 53, 73; social realism as response to, 125
modernity, 73; text as conveyor of, 104
montuvio, 66, 122, 127
myth, 73; and atemporality, 74; authority of, 120; Christian and Jewish, 77, 84; and history, 119; indeterminacy of, 119; in the jungle, 76; of *mestizaje*, 87; of national identity, 120; and time, 77, 82
mythification: of rebel hero, 108

narrative: authority in, 38; continuity and nothingness in, 83; credibility in, 33–34; epic conventions in, 107; and history, 9, 104–5; and ideology, 7, 10; multiple perspectives in, 90, 105; and mythification, 108; oral (*see* orality); as "neurosis," 160 n. 4; popular voices in, 11, 69; totalization in, 9, 101, 104, 181 n. 26; unfinished, 101
narrators, unidentified: in *Bruna, soroche y los tíos*, 110; in "The Man Who Was Kicked to Death," 32; in *Polvo y ceniza*, 108; in *Los Sangurimas*, 68
national anthem (of Ecuador), 96
native Ecuadorians: anthropomorphism and, 44; national identity and, 111; Amautas, 54; Andeans, 25, 45; Aragundis, 42; Cañaris, 51; Shuars, 171 n. 17
natural disasters: in history, 39; in *Huasipungo*, 44, 51
naturalism, in dialogue, 41
nature: as adversary, 49, 76; feminization of, 48, 120; Indians as, 44; as self-image, 49; symbolizing freedom, 64
Nazis, 10, 25

Neruda, Pablo, 20, 93; *Residencia en la tierra*, 20
Nietzsche, Friedrich, *The Will to Power*, 82–83
Nivel, 93
noche de los asesinos, La (Triana), 124
Nord-Sud, 21
Nuestro pan (Gil Gilbert), 8, 41, 48–49; anthropomorphism in, 55; heteroglossia in, 13; non-linear time in, 48; plot summary of, 170–71 n. 16

Ojeda, J. Enrique, 25
Olivier, Laurence, 121
One Hundred Years of Solitude (García Márquez), 8, 65–73; humor in, 95–96; mythic time in, 183 n. 23; as popular history, 119; precursors of, 53, 65; as socialist realism, 164 n. 29
O'Neill, Eugene, 8, 76, 77; *The Emperor Jones*, 8, 75–77, 79-82, 84
Ong, Walter, 162 n. 15
OPEC, 40
orality, 11, 162 n. 15, 179 n. 4, 181 n. 26; in conflict with official history, 13, 68, 105; as counter-hegemonic, 104; and epic, 107; in *The Grapes of Wrath*, 59–61; and history, 112, 120; open-endedness of, 105; in *Los Sangurimas*, 67–68; as source of magical realism, 120, 122; versus textual authority, 61, 72, 103
Ortiz, Adalberto, 126
Ortner, Sherry, 48, 49

Pachacamac, 14, 46
Palacio, Pablo, 8, 29–38; and Marxist economic analysis, 29-30; in *Polvo y ceniza*, 109; "The Man Who Was Kicked to Death," 31–38, 109; *Vida de ahorcado*, 29
Pareja Diezcanseco, Alfredo, 29, 57
Paris, 21, 24, 126, 165 n. 33
Parkinson Zamora, Lois, 92, 99
patriarchy: Abraham, 67; novels of, 65
Paz, Octavio, 24, 25; *Piedra de sol*, 119
Pearl, The (Steinbeck), compared to *Huasipungo*, 56, 57
Pearl Harbor, 119
Picasso, Pablo, 26
Piedra de sol (Paz), 119

Pirandello, Luigi, 19, 165 n. 45
Plato, 101
Play by Play (Goldemberg), 92
Poe, Edgar Allan, 37; "The Imp of the Perverse," 116
Polvo y ceniza (Cárdenas [*Dust and Ashes*]), 9, 11, 103–18; banditry in, 116; fragmented time in, 110; intertextuality of, 109; mythification of hero, 108; non-chronological history in, 105, 107; oppositional narratives in, 105; Russian Revolution in, 116–17
popular art, and high art, 160–61 n. 11; 183 n. 15
Propp, Vladimir, 125
psychological perception, 160–61 n. 4
Puech, Henri-Charles, 74; on atemporality, 81; on Christian mythology, 77

Quechua, 12
Quichua, 12, 46, 111, 162 n. 21
Quintessence of Ibsenism, The (Shaw), 123
Quito, 40, 126

Rabassa, Gregory, 127
Raglan, Lord, 120
Rama, Angel, 12; on linguistic subcultures, 161 n. 14
realism: autocthonous, 121; in early twentieth-century Ecuadorian novels, 30; grotesque, 178 n. 29; and ideology, 9; insufficiency of, 101; mythic, 159 n. 1; as source of magic, 121; Zolaesque, 29. *See also* anti-realism; magical realism; marvellous realism; social realism; socialist realism
regionalism, 40
reino de este mundo, El (Carpentier), 19–20, 25, 159 n. 1
Residencia en la tierra (Neruda), 20
Reverdy, Pierre, 21
Ricoeur, Paul, 83
Rimbaud, Arthur, *Illuminations*, 25
Rivera, José Eustasio, *La vorágine*, 121, 122
Robles, Humberto, 26, 27, 30; and mythic realism, 159 n. 1; on "traditional vanguardists," 163 n. 9
Robles, Mercedes, 106

Rodríguez Lara, General, 91
Rumiñahui, 51
Russian Revolution, 116–17

Sábato, Ernesto, 21
Sacoto, Antonio, 30
Sangurimas, Los (de la Cuadra), 8, 11, 65–73; heteroglossia in, 13; magical realism in, 53; as precursor to *One Hundred Years of Solitude*, 65; orality in, 67–68; translation issues in, 126–28
Scliar, Moacyr, 92, 95, 113; on betweenness, 101; on transformation and survival, 99–102; *The Strange Nation of Rafael Mendes*, 92, 95, 99–102, 113; *The Volunteers*, 178n. 25
Scott, Sir Walter: *Ivanhoe*, 112, 171–72n. 33
Secret of Dr. Honigberger, The (Eliade), 82
secuestro del general, El (Aguilera Malta), 13, 54
Shakespeare, William, 99; *Hamlet*, 116
Shaw, George Bernard, 7, 123; *The Quintessence of Ibsenism*, 123
Shepard, Sam, 124
social magic realism, 27, 56
social mobility, 14
social realism, 12, 30; *Don Goyo* as, 51; as factor in magical realism, 120; in *Huasipungo*, 56; in *Nuestro pan*, 56; as reaction to literary modernism, 125; simple models in, 47; and socialist realism, 164n. 29
Socialist Party, 25
socialist realism, 25; and Gallegos Lara, 26; and the "knowable," 121; strict definition of, 164n. 29
Sollors, Werner, 94
Soupault, Philippe, 22
Spielberg, Steven, 10
Stalinism, 25
Steimberg, Alicia, 91, 98, 113–15; satirizing "male" narrative forms, 113–14; "Cecilia's Last Will and Testament," 100; *La loca 101*, 91, 98, 113–15
Steinbeck, John, 8; *The Grapes of Wrath*, 8, 46, 57–64, 172n. 34; *The Pearl*, 56, 57

Strange Nation of Rafael Mendes, The (Scliar), 92, 95, 99–102, 113
surrealism, 19–24, 28; and anti-realism, 37; as "foreign" idea, 19; in Latin America, 24; as literary movement, 21, 24; and para-surrealism, 22, 24; and ultraism, 22
Szichman, Mario, "Remembrance of Things Future," 113

telenovelas, 16, 163n. 23
tigre, El (Aguilera Malta), 8, 74–84; compared to *The Emperor Jones*, 76; compared to *Moby Dick*, 80; heteroglossia in, 13
time: ahistorical, 65; cosmic, 81; cyclical indigenous, 54; fragmented, 110; linear Christian, 76; and myth, 74, 77, 183n. 23; non-linearity of, 48
Tobacco Road (Caldwell), 41
translation: and ambiguity, 32, 44, 165–66n. 53; and cultural specificity, 126, 127; and indeterminacy, 128; and Latin-based words, 127; meaning-based, 127; slang and idioms in, 128; substitution in, 184n. 1
Triana, José: *La noche de los asesinos*, 124
Trotsky, Leon: *Literature and Revolution*, 161n. 11
Turbay Ayala, Julio César, 87
Twilight Zone, The, 124, 176n. 23

Ubidia, Abdón, 126
Ulysses (Joyce), 53
Uncle Tom's Cabin (Beecher Stowe), 100
Uslar Pietri, Arturo, 21

Valenzuela, Luisa: *The Lizard's Tail*, 174n. 16
Vallejo, César, 21
van der Leeuw, G., 176n. 22
vanguardism, 19, 30, 163n. 9; replaced by social realism, 27
Vargas Llosa, Mario, interview with Carpentier, 23
Velasco Ibarra, José María, 166n. 1
Venezuela, 23, 24
Vida de ahorcado (Palacio), 29
Volunteers, The (Scliar), 178n. 25

Vonnegut, Kurt, 160n. 4
vorágine, La (Rivera), 121, 122

Waag, C. Michael, 54; on autocthonous realism, 121; on *Don Goyo*, 122
Waiting for Godot (Beckett), 124
Whitten, Norman E., Jr., 13
Wilder, Thornton, 57
Williams, Raymond, 46, 106, 121, 123
Wordsworth, William, 40

writing: as legal authority, 72, 103; mysteries of, 42; and power, 41, 61; versus speech, 61, 66, 72, 104–5, 108–9, 119–20. *See also* language

Yánez Cossío, Alicia, 9, 11, 13; *Bruna, soroche y los tíos*, 9, 11, 103–18
Yawar fiesta (Arguedas), 45, 46

Zaldumbide, Gonzalo, 27